P9-DZO-183

Policing Hatred

CRITICAL AMERICA

General Editors: Richard Delgado and Jean Stefancic

White by Law: The Legal Construction of Race
Ian F. Haney López

Cultivating Intelligence: Power, Law, and the Politics of Teaching
Louise Harmon and Deborah W. Post

Privilege Revealed: How Invisible Preference Undermines America
Stephanie M. Wildman
with Margalynne Armstrong, Adrienne D. Davis, and Trina Grillo

Does the Law Morally Bind the Poor?
or What Good's the Constitution When You Can't Afford a Loaf of Bread?
R. George Wright

Hybrid: Bisexuals, Multiracials, and Other Misfits under American Law
Ruth Colker

Critical Race Feminism: A Reader
Edited by Adrien Katherine Wing

Immigrants Out!
The New Nativism and the Anti-Immigrant Impulse in the United States
Edited by Juan F. Perea

Taxing America
Edited by Karen B. Brown and Mary Louise Fellows

Notes of a Racial Caste Baby:
Color Blindness and the End of Affirmative Action
Bryan K. Fair

Please Don't Wish Me a Merry Christmas:
A Critical History of the Separation of Church and State
Stephen M. Feldman

To Be an American: Cultural Pluralism and the Rhetoric of Assimilation
Bill Ong Hing

Negrophobia and Reasonable Racism:
The Hidden Costs of Being Black in America
Jody David Armour

Black and Brown in America: The Case for Cooperation
Bill Piatt

Black Rage Confronts the Law
Paul Harris

Selling Words: Free Speech in a Commercial Culture
R. George Wright

The Color of Crime: Racial Hoaxes, White Fear, Black Protectionism, Police Harassment, and Other Macroaggressions
Katheryn K. Russell

The Smart Culture: Society, Intelligence, and Law
Robert L. Hayman, Jr.

Was Blind, But Now I See: White Race Consciousness and the Law
Barbara J. Flagg

The Gender Line: Men, Women, and the Law
Nancy Levit

Heretics in the Temple: Americans Who Reject the Nation's Legal Faith
David Ray Papke

The Empire Strikes Back: Outsiders and the Struggle over Legal Education
Arthur Austin

Interracial Justice: Conflict and Reconciliation in Post–Civil Rights America
Eric K. Yamamoto

Black Men on Race, Gender, and Sexuality: A Critical Reader
Edited by Devon Carbado

When Sorry Isn't Enough:
The Controversy over Apologies and Reparations for Human Injustice
Edited by Roy L. Brooks

Disoriented: Asian Americans, Law, and the Nation State
Robert S. Chang

Rape and the Culture of the Courtroom
Andrew E. Taslitz

The Passions of Law
Edited by Susan A. Bandes

Global Critical Race Feminism: An International Reader
Edited by Adrien Katherine Wing

Law and Religion: Critical Essays
Edited by Stephen M. Feldman

Changing Race: Latinos, the Census, and the History of Ethnicity
Clara E. Rodríguez

From the Ground Up: Environmental Racism
and the Rise of the Environmental Justice Movement
Luke Cole and Sheila Foster

Nothing but the Truth:
Why Trial Lawyers Don't, Can't, and Shouldn't Have to Tell the Whole Truth
Steven Lubet

Critical Race Theory: An Introduction
Richard Delgado and Jean Stefancic

Playing It Safe: How the Supreme Court Sidesteps Hard Cases
Lisa A. Kloppenberg

Why Lawsuits Are Good for America:
Disciplined Democracy, Big Business, and the Common Law
Carl T. Bogus

How the Left Can Win Arguments and Influence People:
A Tactical Manual for Pragmatic Progressives
John K. Wilson

Aftermath:
The Clinton Impeachment and the Presidency in the Age of Political Spectacle
Edited by Leonard V. Kaplan and Beverly I. Moran

Getting over Equality: A Critical Diagnosis of Religious Freedom in America
Steven D. Smith

Critical Race Narratives: A Study of Race, Rhetoric, and Injury
Carl Gutiérrez-Jones

Social Scientists for Social Justice: Making the Case against Segregation
John P. Jackson, Jr.

Victims in the War on Crime: The Use and Abuse of Victims' Rights
Markus Dirk Dubber

Original Sin:
Clarence Thomas and the Failure of the Constitutional Conservatives
Samuel A. Marcosson

Policing Hatred: Law Enforcement, Civil Rights, and Hate Crime
Jeannine Bell

Policing Hatred

Law Enforcement, Civil Rights, and Hate Crime

Jeannine Bell

NEW YORK UNIVERSITY PRESS
New York and London

To my parents, John and Jeanette Bell

NEW YORK UNIVERSITY PRESS
New York and London
© 2002 by New York University
All rights reserved.

Library of Congress Cataloging-in-Publication Data
Bell, Jeannine, 1969–
Policing hatred : law enforcement, civil rights, and
hate crime / Jeannine Bell.
p. cm. — (Critical America)
Includes bibliographical references and index.
ISBN 0-8147-9897-7 (cloth : alk. paper)
1. Hate crimes—United States.
2. Criminal law—United States—Decision making.
3. Police—United States—Decision making.
4. Civil rights—United States. I. Title. II. Series.
KF9345 .B45 2002
345.73'025—dc21   2002001427

New York University Press books are printed on acid-free paper,
and their binding materials are chosen for strength and durability.

Manufactured in the United States of America
10 9 8 7 6 5 4 3 2 1

Contents

Tables

Acknowledgments

I have benefited enormously from what I've learned while watching others.

I owe a great debt to the members of the "Anti-Bias Task Force," who allowed me to observe them. For several months they bore my nearly constant presence with patience and good humor. Their openness and willingness to include me in many of their activities during the time I spent observing the unit was essential to this account of what police do.

I planned this project soon after the passage of the Hate Crime Statistics Act. It began as a Ph.D. dissertation and was supported by generous grants from the University of Michigan Political Science Department's Gerald R. Ford Dissertation Fund and grants from the Horace H. Rackham School of Graduate Studies.

I am grateful for the extraordinary advice on this book given to me by the five faculty members who served on my dissertation committee. Kim Lane Scheppele, Martha Feldman, Rick Lempert, John Kingdon, and Mark Brandon deserve particular thanks not only for their wonderful insights based on an exceptionally close reading of the manuscript but also for their remarkable enthusiasm about the project. All were generous in giving their time in support of this project and of me. I owe special thanks to my committee co-chair, Kim Lane Scheppele, who has shaped my scholarship in immeasurable ways. Much of what I know about public law and political science, I learned from Kim.

One's help sometimes comes from unexpected places. I am very thankful to David Bayley, of SUNY Albany, who has provided tremendous assistance from beginning to end. Over the past several years David was never too busy to take a call, answer a question, or give advice.

I extend special thanks to a small and fearless band of friends from graduate and law school. Myriam Jaïdi, Ronie Garcia-Johnson, George Lovell, Sherry Martin and Debbie Meizlish were tirelessly supportive during the project and made time in their busy schedules to provide comments on drafts of the book. I would also like to especially thank several of my colleagues at Indiana University: Kevin Brown, Yvonne Cripps, Steve Conrad, Sarah Hughes, Dawn Johnsen, Donald Gjerdingen, Seth Lahn, Aviva Orenstein, and Susan Williams.

Several Indiana University graduate and law students furnished extremely useful research assistance for the book. I am especially grateful for the help of those Indiana University School of Law librarians and staff members who cheerfully unearthed a wealth of books and articles, often at a moment's notice. The O'Byrne research fund and Indiana University Law School summer research grants provided financial support for work on the book.

At New York University Press, I wish to thank Jennifer Hammer, who has provided great assistance at every stage of the publication process. Her warmth, good cheer, and generosity has made the process so much smoother. The Critical America series editors, Richard Delgado and Jean Stefancic, also contributed wonderful comments on the book manuscript. Richard in particular deserves credit for expressing interest in the manuscript and bringing it to the attention of editors at New York University Press. Betty Seaver deserves special thanks for her editorial assistance. I also wish to thank the four anonymous reviewers whose discerning comments significantly helped me strengthen the book's substance.

And finally, I extend my deepest appreciation to my family, John, Jeanette, and Jerilyn Bell, and to Tony Miles. Like many family members who have watched books take over someone's life, you were patient, and gave me crucial support.

1

Introduction

The brutal killing in Texas of James Byrd, a Black man, brought hate crimes to the fore of the public agenda in the late 1990s. In early June of 1998 three White men chained Byrd behind a truck and dragged him to death. Byrd's killing was widely recognized as a "hate" or bias crime. A bias crime is one motivated by prejudice toward one of the victim's characteristics, such as race, color, ethnicity, religion, or sexual orientation, and the perpetrator of the crime usually does not share that characteristic with the victim.[1] In the wake of Byrd's murder, many activists called for passage of stronger hate crimes legislation.

Another incident, though far less publicized, occurred the year before Byrd's murder. The episode began early in the morning of July 24, 1997, in Elk Creek, Virginia, at an informal gathering at which Louie J. Ceparano, Garnett Paul "G.P." Johnson, two other men, and a woman were drinking. Ceparano pinned down Johnson on his back and one of the others heard him say as he stood over him, "We're going to take G.P. out there and put him on that white cross and burn him." Ceparano snapped the watch off Johnson's wrist, remarking, "You won't need the watch where you're going, they've got their own time down there." Ceparano and another White man then dragged Johnson outside, doused him with gasoline, and set him afire. One of the White men then moved Johnson's body to a nearby sandy ridge and beheaded it. The accused killers were White; the victim, Black. One witness remembered Ceparano calling Johnson a "nigger" during the party.[2]

When news of G. P. Johnson's death spread to the rest of the country, many believed that the difference in race between the victim and the perpetrators, the use of racial slurs prior to the crime, and the brutality of the murder marked the crime as a potential hate crime. Yet Johnson's death was not prosecuted under Virginia's hate crime statute. The Grayson County sheriff responsible for investigating the crime

1

concluded that because of the relationship between the two men— Johnson and Ceparano were said to have been friends—the evidence did not point to race as the cause of the crime.[3] Police officers' exercise of this type of discretion—the power to determine what is and is not a hate crime—is the focus of this book.

The Power of Police Officers in Hate Crime Cases

Abstract discussions of speech rights and nonempirical discussions of the efficacy of hate crime laws have dominated the debate over hate crime. Up until this point, scholars have ignored the extraordinary power of police to classify incidents as particular types of crimes. Police officers have the power to decide whether, and in which circumstances, the criminal law will be used. In the vast majority of possible bias crimes that are committed each year, a decision by police not to invoke the law determines to a great extent that the incident will not be pursued as a hate crime. Advocates and politicians who push for stronger hate crime legislation in the wake of gruesome bias-motivated crimes often fail to recognize and account for this broad police discretion. As one scholar has put it, "[P]olice decisions not to invoke the criminal process largely determine the outer limits of law enforcement."[4]

Police decisions and the criteria officers use to make them are crucial for the administration of the criminal law, and ultimately, for justice. To grant police, the first gatekeepers in the criminal justice system, the power to set the limits of law enforcement is to allow their decisions to limit the options available to all of those—like prosecutors, judges, juries, probation officers, and parole boards—who exercise their discretion downstream in the system. Control over the initial classification of incidents also means that police wield the power, often unreviewed by others in the criminal justice system, to determine those situations in which the law will be applied.

Deciding how and under which circumstances to apply any law is fraught with difficulty. This book does what scholarly treatments of hate crime law have not done up to this point. It analyzes in depth how hate crime law works in a large city, based on extensive interviews with those who must enforce hate crime law. For several months, I was a participant observer of a specialized hate crime unit in a metropolitan city and enjoyed access to detectives, their case files spanning two decades, and most of their records.

Before this research, anecdotal evidence from other cities suggested reluctance by police to enforce hate crime law.[5] Police may resist activists' and community leaders' calls for hate crime charges because they find hate crimes ambiguous or are uncertain about what may constitute evidence of motivation.[6] There is a disincentive for police to identify crimes as bias-motivated. Large numbers of hate crimes can lead to media reports that a city is not racially tolerant and detract from its image.[7] The publicity that such cases draw and the marker of racial intolerance that comes with identifying hate crime create a reason for police and other local officials to deny such events happen in their city or town.[8]

If we care about whether hate crime law works, we must understand the nature of police discretion. Street-level enforcers of these laws can effectively nullify hate crime statutes through nonenforcement, thereby reducing the statutes to an empty symbolic gesture.[9] This raises a number of concerns: If the police do not enforce hate crime laws, why not? Can we assume that police officers refuse to enforce bias crime legislation because statutory ambiguity leads them to think that it is "feel-good" lawmaking that legislators do not really want enforced? Is police nonenforcement localized and geared to certain situations (e.g., cases involving violence against Asian Americans) that they believe are less of a problem in order to conserve scarce resources?[10] Does victims' reluctance to prosecute play a role in the nonenforcement of hate crime legislation? Finally, do police practice nonenforcement, as existing research would lead one to assume, because they do not really think these actions are crimes? If any of these questions can be answered affirmatively, as earlier studies of low-level crimes suggest they might be, then hate crime laws are not having their intended effect. If this truly is the case, victims and their advocates are unwise to put their faith in them, and constitutional critics of hate crime laws can rest easy.

Hate crimes are different from other crimes in that they give more power to police. The level of discretion that comes with the identification and charging of hate crimes differs substantially from that in other areas in that some bias incidents have the potential to have either extremely high or low visibility. Hate crime identification differs from, say, the enforcement of traffic laws because it can occur under intense public scrutiny.[11] Even if the media do not report it, other members of the affected community are likely to know of some hate crimes and pressure police for a bias or nonbias classification.[12]

Other hate crimes suffer from extremely low visibility. Most hate crime statutes require bias motivation as well as an underlying criminal offense. Murder, nonnegligent manslaughter, forcible rape, aggravated and simple assault, intimidation, arson, destruction, and damage or vandalism of property can all be hate crimes if motivated by bias.[13] Acts of bias-motivated vandalism such as the stoning of residents' windows and the damaging of their cars—crimes where the underlying criminal offense is relatively minor—even when severe, rarely garner publicity. Hate crime statutes therefore present officers with more options because the decision not to charge an offender with a hate crime does not necessarily mean that the offender will escape punishment. Since bias-motivated incidents can be dealt with as "ordinary" crimes without being labeled as hate crimes, officers are more vulnerable to community pressures not to identify crimes as bias-motivated.

Police-Minority Interaction

Another reason to examine with particular care how police enforce hate crime law is that with hate crime, stereotypical assumptions about criminal law roles are reversed: most of the perpetrators are White, and most of the victims are non-White. Current data showing racial profiling of minorities by police officers as well as data regarding the excessive use of force by the police suggest that the police relate differently to and cannot be trusted to protect communities of racial minorities. The possibility that officers may not enforce the law when minority victims have been attacked is magnified by the power that relatively low-level officers—often not subject to public scrutiny—have to define hate crime.

Nonenforcement is an issue in antigay and -lesbian hate crimes, as well. Gays and lesbians have suffered both physical and emotional abuse at the hands of the police. One study found that 23 percent of gay men and 13 percent of lesbians had been harassed by the police at least once in their lives because of their sexual orientation.[14] The history of police-minority interaction, combined with documented officer indifference toward hate crime law, creates a legitimate concern that police officers may not be properly enforcing the law.

Hate Crime Victimization

Consider also the problem of hate crime victimization. One justification offered for enhanced penalties for hate crime is that hate crime victims and the larger community suffer greater harm when hate crimes are committed.[15] Empirical studies that compare non-bias-motivated crime victims with bias crime victims have shown that victims of bias-motivated violence suffer longer and more intensely than victims in other groups.[16] One national survey compared individuals who were victimized by personal crime with people who had not been victimized by crime. Victims in this survey included victims of crime not based on prejudice, those victimized by ethnoviolence, acts motivated by prejudice against one's group, and those who had been victims of group defamation, insults based on the victim's background or that of persons with whom he or she identified.[17] This survey revealed that of the four groups, ethnoviolence victims reported the greatest symptoms of post-traumatic stress and had made the greatest number of social and behavioral changes as a result of the incident.[18]

Another study examined victims who had reported bias-motivated and non-bias-motivated aggravated assaults to Boston police between 1992 and 1997. Controlling for the effects of factors like previous victimization, the quality of police response, and socioeconomic factors, the researchers examined sixteen psychological and twelve behavioral factors for differences between the victims of bias-motivated and non-bias-motivated violence. They found that the victims of bias-motivated aggravated assault experienced particular types of psychological stress for more prolonged periods and more severely than non-bias victims.[19] One of the study's most telling conclusions concerned the impact on hate crime victims of law enforcement's response. The study found that the police response can be "pivotal" to the psychological stress of victims, and that "the ability of police officers to address incidents of assault in a responsive and effective manner can significantly reduce the potential for psychological stress" for crime victims.[20]

This research on bias crime victimization supplies special reasons to inquire about police treatment of victims of bias-motivated violence. The trauma that victims of bias-motivated violence experience compels a response that is different from the normal police response to low-level crime: nonenforcement of the law. If investigating bias-motivated crime in a particular area can lead to a decline in that type of crime, the increased psychological effect of bias-motivated violence on victims suggests that allowing the police to ignore hate has even greater consequences than allowing the police not to enforce other types of laws.

Police Interpreting Higher Law

Studying police methods of bias crime classification also expands our knowledge of the range of actors in the law enforcement community with the power to interpret so-called higher law, such as the First Amendment. Though the Supreme Court has settled the constitutionality of bias crime statutes, much disagreement in the legal community remains over what counts as proper evidence of bias motivation and whether motivation can consist of "just words." In the absence of an agreed-upon definition of what counts as evidence of bias motivation, as the police gather evidence in hate crime cases, they are required to interpret the First Amendment. Significant differences between prosecutorial and police understandings of protected speech and unprotected conduct suggest that the police exercise much influence enforcing the law, and that judges and lawyers are not the only actors within the criminal justice system with powers of meaningful interpretation of the First Amendment. Police officers' interpretations in this area matter because of the critical role they play in screening the disputes that come to court, and thus their ability to decide when hate is a crime.

Whether hate crime law works and if law matters to ground-level enforcers can be examined through an empirical study of enforcement. Activists have appealed for changes in hate crime law in the wake of highly publicized crimes like the murders of James Byrd and G. P. Johnson.[21] Whether such changes are necessary should also depend on empirical assessment. The issue of whether hate crime law matters and whether it works is inextricably linked to how it is enforced. Appeals to law are useful only if the law is meaningfully carried out by those charged with its enforcement. The critical role of motivation in hate crime law combined with the responsibility police have to determine the existence of motivation through their collection of the evidence means that closely examining the police may help us decide whether hatred is an area that the law can regulate effectively and whether bias crime legislation is the proper vehicle.

The Setting

This book evaluates how law works "on the ground," based on observations and interviews with victim advocates and those responsible for enforcing hate crime, prosecutors and police officers in "Center City," a large city in the United States. The study spanned the nine-month period from September 1997 to June 1998.

I have changed the city's actual name and some of its identifying details to preserve the anonymity of those I observed and interviewed. I promised anonymity to ensure that my respondents would feel free to reveal information that they might otherwise have been reluctant to disclose. Because of the small number of individuals responsible for prosecuting hate crime cases, some of my respondents would be readily identifiable if I were to use the city's actual name. I also wished to protect those who served at the pleasure of elected officials from job-related reprisals that could occur if what they said were revealed publicly.

Taking seriously this promise of confidentiality meant that in particular cases I have also disguised citations that would reveal the city. These include statute numbers for the state hate crime law and the actual names of the newspapers I cite. Given technological advances that put full-text computer searches of statutes at nearly everyone's disposal, I describe rather than quote statutes directly.

Newspapers have been given the following fictitious names: *Center City Daily News, Center City Tribune, Gertown Voice, Bayview City Herald,* and *Grangeville Star.* The *Center City Daily News* is a well-respected city daily, not only in Center City but also in many of the small towns around it. The *Center City Tribune,* the second-largest newspaper in the city, is a tabloid with a wide circulation. The *Gertown Voice* is a weekly community newspaper available only from stores in the Gertown neighborhood. Finally, the *Grangeville Star* and the *Bayview City Herald* are newspapers based in other cities that devote some coverage to life in Center City.

Demographics of Center City

Though I cannot provide the city's actual name, a few details about the city will provide a necessary context. Center City is a metropolitan city of between 500,000 and 900,000 residents. As its name implies, it serves as the center of business and industry for many of the smaller localities surrounding it. In 1990 the percentage of persons living below the poverty level in Center City was more than twice the statewide percentage, and the unemployment rate was higher than the state's average as well.[22] In 1990 more than 60 percent of Center City's residents were White. At that time, African Americans were the largest minority group in Center City, followed by people of Hispanic and Asian origin.[23] The city's history is described in Chapter 3.

I spent most of my time collecting data as a participant-observer of the detectives in the city's specialized hate crime unit, which I refer to by the fictitious name "Anti-Bias Task Force" (ABTF). From September of 1997 to February of 1998, the police department granted me open access to detectives in the unit, all of the unit's case files during its two-decade history, and most of the unit's records. I also had full access to the unit's office suite and the opportunity to observe the officers at work. I accompanied them on surveillance, watched them conduct investigations, and went with them to court, training, and meetings. A more detailed description of the study's methodology is discussed in the appendix.

Preview—What Cops in Fact Do

My research shows that hate crimes are made rather than solved. They are constructed, pieced together, and pass through several stages before hate crime charges can be brought against a suspect. Incidents are first constructed through investigation. Investigation is a complicated process in which officers use official procedures, routines, and practices to identify suspects and, generally speaking, "get to the bottom of things" as they sort out which individuals are lying and which are telling the truth. Getting to the truth is by no means an easy process because significant barriers from within and from outside the unit interfere with investigation. The most significant of these barriers consists of the political consequences for labeling an incident a hate crime. Policing hatred is a form of policing the community as police officers arrest members of the White majority for assaults and property damage done to minorities. The "politics of hate" influences nearly every stage of the process, including what gets reported, the help the unit receives to investigate incidents, whether witnesses come forward, whether the community and City Hall pressure the unit to investigate or not to investigate, and finally, the action the district attorney will take on a case. If an incident makes it through the investigation process without being dropped or classified as unfounded, it must then make it over a different set of hurdles when prosecutors and the courts come into play.

And what is the role of law? Though police are not completely free to ignore its dictates, the fate of law on the books is greatly influenced when the police readily use their power to infuse it with their own meanings. Though limited by social factors, such as training and routines, police discretion remains a key force in the decision to charge. Police possess as much power as they do for two related reasons. First, though the police have comparatively little power after cases leave their hands, the vast majority of reported crimes do not get evaluated by prosecutors. Because police encounter incidents first, they serve as gatekeepers with the discretion to discard incidents that prosecutors and judges will never see. Second, police discretion not to enforce hate crime law has low visibility. Detectives may deflect attention from their decisions by choosing a lower visibility way of not enforcing the law. Detectives' power to investigate crimes allows them to construct facts and define what the law is in a way that make sense to victims.

Defining the law in a way that serves victims is not the story we are used to hearing about police treatment of minorities. This book examines police-minority interaction in an entirely different context. Rather than focusing on patrol, it examines the use of race by detectives, including those who are women, Latino, Black, Asian, and/or gay. I found that many of the officers do the best they can to find justice for minorities who are victims of "the haters," as the detectives refer to perpetrators of hate crime. Rather than denying that hate or bias is a problem in Center City, the detectives identified conflict as racist, anti-Semitic, and anti-gay and -lesbian. Some of the White officers doing this work suffered personal and professional costs as a result. In some cases they lost the respect of the community in which they worked, and many were ostracized by the community of police officers.

How did the detectives decide whether hate crime law should be used? They adopted a series of routines and practices that allow them to separate the many non-bias-motivated crimes that they encounter from the bias-motivated ones. The practices that allow them to negotiate ambiguity in the law and in the actual crimes include the use of categorization and the examination of context when they evaluate events. As I discuss in more detail in chapter 7, the police officers rejected cases that fell into particular categories and closely scrutinized the context of the crime. These practices and others used during investigation allow the police to apply a working definition of hate crime.

Descending from the realm of high theory and the statute books and looking empirically at how the police actually enforce hate crime law reveal that First Amendment scholars and commentators in this area are asking the wrong questions and worrying about the wrong issues. Hate crimes are not ways for perpetrators to express their views but instead are used by dominant groups to maintain social hierarchy. Hate crime in Center City and many areas of the United States frequently occurs as people enter and leave their neighborhoods and as a result of "move-in" violence directed at people of color who have resettled in all-White areas. Like the southern judges who enforced the Supreme Court decision in *Brown v. Board of Education*, officers enforcing hate crime law are pitted against White residents who wish to remain in control of the face of their neighborhood. In this sense, enforcing civil rights is a form of policing the boundaries of small communities. The unit's enforcement of hate crime law not only speaks to the ability of police officers to enforce hate crime law but also testifies to the support of the principles embodied in civil rights decisions handed down nearly half a century ago. The book describes the difficulty of enforcing the promise of 1960s Supreme Court civil rights decisions governing the right to travel[24] and the right of equal access to housing.[25]

Organization of the Book

The rest of this work proceeds as follows. Chapter 2 describes the disciplinary questions that this book is designed to address by examining the framework of police decision-making. Chapter 3 provides a social history of Center City and describes how the city developed public policy and a legal response to bias-motivated violence. I turn to detective work in chapter 4, exploring how detectives investigate hate crimes. The difficulties of investigating crime in an area mobilized against the law and the forces in the community that complicate investigation are the focus of chapter 5. Police culture and police approaches to race and investigation are the subject of chapter 6. Chapter 7 focuses on officers' practices as they determine legal outcomes, including whether incidents should be charged as civil rights violations. Chapter 8 describes what happens after an incident leaves the detectives' hands, including the influences that other legal actors—the courts, district attorneys, and assistant attorneys general—have on whether suspects are charged with hate crimes. The book concludes with chapter 9, which details two policy recommendations regarding the discretion of ground-level enforcers and implementation and enforcement of hate crime law.

2

The Framework of Police Decision-Making in Hate Crime Cases

The Special Challenges of Enforcing Hate Crime Law

For both procedural and practical reasons, in hate crime cases the police play a critical role as criminal justice gatekeepers. Most bias-motivated violence and intimidation statutes have two parts. First, they require an underlying crime. Second, they require motivation in part by a proscribed hatred.[1] Thus, in order to charge individuals under these statutes, prosecutors must show evidence of bias motivation. As is so for most other crimes—murders, burglaries, rapes—it is the police who are responsible for investigating, building a case, and later identifying and classifying bias crimes. If the police determine a case to be a hate crime, they can request that criminal civil rights charges be issued. If they do not, it is unlikely that the suspect will ever be charged with bias crime violations. This task of classifying and identifying, or rather naming, is a powerful one. Since most bias-motivated incidents are first placed in other crime categories such as battery, assault, and vandalism, bias crimes do not exist in practice until the police say they do.

Enforcing bias crime legislation would be much easier if identifying bias crime were like identifying "regular" (i.e., non-bias-motivated) homicide.[2] When the police find a dead person—so long as they can determine that the individual's death was not accidental, and that he or she did not die as a result of natural causes, or by his or her own hand—they know by definition that a homicide has occurred. While both the type of homicide (murder or manslaughter) and the degree (first or second) may be in doubt, homicide is the only way to classify the death of one person caused by another. Identifying bias crime is more complicated on two levels: the factual and the political. Bias crimes require police officers to examine not only what happened, but also *why* it happened. Furthermore, the search for what happened is complicated by contested stories and by victims who are sometimes afraid to acknowledge the bias nature of the crime for fear of revictimization.

The job of classifying crimes as bias-motivated is also complicated by having to conduct hate crime investigations in a politically charged atmosphere. Some hate crimes can receive a significant amount of publicity. As a result, residents of the communities in which the crimes occur may worry about the police classifying crime as bias-motivated because they do not want their community to be seen as racist. Community leaders may appeal to their political allies, who in turn pressure the police chief not to prosecute the incident as a hate crime. At the same time, victim advocates may pressure the hate crime unit for a bias classification.

Consider the following real case from Center City. This example, taken from the files of the bias crime unit I studied, dramatizes many of the political dilemmas involved in bias crime investigation and classification. The case occurred in a community known for White-on-Black hate crime. The police were called when a fifteen-year-old White youth was shot in the buttocks. He asserted that he had been shot by a group of Black men. Community activists from the mostly White community demanded that the incident receive special attention from the bias crime unit to show that White victims receive the same treatment from the police as Black victims.

Detectives from the hate crime unit were called in to decide whether the state's hate crime law would be used. They interviewed White neighborhood activists who considered the crime a hate crime and demanded that the police bring the perpetrator to justice. The detectives also spoke with informants who, like many of the neighborhood's minority residents, insisted the incident was the result of drug deal gone bad, and therefore it should not be labeled a hate crime. The labeling of the crime had consequences for the victim, the defendant, and the community, as well as for the unit, whose credibility was at stake in the investigation. The police alone were faced with the task of official classification and sorting out the conflicting stories. In the end, the detectives discovered that the youth had placed a pistol in his pocket for protection during a meeting with drug dealers. During the transaction, the gun had discharged accidentally.

Making Decisions: The Policeman as Policy-Maker

Scholars of police decision-making have recognized the importance and inherent power of the decisions that the police make. Police have been characterized as policy makers and bureaucrats, responsible for making enforcement policy.[3] Because their day-to-day jobs are characterized by a high degree of discretion and autonomy, police often determine the amount and quality of benefits and sanctions to be dispensed to the public.[4] Like low-level bureaucrats in many other contexts, they work in environments with few controls, inadequate resources, and indeterminate objectives. Thus, police engage in political decision-making when they manage the conflicting goals inherent in dispensing the benefits of citizenship.[5]

Police discretion is shaped by the officers' work environment, their role in enforcing the criminal law, and statutory ambiguity. Police may take advantage of their work environment to satisfy their own personal and institutional goals.[6] Organizational pressures may provide incentives for police to fail to comply or to comply only minimally with the law. Police may not enforce the law because efficiency demands that limited resources be allocated to activities they believe more deserving of official action.[7] Institutional norms may support nonenforcement of particular laws against subgroups of the community, or in cases when the victim does not wish or refuses to aid in the prosecution of the crime.[8] Personal goals, such as protecting public respect for the police, may also lead the police not to enforce the law.[9]

Connected to the issue of officers' personal goals is the individual officer's own idea about how laws should be enforced. Police use their discretion to achieve what they perceive to be the law's substantive aims.[10] Officers may avoid invoking the law when they believe its application would be inappropriate or unfair. Aside from constraints imposed by limited resources, officers may ignore violations if they believe the application of the law will be ineffective or wasteful or if the cost of invoking the law will outweigh its benefits.[11] For instance, officers may turn a blind eye to informants' drug use for fear that informants will no longer be able to provide them with information if prosecuted.[12] Officers may also treat some deviations from lawful behavior such as drunkenness or speeding as trivial because they believe that the errant behavior is not serious or that a warning will suffice.[13]

In some cases the ambiguity of the police officer's role fosters discretion. Task-oriented ambiguity stems from charging the police with both the duty to enforce the law as well as the duty to preserve order. There is a tension between the duty to enforce the law and the duty to maintain social order.[14] In its purest sense, the rule of law requires rigid adherence to the letter of the criminal law, with conflicts and ambiguities to be resolved by consultation with the rules themselves.[15] The rules themselves, however, may not resolve the ambiguity. In practice, police officers encounter a variety of complex situations and must exercise their discretion to make decisions and rapid judgments based on their experience of what they consider appropriate rather than what is required by the logic of the rules.[16]

The job of the police officer is further complicated by ambiguity in the statutes and ordinances that police are charged with enforcing. Many statutes and local ordinances, though couched in permissive language, often impose a duty to enforce all law.[17] For instance, police must assume that laws, like sexual conduct laws or those that apply to victimless crime, for example, were created to reflect the ideals of society and not to be enforced.[18] Further ambiguity in the task of the police stems from broad language or laws in which the legislature fails to clearly define the conduct being proscribed.[19] In addition, laws such as those prohibiting gambling have loopholes that legislatures decline to eliminate for fear that doing so might inadvertently encompass legal behavior.[20]

Though all police officers have discretion, the contours of police discretion, or the ways in which an officer exercises it, may depend on the role that the officer plays in criminal law enforcement. In police departments uniformed patrol officers are generally responsible for maintaining order and for enforcing the law. Their duties include responding to citizen complaints, keeping the peace, and providing immediate assistance to those who need it.[21] Patrol officers' contact with citizens means that their discretion is located mainly in circumstances in their on-the-spot decisions about whether to invoke the law, and then to arrest violators, to administer a lesser sanction, or to do nothing.

Detectives, who may be located in specialized units responsible for the investigation of a single category of crime or who may investigate all crimes that occur in a particular area of the city, are responsible for investigating crimes referred to them by patrol. The range and scope of the discretion afforded detectives are different from that of patrol officers. In effect, detectives are granted control over information.[22] Detectives' decision-making tends not to be ad hoc. Rather, they create routines to process the information they receive from patrol officers. These routines are shaped by the need to conform to the law and to satisfy the community's pressure, pressure placed on them by others in the police department, and the detectives' own organizational culture.[23] Routines allow the detectives to assign particular meanings to events. This book is about the routines that detectives use to make hate crime.

For detectives, as with other police officers, low visibility leads to little accountability and consequently a large amount of discretion. "Detectives employ the authority of their office, situated strategies, and the low-visibility conditions of their work to obtain and use information provided by citizens."[24] In a job characterized by little supervision, individual detectives have the power to aggressively or minimally investigate cases referred to them. They can, and studies have shown quite frequently that they do, choose not to investigate cases at all.[25]

The Parameters of Hate Crime Law

In most jurisdictions that have some type of hate crime law, police are responsible for enforcing bias-motivated violence and intimidation statutes. These statutes, on the books in forty-one states, generally do one of the following: (1) make bias-motivated violence or intimidation a separate crime—either alone or when it is accompanied by another criminal offense; (2) enhance the penalty for crimes motivated by forbidden prejudices; or (3) define bias crimes as civil rights violations.[26] Most of these statutes prohibit violence or harassment because of a protected status. The most common protected statuses are race, color, religion, and national origin. Some state statutes include disability and gender. Several state hate crime statutes include sexual orientation as well.[27]

Bias-motivated violence and intimidation statutes are not the only hate crime statutes that police enforce. Depending on the incident and the law in the jurisdiction where the crime was committed, prosecutors may charge individuals who have committed a bias-motivated crime under a statute that prohibits cross burning, an institutional vandalism statute that prohibits the vandalism and defacement of churches, synagogues, schools, and other institutions, or an antimask statute that penalizes wearing a mask, hood, or disguise while in public.

Regardless of the form that hate crime legislation takes, prosecution under bias-motivated violence and intimidation laws or the enactment of additional penalties require evidence that bias-motivated the crime. Evidence of motivation may take a variety of forms. For bias-motivated assaults, for example, such evidence could consist of statements made by the perpetrator prior to or during the attack. Evidence could also be in the form of a pattern of unexplained attacks of a similar type by the perpetrator. The perpetrator's membership in a hate organization could also be used as evidence that the crime was motivated by bias. Evidence of bias-motivated intimidation or property damage could include words or symbols left by the perpetrator. Because statements or symbols that serve as evidence of motivation are "speech" or expression in hate crime cases, critics of hate crime legislation believe that such laws violate perpetrators' First Amendment rights.

A Constitutional Fine Line

The police enforcing hate crime law must grapple with the fine constitutional line between hate crime and hate speech. The Supreme Court cases in this area are confusing and, some argue, contradictory.[28] The Court's decision in a 1992 case, *R.A.V. v. City of St. Paul*, suggested that hate crimes are difficult to identify because they are so closely linked to politically protected speech.[29] That case examined the conviction of Robert Viktora, who burned a cross on the front lawn of the Joneses, a Black family who had recently moved to an all-White neighborhood. Viktora was convicted under the St. Paul Bias Motive Crime Ordinance, which prohibited the placement of any object, such as a burning cross or a swastika, that one has reason to know arouses anger or alarm in others on the basis of race, color, creed, or gender.[30] He challenged his conviction on First Amendment grounds, arguing the statute was overbroad and impermissibly content based. On appeal, the Minnesota Supreme Court rejected the defendant's claim but limited the ordinance to expressions of fighting words within the meaning of *Chaplinsky v. New Hampshire*.[31] In *Chaplinsky* the United States

Supreme Court declined to extend First Amendment protection to "fighting words" or "words which by their very utterance inflict injury or tend to incite an immediate breach of the peace."[32]

The U.S. Supreme Court reversed the Minnesota Supreme Court's decision. Justice Scalia, who wrote the majority opinion, argued that by not criminalizing all fighting words, the Minnesota statute was clearly attempting to isolate certain words based on their political content.[33] Calling the statute's singling out of fighting words based on race, color, creed, and gender "viewpoint discrimination,"[34] Scalia insisted, "St. Paul has no such authority to license one side of a debate to fight freestyle, while requiring the other to follow the Marquis of Queensberry rules."[35] The Court also held that the city's desire to communicate to the minority population its condemnation of the message in bias-motivated speech was insufficient to justify a content-based ordinance.[36] Although the Court found St. Paul's interests compelling, it deemed the ordinance not reasonably necessary, maintaining that "[a]n ordinance not limited to the favored topics . . . would have had the same beneficial effect."[37]

Less than one year later, apparently in light of much confusion among the states' high courts on the constitutionality of penalty enhancement statutes,[38] the Court elected to rule on another bias crime case, *Wisconsin v. Mitchell.*[39] In this case, after viewing the movie *Mississippi Burning*, the defendant, Todd Mitchell, who was Black, incited a group to attack a fourteen-year-old White youth.[40] Mitchell was convicted under Wisconsin's bias crime statute, which provided that the penalty for crimes be increased if the victim was selected because of the actor's belief or perception regarding the victim's race, religion, color, disability, sexual orientation, national origin, or ancestry.[41] Because the jury found that the victim had been selected because of his race, Mitchell's sentence was increased to the maximum penalty: seven years.[42]

Mitchell challenged his conviction on Fourteenth Amendment grounds, arguing that the Wisconsin statute was overbroad, and that providing enhanced penalties whenever a defendant intentionally selects a victim on the basis of race, violated First Amendment rights.[43] On appeal, relying on *R.A.V.*, the Wisconsin Supreme Court held that the statute violated the First Amendment by punishing offensive thought and by chilling speech.[44]

In a move that surprised many, in *Wisconsin v. Mitchell*, the Supreme Court reversed the Wisconsin Supreme Court's decision, insisting that both the punishment of Mitchell's discriminatory conduct and the use of Mitchell's speech as evidence of discriminatory motive was permissible.[45] The Court held out as examples two other contexts where the perpetrator's motive was considered—the sentencing of aggravated crimes, and state and federal antidiscrimination law.[46] To assign a harsher penalty when the defendant has selected his victims for discriminatory reasons is consistent with other contexts and does not violate the First Amendment.[47] The Court insisted that the state of Wisconsin's desire to prevent harm caused by bias-motivated conduct provides evidence that the penalty enhancement statute is not based on disagreement with the offender's protected beliefs.[48]

It seems clear that in deciding to uphold the use of speech as evidence of motivation, the Court did not intend to allow jurisdictions to criminalize pure hate speech. In *Wisconsin v. Mitchell* there are two signs that pure hate speech remains protected. First, the Court explicitly declined to overrule two of its earlier cases that provided protection for hate speech, *R.A.V.* and *Dawson v. Delaware*. Relative to the former, the Court declined to overrule *R.A.V.*, declaring that the ordinance at issue "was explicitly directed at the expression" (that is, speech or messages).[49] Here, the Court seems to try to draw a line between punishing the speech and punishing motivation.

Second, the Court appeared to suggest that First Amendment protection exists for hate speech or, at least, the expression of biased ideas when it argued, "[A] defendant's abstract beliefs, however obnoxious to most people, may not be taken into consideration by a sentencing judge."[50] The Court supported this proposition with *Dawson v. Delaware*, a case decided the term before, in which the Court held that the introduction of evidence that the defendant was a member of a White supremacist gang violated his First Amendment rights.[51] One principle that emerges from these cases is that the state may punish discriminatory conduct but may not single out hate speech for punishment. Thus, as long as it is discriminatory *conduct* being punished, speech may be used as evidence of motivation.

Can the Police Unravel Motivation?

The constitutional enforcement of hate crime law thus involves the police searching for motivation rather than charging individuals with hate crimes merely for using racist or other bias-motivated speech. In analyzing how enforcers of hate crime law really behave, some critics of hate crime legislation have questioned the ability of those enforcing these laws to uncover perpetrators' motivation. Several of these scholars suggest that bias motivation is something hidden, difficult to disentangle, or otherwise impossible to discern. One writes, "Assessing motive presents more than the problem of somehow reading the defendant's mind, for the defendant himself may not know his true motive. Social psychology is full of research that demonstrates people are unaware of what is truly influencing their behavior."[52] In critics' eyes the slippery nature of bias motivation means that law enforcers will be forced to search for evidence of the crime's motivation by looking to cues from words or associations that are protected by the First Amendment.[53]

The search for evidence of bias motivation would most logically begin with what was said during the crime. Critics are fearful that enforcers will use the defendant's biased utterances (or symbols, in the case of property crimes) during the commission of the crime as the only evidence of bias motivation. They argue that if enforcers use words alone as evidence of bias motivation, this punishes the defendant for saying the words, thereby obviating the First Amendment protection for bigoted beliefs.[54] Susan Gellman, a staunch critic of bias crime legislation, implies that the arbitrariness of racial epithets make it nearly impossible to separate bias crimes from those not motivated by bias.[55] With enforcers scrutinizing the words uttered during the incident as evidence of hate motivation, critics worry that many with constitutionally benign motives would be penalized under hate crime laws because enforcers are not able to disentangle criminal action from protected expression of speech or thought.[56]

Critics of hate crime legislation raise an important issue here. *Wisconsin v. Mitchell* is silent on the question of whether it is acceptable to charge persons with hate crime in cases where words are the *only* evidence of motivation. Allowing an additional punishment just for using hate speech when committing an assault, seems inconsistent with the protection for hate speech the Court granted in *R.A.V.* and *Dawson*.

To bolster the argument that hate crimes are impossible to identify, critics' articles are replete with "hard cases" that seem clearly unintended by the law but have been allegedly punished as hate crimes.

Gellman provides an example that she says will fall within the ambit of the bias crime statutes, even though the alleged perpetrator had benign motives. Her hard case involves a "racial champion," White woman A, who, hearing White woman B calling C, an African American child, a racist name, threatens B in an attempt to protect C.[57] Gellman suggests that under many hate crime statutes ambiguous cases like the one she created could be prosecuted as hate crime. One real case, widely cited by critics, involved a Black Florida man who was charged with a hate crime after he called a policeman trying to break up a domestic disturbance a "cracker."[58] That defendant, one critic writes, "clearly was not motivated to commit his crime because of the policeman's race . . . His name-calling is not being used as evidence he was hate motivated. Instead, he is being prosecuted for evidencing prejudice by calling the officer a racial epithet."[59] Hate crime charges against the man were later dropped.[60]

In addition to charging ambiguity and unintended consequences, critics of bias crime legislation charge that the problem with classifying some crimes as bias-motivated and others as not bias-motivated creates another First Amendment problem: one of overbreadth leading to the chilling of speech, thought, and association. Although the Court rejected this argument as too attenuated in *Mitchell*, scholars have expressed the concern that enforcers will investigate not just the defendant's words or actions during the crime but also "all of his or her remarks upon earlier occasions, any books ever read, any speakers ever listened to, or associations ever held."[61] The Court did not specify in *Mitchell* how far back one might go in seeking evidence of motivation or what might count as evidence of motivation in a bias crime case. One scholar worries that racist jokes will be used as evidence of guilt.[62]

That police have criteria for identifying bias motivation does not satisfy those concerned about the enforcement. James Jacobs criticizes the extensive criteria used by officers in the New York City's Bias Investigating Unit, writing that they are "so broad and loose that practically any intergroup offense could be plausibly labeled a hate crime."[63] Jacobs also complains that the criteria do not tell officers how much to weigh the testimony of thin-skinned victims, who, he insists, may be especially sensitive to "any negative encounter with a member of another group."[64] The victim's perspective is also in doubt because, as Jacobs points out, the victim may himself be "a racist, homophobe, or holder of another bias."[65] The combination of inadequate criteria and police discretion to enforce the laws is not lost on other critics, who frequently raise the question of selective or differential enforcement of hate crime legislation against minorities.[66]

Empirical Difficulties: Policing Free Speech or Enforcing Bias Crime Legislation?

As discussed above, hate crime laws themselves are difficult to enforce because motivation is an element of the crime, and most hate crime statutes contain no definition of what constitutes evidence of bias motivation.[67] Nor do state statutes supply a procedure for identifying motivation or criteria for acceptable evidence of motivation. Police officers must guess at what counts and what will hold up in court.

The social-psychological literature also suggests that identifying motivation may present problems. The work of several scholars argues that motivation is quite complex and that perpetrators may act out of a variety of motivations.[68] One study of perpetrator motivation implies that police officers' search for motivation is made more difficult by the different types of motivation. The study identified four types of hate crimes: (1) those motivated by resentment; (2) those done "for the thrill of it"; (3) reactive hate crimes; and (4) mission hate crimes.[69] Hate crimes motivated by resentment increased in the 1980s as downward mobility led many people to look for someone on whom to blame their misfortune.[70] Those who commit hate crimes for the thrill perform utterly random attacks for the enjoyment and exhilaration of making others suffer.[71] Reactive hate crimes are motivated by the personal threat posed by outsiders' entrance into a previously homogenous area.[72] Finally, the rarest type of hate crime, mission hate crimes, often perpetrated by members of organized hate groups, are characterized by a desire to rid the world of all members of a particular group.[73] In the perpetrator's mind, members of the targeted group are subhuman and must be eliminated to prevent them from destroying the perpetrator's culture, economy, or purity of racial heritage.[74]

Successful investigation depends on the ability to tailor the investigation to the type of hate crime committed.[75] For example, a hate crime motivated by excitement is likely to be committed by a group of young, White men without criminal records who live in an area different from the one in which the crime occurred. By contrast, perpetrators of reactive crimes, whose bigotry is more likely to be known, tend to live in the same area in which the crime was committed.[76]

The victim's behavior and officers' occasional inability to use victim testimony as a reliable account of the event can further confound officers trying to identify bias motivation. Victims may refuse or be unable to recognize that a hate crime has occurred, which may slow bias crime identification.[77] Victims often look to reasons other than their membership in a particular group to explain their victimization since, if their attack was based on their group identity, they can do nothing to reduce their chances of future victimization.[78] The common problems with victims' accounts—that they may be mistaken, that they may hold personal biases that affect their judgments, that they may have misperceived the incident—take on heightened importance when the perpetrator's motivation is a crucial element of the crime.[79]

The final, and most nuanced, difficulty with enforcement patterns is a problem with under, rather than over, enforcement of the law. One scholar argues that enforcers may be applying hate crime law only to a narrow range of cases in which "it appears the defendant felt and acted upon personal hostility or animus toward the victim's social group."[80] In doing this, enforcers may be ignoring cases in which opportunistic perpetrators selected victims because the victims' protected characteristics increase their vulnerability.[81] For example, an opportunistic perpetrator may select victims of a particular race because he or she believes that this group is less likely to report the crime to the police. Under this reasoning, police might also ignore cases in which the perpetrator chooses to commit a crime in order to provoke a reaction, such as someone who vandalizes a synagogue in order to shock the congregation.[82] If officers are restricting their application of hate crime law in this way, they may be missing crimes that would be important to classify and capture under hate crime law.

The evidence from the field gives cause for further concern regarding what enforcers are actually doing when they enforce hate crime. One study, by Elizabeth Boyd, Richard Berk, and Karl Hamner, of detectives who classify hate crime in a large police department revealed that police resist enforcing hate crime law. According to this study, the general perception among the majority of officers was that "only a few crimes could 'really' be called hate motivated, such as a cross burning on the lawn of an African American family or the organized activities of the KKK or Aryan Nation."[83] The authors of the study found that police at all levels—patrol officers, detectives, and commanding officers—expressed resentment of the departmental policy giving priority to hate crimes. Officers in the study dismissed hate crimes as "overkill," "mostly bull," "a pain in the ass," "media hype,""a giant cluster fuck.'"[84] Even those who did think that hate crimes were a problem did not feel that hate crimes deserved priority over what they considered "real" crime: burglary, theft, and rape.[85] The detectives' belief that hate crimes did not really happen in the city translated into two different, though equally disturbing, types of behavior. Detectives in "Division A" categorized only cases marked by the clearest signs of bias as "normal hate crimes," such as cases with racial epithets, those with symbols of hate, and those involving hate groups. The detectives in "Division A" rejected all cases that did not have those features.[86] Those in "Division B" ignored the issue of motivation altogether. They focused solely on the facts of the crime, classifying incidents as hate crimes without inquiry into whether they were actually motivated by bias.[87]

The behavior of both groups of detectives has troubling implications for the enforcement of hate crime law in all applicable situations. In "Division B," cases which are not bias-motivated may be identified as hate crimes. This is a problem both for the area's statistics and for the prosecution of hate crime cases. The detectives in "Division B" left it up to the district attorney (DA) to determine the perpetrator's motivation.[88] If the detective has conducted little or no inquiry in this area, the DA may have little evidence from which to draw conclusions regarding the perpetrator's motivation. In "Division A," adopting the normal hate crime typification may mean that detectives miss crimes that do fall under the law but that do not contain extreme manifestations of bias.

Another study, of bias units in New York City and Baltimore, raises different questions about the enforcement of hate crime law. The authors indicate that in a number of cases the primacy of the element of bias was ambiguous and that often the police have to deal with cases that seem to contain bias as a secondary motivation or an additional motivation. Another issue that affects the classification of an incident includes the weight the officers accorded the victim's perception relative to other factors and whom to believe when there are conflicting stories.[89] These issues are important, but unfortunately the study does not describe in detail how police address them.

News reports from around the country seem to support the idea that officers find the situations in which hate crimes occur ambiguous.[90] One detective from the New York City Police Department is quoted as saying, "I hate these cases because they become real mysteries. . . . [E]verybody jumps on the bandwagon but nobody has the facts."[91] In cases that are ambiguous, officers question whether the perpetrator's motivation is bias or a prank and whether the incidents are aimed at a particular victim. Are such ambiguous cases the exceptions or, as many critics of bias crime legislation would have us believe, the rule? Is it possible for police to sort out these difficulties? The existing literature is silent on the matter.

Conclusion: Unanswered Questions

The literatures evaluating constitutional principles and police behavior outlined above raise important questions about hate crime law enforcement that social scientists and legal scholars have largely failed to consider. Part of this failure results from the characteristic focus of each group. In evaluating statutes and laws, many legal scholars assume that "higher" law—constitutional law—resides exclusively in courts, and thus the power to enforce this type of law belongs only to judges and prosecutors. With the exception of the Fourth Amendment context, legal scholars rarely investigate how law is enforced "on the ground" by street-level bureaucrats such as the police. Disregarding what happens in low-level enforcement leaves most constitutional critics free to conclude on the basis of anecdotal evidence or in imagined worst-case scenarios that one cannot separate bias-motivated actions from politically protected expression, and therefore that hate crime laws should be abolished. Their claims of impossible enforcement of these laws have not been tested empirically in light of any actual cases. Are police making the distinction between politically "protected expression" and bias motivation? The constitutional literature does not tell us and does not even think to ask the question in anything but a hypothetical way.

Police scholarship is better at evaluating enforcement because it discusses the power of the police not to enforce the law and because it tells us more about the crucial role the police play as criminal justice gatekeepers. It too, however, has very serious failings. First, the literature's detailed picture of police culture and police decision-making says little about the force and power of law and the extent to which law on the books binds police officers. How much law do police know? What role does the law play in their investigation? What are the scope and contours of police discretion with respect to the law? The social science literature is largely silent on this issue.

The nonenforcement literature raises serious normative problems of interest. Many scholars portray nonenforcement of the law benignly, as a good thing. Police use it to cut down inefficiencies in the law, to level social and cultural inequalities, and to protect us from laws that legislators have passed that we as a society do not want enforced, at least not in those circumstances (or against *that* group of people). An officer's deciding, for example, that he will use the loitering law to arrest only "suspicious characters" and not "bums" is clearly a form of deciding what the law is. [92]

Many political scientists and legal scholars, particularly those who study constitutional law, however, find the idea of a nonelected group of individuals making law quite a bit more problematic than police scholars appear to.[93] If the United States Supreme Court has tenuous lawmaking authority to second guess or correct the mistakes of legislatures, then police officers, who have little knowledge of the law and usually much more distant relationships to elected officials, have even less. If police officers are enforcing hate crime laws specifically designed to combat bias-motivated violence only when they themselves (and not the statute) deem hate crime laws should be so used, perhaps our state and local governments are not functioning as democratically as we think they are.

As an empirical study of how hate crime law is enforced, this book addresses the questions left unanswered by the First Amendment literature on hate crime and the scholarship on police decision-making. In attempting to fill the significant gap in both literatures created by the problem of hate crime enforcement, this book evaluates how police deal with complexity and vagueness as they enforce hate crime law. I identify not only the procedural structures that police adopt to cope with the vagueness of hate crime law but also the informal routines and practices that they use to give meaning to legal abstraction.

As a study of how hate crime law is enforced, this book provides a wide-angled view of the system out of which actual hate crime charges emerge. This system includes those in the criminal justice system—

police, prosecutors, judges and juries—as well as residents of the communities in which these incidents take place, members of the advocacy community, and the news media. Each of these actors has some role in making hate crime. By capturing the struggles and the influence of all of these actors, this book is also a description of politics and, ultimately, power—the power of police to define racism, anti-Semitism, and antigay and -lesbian bias, the powerlessness of victims, and the power of communities allied against the enforcement of laws designed to protect victims' civil rights.

3

Integration and Hate Crime
The Institutionalization of Civil Rights Law

In 1990 the Joneses, a Black family, moved into a house in a mostly working-class White neighborhood in St. Paul, Minnesota. In the first month after the Joneses moved in the tires of their car were slashed. The second month, the tailgate of their brand new station wagon was broken. A few weeks later, a young White man called the Joneses son a "nigger" as he was walking down their street. Three months after they moved in a large cross was burned in their front yard. Later the same night, another cross was burned in front of the apartment building across the street from their house. As one of very few Black families in the neighborhood, the Joneses were frightened and felt very vulnerable. The local police to whom they turned for protection did little to help them.[1]

In most cities incidents of harassment such as that directed at the Jones family would be referred to police officers assigned to the area in which the incident occurred and, like most low-level crimes—crimes without serious injuries—would not be investigated. Though the FBI pressures state and local police departments to report hate crimes, they are not required to have specialized hate crime units. Departments have complete discretion over the institutional mechanisms they create to enforce hate crime law. In fact, perhaps fearing that a hate crime unit's statistics will dramatize the level of racism, homophobia, and anti-Semitism in a city, departments rarely establish specialized hate crime units. Fewer than 10 percent of police departments of more than one hundred officers have a specialized unit staffed by full-time personnel devoted to the investigation of bias crime.[2] Most police departments, even those in jurisdictions with hate crime laws, have not established specialized units devoted to enforcing hate crime laws or collecting hate crime statistics.

In the 1970s minorities moving into all-White neighborhoods in Center City began to experience harassment similar to that which the Jones family experienced. In response, the Center City Police Department (CCPD) established a specialized detective unit called the Anti-Bias Task Force (ABTF). The only job of the ABTF was to investigate bias-motivated incidents. Two years after the unit was established, the state passed a law specifically aimed at bias-motivated violence. After a general introduction to the problem of integration and hate crime, this chapter addresses the development, use, and acceptance of hate crime law, exploring the particular circumstances that led to the laws and the policy positions that the city adopted.

Bias Crime and Integration

The Fair Housing Act of Title VIII of the Civil Rights Act of 1968 was enacted to ensure all citizens the right to live in the neighborhood of their choice.[3] Decades after the passage of the act and other laws attempting to prevent and punish housing discrimination, that right meant little to many minorities attempting to integrate neighborhoods. Despite court decisions[4] and state and federal laws forbidding discrimination in the sale or rental of housing, and the section of the Fair Housing Act specifically aimed at punishing racially motivated intimidation of individuals in their homes,[5] in many areas Whites remained determined to keep minorities from living in "their" neighborhoods.

"White flight" and White Americans' lack of desire to live with Blacks have been cited as an important cause of substantial residential segregation—and thus the failure of the Fair Housing Act's integrationist aim in many cities. The impact of White violence on residential segregation is far less discussed. In neighborhoods around the country, some of the White residents who remained in "their" neighborhoods resorted to violence—bombings, arson, battery, vandalism, and harassment—to drive the intruders away. In Cleveland, Detroit, Boston, Chicago, and other cities, minority newcomers to neighborhoods faced organized violent opposition to their presence as residents sought to "collectively establish and enforce an extralegal 'right' to practice racial discrimination."[6]

Neither civil rights law designed to protect the rights of minorities integrating all-White neighborhoods nor the local police have been of much help to those who faced violence. For instance, in 1976 Alva and Otis Debnam were met with a constant barrage of bottles, bricks, and rocks thrown through the windows of their new home after they moved to an all-White neighborhood in Boston. Their car was fire-bombed, and they were harassed by White youths who shouted racial epithets. The local police responded when called but insisted that unless the Debnams provided them with names, addresses, or at least detailed descriptions of their assailants, there was nothing the police could do.[7] The violence families like the Joneses and the Debnams experienced not only encouraged minorities who moved in to leave but also helped deter other minorities considering moving to White neighborhoods.

In the 1990s, with the increasing passage of local and state hate crime laws, incidents of violence directed against minorities in and around their homes began to be recognized as hate crimes. Though the link between resistance to integration and hate crime is not widely recognized by scholars, in several cities a significant percentage of the reported hate crime citywide occurs in "changing" neighborhoods. For instance, in Chicago between 1985 and 1990, half of the 1,129 incidents reported as hate crimes occurred in ten communities undergoing racial change.[8] In Los Angeles, 60 percent of the racially motivated hate crimes reported to the city's Human Relations Commission were directed at Blacks, and 70 percent occurred at the victim's residence. Often referred to as "move-in" violence, research describes similar violence faced by Blacks moving into White neighborhoods in the 1980s and 1990s in Philadelphia, Boston, and New York City.[9] For example, a study of 365 cases investigated by the hate crimes unit of the Boston Police Department revealed that the third-most-frequent reason for hate crime was "moving to a neighborhood."[10]

Empirical work has shown a link between racially motivated crime and changing demographics. One study of bias-motivated crime in the 1980s and 1990s in New York City found that increases in anti-Black, Latino, and Asian crime tracked moves of each of these groups into White strongholds.[11] In this study the cause of such an extreme reaction to neighborhood change was not known but the researchers speculated that racism, nostalgia, and self-interest, "in conjunction with exclusionary sentiment and tacit support (or active encouragement) of neighbors leads to a heightened propensity for action when neighborhoods are threatened."[12]

A number of other researchers have documented community support for racist acts committed by the perpetrators of anti-integrationist violence.[13] The rhetoric of many the White ethnics—Jews, Italians, Irish, and Poles—who dominate these neighborhoods shows that they view the communities in which they live as belonging to their own ethnic or racial group, and thus resent the influx of Blacks and other minorities. Many either tacitly or openly endorsed violence aimed at forcing out newcomers and discouraging others from moving in. Perpetrators could thus engage in acts "in defense of their neighborhood" encouraged by neighbors who either looked the other way or directly supported them.[14]

Racist harassment aimed at people in their residences can include assaults, vandalism, threats, cross burnings, and arson. Unless the police department has established a specialized unit to deal with the crimes, they are investigated by district or "sector" detectives, who are responsible for investigating most crime in the area in which it occurred. If the incident is referred to these detectives, the incident is unlikely to be investigated. There are two reasons for this failure. First, studies show that only about one-half of the incidents reported to the police receive more than minimal investigation.[15] Second, from a law enforcement perspective, many incidents that new residents encounter are low-level crimes, and the detectives to whom they are referred are responsible for investigating a host of other incidents—burglaries, assaults that result in serious injuries, drug crimes—to which the police assign a higher priority. In the unlikely event the incidents were investigated and suspects were caught, or if the city or state does not have a specialized legal mechanism for prosecuting these incidents, then they would be prosecuted under the criminal law prohibiting assault, trespass, vandalism, and the like, not as hate crimes.

Segregation in Center City

The story of the development of hate crime law and the creation of a bias unit in Center City begins with the backlash against integration. The bias unit was formed in 1978 in response to the social unrest that began in the mid-1970s in Center City. The roots of the social unrest lie in demographic shifts that began occurring in the 1950s and 1960s, when many of the city's White upper-middle-class professionals, fleeing crime, high taxes, and high rents moved from the city to the bordering suburbs, bedroom communities, and small towns. The White professionals who moved out left behind many working-class Italians, Jews, and Irish. Unemployment was particularly high among those working-class Whites who could not afford to leave Center City, where they were concentrated in several ethnic neighborhoods.

Like many other large cities, Center City has a long history of residential segregation along ethnic lines. Many ancestors of the Jews, Poles, Irish, and Italians who had composed a majority of Center City's residents by the late 1960s had immigrated to the city in the mid-1800s, settling in ethnic enclaves. Over decades, the locations of the ethnic enclaves changed; some groups who gained prosperity moved to better areas of the city, while newly arrived immigrants from Asia and Latin America and Blacks from the American South moved into the spaces that departing Whites left behind. Even in the 1960s, however, residential segregation remained quite rigid. Different ethnic groups dominated particular areas of the city. Several areas were mainly Irish, and a couple of neighborhoods were Italian and Hispanic. By the 1970s, one neighborhood that had once been Irish and Jewish had become primarily African American. Despite some resentment at being unable to leave the city, White ethnic residents in these areas were fiercely loyal to their close-knit, homogeneous communities. In fact, these ethnic neighborhoods were more like tiny cities or boroughs within Center City, with their own shopping areas, restaurants, churches, sports teams, citizens' councils, and newspapers. City dwellers, especially minorities, kept to their own sections of town.

Center City residents were fierce defenders of intrusions into their turf. Center City Italians, for example, would walk blocks out of their way to avoid the Irish section of town. If one were caught in the "wrong" section, one had either to be able to run or know how to fight. Reflecting the city's ongoing racial tension, the president of the Center City NAACP remembered what African Americans experienced in the 1950s:

> You'd always have to fight your way back home. . . . The Irish kids out there said that that's their turf and the young Blacks said it's the public's turf and so from the time I was a kid hopping the streetcar to go out to the City Point we'd always fight our way back. The only difference between then and now was that it wasn't as violent and they didn't use knives and guns.[16]

The minority population in Center City rose significantly between 1950 and 1970. Family members advised new arrivals which neighborhoods they must avoid, at all costs. One woman, who never went to the stores in her neighborhood, told a reporter that she had also adjusted her route to work, driving twenty minutes out of her way to avoid a certain neighborhood. A White coworker took her home once, when her car was being repaired, and drove through the neighborhood. "A bunch of kids started jumping all over the car. . . . That woman never did offer me a ride again," she said.[17]

Despite these types of incidents, Center City experienced little large-scale social unrest until a federal judge ordered that schoolchildren be bused to end the de facto segregation of Center City schools in the early 1970s. As it had in cities throughout the country, school desegregation sparked several incidents, many of them violent, in Black and White neighborhoods throughout the city. Whites, Blacks, and other minorities traveling though one another's neighborhoods ran the risk of being stoned at best, killed at worst.

In "Gertown," a working-class Irish neighborhood, residents opposed to school desegregation organized numerous marches and protests against the court-ordered busing. Newspapers and television cameras captured pictures of residents throwing rocks at school buses. To deal with the violence, the police department created a special police unit, and at one point, state troopers had to be called in to protect schoolchildren. Though Gertown's opposition was the most widely publicized, residents in other neighborhoods in the city were opposed to school desegregation, too. The outward signs of the opposition to busing died down within two years, but residents of Gertown and other small, close-knit ethnic communities remembered what they called "forced busing" and remained bitter about it for years to come.

The Backlash against Housing Desegregation

At roughly the same time that school desegregation was taking place, African Americans and other minorities began moving into all-White areas. White flight, caused in part by school desegregation and the city's mounting crime rate, increased. As in cities and suburbs across the country in the mid-seventies, blockbusting was common. Homeowners were induced by opportunistic real estate agents to sell their homes quickly for fear that as the neighborhood "darkened," their homes would be worth less and less. Many of the Whites who remained reacted violently to changes in the racial composition of the neighborhoods. Within days and sometimes hours of moving into all-White neighborhoods, Center City minorities were subjected to harassment. Eggs or rocks were thrown at newcomers' houses, they were physically assaulted, racial taunts were directed at family members, some of their houses were firebombed, and many suffered multiple acts of vandalism to their cars.

The experiences of one Black resident and her family vividly illustrate what happened when minorities moved into working-class White neighborhoods in Center City. Mrs. "A" wrote the mayor:

> Dear Sir,
>
> In this letter I am stating grievances that I wish to grieve against the local neighborhood racist hoodlums, and the policemen who work in District A. . . . For the last two years until now there has been continuous harassment from racist hoodlums. They constantly threaten us every day of the week.[18]

In her letter, Mrs. A described incidents spanning nearly two years— rocks thrown through the windows of her family's home and car, nightly verbal harassment from the neighborhood, and countless threats, including one to burn down the family's home. Calls to the local police responsible for investigating the crime were fruitless. The local police, the victim asserted, were slow to respond. The officers, she wrote, "had shown us that they want no part in the investigation or apprehension of these hoodlums." Secure in the knowledge that the police would do nothing, the neighborhood youth perpetrators were not afraid of them. "Many of these hoodlums have gone as far as to open our gate and walk right into our yard, ring our doorbell and tell us to call the police." She asked:

> To whom can I beg for legal protection. Mayor, you inferred in many of your pre-election speeches that all citizens in Center City would have adequate police protection when they feared that their lives were in danger, regardless of their ethnic background. Perhaps the local law enforcers who work in District A misunderstood your statements, because they have made me feel that I have no right to assume that investigating the

incidents of verbal harassment and vandalism to my property is their responsibility to me. I have called the police in District A numerous times for their assistance and several times they did not respond.

Mrs. A's experiences were not unusual. Minorities moving into Center City would move in only to be "crimed" out. Homeowners replaced windows one day, only to have them broken the next evening. Coping with the expense as well as the fear caused by the harassment was too much for many families. Those in market-rate housing moved; those in public housing requested emergency transfers out of White developments. The Center City Public Housing Office (CHO), the authority in charge of public housing, moved 250 Blacks into two all-White housing developments in the early seventies. A decade later, only two remained.[19]

After a number of well-publicized incidents of racial harassment in housing developments that nearly started riots, the commissioner of police asked his staff to investigate the scope of the city's racial unrest. Drawing their sample from police reports, staff members interviewed victims of incidents that had occurred in housing developments. For many in the police department, the results were unanticipated: the problem was much more extensive than they had imagined. One member of the ABTF recalled conducting interviews with victims and discovering that additional incidents, some of which were serious, had occurred and had not been reported to the police.

> There were lots of incidents that no one knew about, racial violence in neighborhoods.
> I went to the Reports Bureau. I looked at all the reports marked "racial incident." . . . I saw a pattern developing. This was just the tip of the iceberg. There was a discernible pattern. I'd call people and ask if I could talk to them. They were very frightened. It was very ugly.

After investigating several incidents, staff members found that other minorities moving into White neighborhoods had had experiences similar to that of Mrs. A. The neighborhood police officers had been slow to respond and, when they did, were diffident and unhelpful.

The slow response that Mrs. A and other victims of racially motivated violence experienced was emblematic of the treatment of low-level incidents—vandalism, simple assaults, and similar crimes—in Center City and other cities that respond to crimes according to their severity. Like police departments across the country, the CCPD used a

Computer Aided Dispatch (CAD) system that automatically ranked requests for police services relative to the threat of physical injury or death. Crimes in progress, such as homicides and rapes, were given the highest priority (priority one) and received the quickest response. Thefts and stolen cars were priority two, and calls about unruly neighbors, vandalism, and abandoned cars were the lowest priority, priority three. In Center City, as in other places, many of the incidents that hate crime victims reported consisted of vandalism and verbal threats. Bias-motivated violence rarely involved serious physical injuries and frequently was accorded the lowest priority by the system and the neighborhood precinct.

The department's deployment of officers prevented hate crime victims from receiving services. For efficiency, as in many police departments, the city was geographically divided into districts. Each district contained a station staffed with patrol officers, supervisors, and detectives who were primarily responsible for crime control and responding to calls for service from within their district. Officers had some choice over the district to which they were assigned. In the all-White neighborhoods where many of the bias-motivated incidents in the 1980s and 1990s had occurred, most of the officers who responded to minorities' calls were White. Some of these officers were slow to respond and did little to help because they themselves lived in the neighborhoods and shared the residents' sentiments about the minorities moving in and found it easier to excuse the violence. Others, who may not have condoned the violence, may have done little so as to protect public support for the neighborhood police.

Special Procedures for Bias-Motivated Violence

After a number of widely publicized incidents, the CCPD created a number of special procedures for the treatment of bias-motivated crime, which included referring such crimes to a specialized unit, the ABTF. The stock story about the unit's origins and the departmental changes that appears in the media is that knowledge of the full extent of the problem led to changes in the policy and the creation of a specialized unit. There may have been another, much less flattering, reason that the department established the unit. Several detectives maintained that the department created the unit because a Black family whose house was firebombed by Whites sued the department and the public housing agency, asserting that both entities failed to protect minorities. After the police department settled the suit, according to one detective, the police commissioner established the ABTF so that in the future Blacks could not contend that the police had not made an effort to protect them.

Regardless of the department's motives, it took steps to address conflicts that disturbed the peace or infringed upon citizens' right to be free from violence, threats, or harassment. These conflicts, termed "neighborhood disturbances," involved incidents in which there was (1) evidence to support that the victim(s) had been selected because of their race, including incidents and situations precipitated by racial motives, (2) group activity that could incite group conflict or violence, or (3) concerted efforts to deprive others of free access to any neighborhood or community in the city.

The focus on particular types of events was accompanied by an attempt to change the way the department as a whole responded to bias-motivated violence. If an incident was verified as a "neighborhood disturbance," under the new system, it was given the highest priority. Once at the scene, the patrol supervisor was required to take steps to control the situation and to apprehend those responsible. Wary of the possibility that too much police attention could make volatile situations even worse, the department placed emphasis on ensuring that the appropriate number of officers responded. In small incidents where a large police presence could lead to escalation, departmental policy directed patrol supervisors to focus on solving the crime with a minimal number of officers. In all incidents they were required to enlist the help of community leaders to control rumors and dispel vigilante efforts.[20]

Function and Structure of the ABTF

The ABTF, the department's hate crime unit, was designed to coordinate the department's response to racial incidents. The unit was originally conceived as a small administrative unit with neither investigative nor other police powers. The ABTF, which began with just three officers, was responsible for evaluating the performance of those responsible for

responding to incidents and designing strategies for controlling disturbances. It was also supposed to serve as the department's liaison with
other concerned government agencies—the housing agency, the district
attorney's office, and the attorney general's office.

Perhaps because the head of the CCPD wished to keep a close eye on
departmental responses to racial violence, the new unit was very
closely tied to the commissioner's office. A conference room in the
commissioner's suite served as one of the unit's first quarters. Organi-
zationally, the unit was different from the rest of the department, too.
A civilian, who served as special assistant to the commissioner, was put
in charge of the unit and reported directly to the commissioner.

Because of its size and organizational composition, the ABTF did little to change either the structure of authority in the districts or patrol
officers' discretion in incidents that were possibly bias-motivated; officers still responded to the scenes of hate crimes. Patrol therefore had
control over both the services rendered to victims and whether the incident would be referred to the ABTF. Even if the incident were referred
to the ABTF, investigation of the incident was still done by the district
detectives because the officers in the ABTF were not detectives.

Even though departmental policy had changed, the district detectives' hate crimes investigations remained problematic for two reasons.
First, racially motivated vandalism and harassment were added to a
caseload that included robberies, thefts, drug crimes, break-ins, and
armed assaults—all of which are generally considered to be much more
serious crimes by police officers. Second, the district detectives relied
on Whites who lived in the neighborhood in which the crimes occurred
for information to solve other crimes. The district detectives thus had a
disincentive to conduct investigations that were certain to antagonize
the White community.

Officers' experiences in the unit's first few years also suggest that the
unit was clearly designed to have an advisory rather than a policing
role. Some insisted that the unit was pure window dressing for the city,
a unit focusing on racial crimes but downplaying the role of race in
Center City neighborhoods. One detective, who joined the unit in its
first few years, remarked cynically:

> We weren't supposed to investigate. Or really we were supposed to inves-
> tigate and prove that it wasn't racial. They didn't want us to make this
> the hate crime capital of the world.

The Unit's Work

Despite having little control over actual investigations, ABTF officers were responsible for contacting victims after incidents occurred. Because the unit's only responsibilities involved aiding victims of bias-motivated crime and because it was not located in any of the neighborhoods, it was able to offer a type of response very different from that the neighborhood police districts had offered. Officers spent their time questioning and listening to victims and providing protection. One Black officer explained that the unit's job in its early days was just to help minorities survive life in their new neighborhoods:

> At that time there were certain parts of the city we couldn't ride through. If a minority bought a house, they couldn't stay there; they'd drive you out. You'd be watching TV and find a can of paint thrown through the window and on your living room floor. So many nights, I spent sitting in someone's house so they could get some sleep, some rest.

In its early years, the ABTF provided services to many victims of bias-motivated violence. During its first full year of operation, more than five hundred crimes were reported to the unit. This was a heavy workload for so few officers. Asked how they could investigate so many cases in a year, a detective responded:

> We didn't think of numbers. We just thought of our job as being able to provide relief for people. Later we got two additional people. But it wasn't until things had started quieting down. We just *worked*.

Though the unit was responsible for investigating cases all over the city, most of the bias-motivated violence was concentrated in areas undergoing racial change. The geographic location of the unit's activities changed with shifts in demographic patterns. In the unit's early years, the late 1970s and early 1980s, its unit activities were concentrated primarily in two mostly White ethnic neighborhoods, "Mulberry" and "Barnsdale," neighborhoods that made up only 16 percent of the city's population yet laid claim to more than half its incidents. Incidents in the Barnsdale neighborhood began to decrease as it became more integrated, but the percentage of cases the unit investigated in Mulberry remained high. From the late 1980s throughout the 1990s, the unit focused its energy on cases occurring in three neighborhoods: Mulberry, "Hillside," and Gertown. These neighborhoods contained less than 20 percent of the city's population, but between 1987 and 1996 more than 70 percent of the unit's cases occurred there. Year after year, in annual reports to the police commissioner, ABTF detectives attributed increases in the numbers of incidents in these neighborhoods to increases in the number of minorities—Blacks, Asians, and Latinos—moving into private housing and public housing developments.

Because a large percentage of the bias-motivated violence occurred in particular neighborhoods, the ABTF was able to develop a proactive response. Some of the unit's activities in this regard included placing officers inside the homes of individuals who had been attacked on many occasions, placing officers nearby in unmarked vehicles to allow for quick response, and using surveillance vans to observe perpetrators' activities without being seen. Such activities resulted in few arrests and even fewer convictions. They were significant, however, because the proactive work resulted in intelligence information, which allowed the ABTF to prevent bias-motivated violence that had been planned against minorities. In addition, they provided information that allowed the housing authority to evict repeat offenders.

A Legal Response to Bias-Motivated Violence

When the unit was formed, the state had no hate crime law. Bias-motivated violence was prosecuted under criminal statutes for vandalism, assault, and harassment. In the unit's second year, the state legislature passed a civil rights law that contained both criminal and civil provisions. Before the bill's passage, members of the attorney general's office, which supported the bill, were concerned that it would not pass; they asked ABTF officers to travel to the Capitol to lobby the legislators. The first supervisor of the unit recalled his trip:

> The AG's office pressed, I took [one of the Black officers in the unit] with me. The first representative who stopped me asked, "You're a cop, why are you supporting this bill?" "I believe it will help end Center City's reputation as a hostile, racist city." I talked to forty-five people.

The bill passed and was signed into law by the governor. It took effect the following year. Though it was the legislature's fourth attempt to pass this type of measure, it did so with little fanfare.

Criminal Civil Rights Violations

Patterned after federal law, the criminal portion of the new civil rights law[21] instituted criminal civil rights violations. The law prohibited individuals by force or threat of force from willfully injuring, intimidating, interfering, or threatening to interfere with those who were enjoying rights or privileges secured by the U.S. or state constitutions. Individuals who violated the law were subject to a fine of not more than one thousand dollars or imprisonment of up to a year, or both. Bodily injury was an important variable under the law. If no injury resulted, violation of the statute was a misdemeanor and the police had no statutory right of arrest unless the offense had occurred in the officer's presence. Punishment was more severe for violations involving bodily injury: a judge could fine a violator up to ten thousand dollars and/or sentence him or her up to ten years in jail.

As in hate crime laws in other states, the various elements of the new criminal bias-motivated violence and intimidation law were vague. No indication was given in the law about (1) what was meant by interference; (2) what evidence was to be used to show that an individual had been attempting to willfully deprive someone of a federally protected right; (3) what rights were protected; and (4) in what circumstances the law was meant to be enforced.

Injunctive Relief

A related statute, passed at the same time as the statute establishing criminal civil rights violations, gave the state's attorney general (AG) the power to request an injunction from a superior court judge when an individual used threats, intimidation, or coercion to prevent someone from exercising his or her federal or state constitutional rights. This injunction would enjoin the perpetrator, under penalty of arrest, from committing further actions that interfered with that person's exercising of rights guaranteed by the state and federal constitutions. It also gave an individual whose constitutional rights had been violated the right to sue for compensatory damages and equitable relief, as well as court costs and attorney fees.

Limiting the Scope of the New Law

Though on its face the new civil rights law was vague, language in the definitions section following the law appeared to limit police and prosecutor discretion. This was accomplished by assigning more specific meanings to several terms. First, the legislature indicated it wished to limit the scope of the law by prohibiting only interference with rights that was accomplished by threat, intimidation, and coercion. It defined interference to include any infringement, encroachment, or disturbance that prevented another person from exercising one of his or her protected rights. Giving the example of a minority person's right to own and enjoy real estate, it stressed that interference did not necessarily involve physical contact. Thus, a racially motivated stoning of someone's house, "even though no damage was done and he does not have to move out of the house," would interfere with that person's rights.

By insisting that to be actionable, interference had to be accomplished by intimidation, threat, or coercion, the legislature implied that spoken and written words could serve as evidence that one had violated this section of the civil rights law. Thus, enforcement implicated First Amendment freedoms. There was, however, a stopping point. The legislature was firm in maintaining that threats must be serious, distinguishable from that which is clearly protected under the First Amendment, such as political arguments or jest. By saying that the seriousness of threats must be evaluated, the legislature seemed to be compelling enforcers of the civil rights law to examine the context of the words spoken. The legislature also indicated that intimidating conduct was to be judged by an objective rather than subjective standard, but it did not have to be so great as to result in terror, panic, or hysteria.

Unlike many hate crime statutes, the state civil rights law did not use the word *motivation*. Nevertheless, in the definitions section of the statute, the legislature wrote that it wanted the criminal (though not the civil) statute to have a distinct motivational element. In this section, it required that the state show that the defendant had manifested *specific intent* to interfere with the victim's protected rights." The victim did not have to know that she or he had the rights. In determining the requisite level of intent, the legislature wrote, a defendant was presumed to intend the natural and foreseeable consequences of his or her actions.

The last part of the definitions section listed selected constitutional rights that the legislature intended that individuals be able to exercise without racially motivated interference. As if to provide a ready reference for law enforcement agents and prosecutors, the section was carefully tailored to the problems that Center City minorities had experienced while moving into White neighborhoods. The legislature recognized rights in several categories, including the following: housing, education, travel and movement, employment, public accommodations, conduct of business, public facilities and governmental services, judicial proceedings, meetings, and speech. In each category, the legislature acknowledged individuals' rights of equal access to benefits and to be free from discrimination. For example, the enumerated housing rights included the peaceable enjoyment of rental housing or home ownership, applying for or looking for housing, freely having visitors at one's residence, and traveling to and from one's residence.

Enforcing the Law

An Expanded Unit with Increased Resources

As a reward for hard work in its first two years, the unit was given full police powers. The first detectives were assigned to the unit in the early 1980s. By 1982, with six officers, the unit was double its original size. The ABTF was also given a small suite of offices tucked away in a corner of police headquarters. The suite consisted of four small, rather dark, wood-paneled offices—an outer office containing the secretary's desk and a makeshift kitchen; an office for the lieutenant; an office shared by the detectives; and another shared by the sergeants. The offices were crammed with telephones, typewriters, computer terminals, desks, and file cabinets. The space seemed an especially tight fit by the late 1990s, when the unit struggled to fit several detectives, four supervisors, a secretary, a clerk and three part-time Asian-language interpreters into space intended for a much smaller unit.

The lieutenant was the leader of the unit and reported directly to the commissioner's office. He was responsible for setting the unit's policy and procedures, speaking to the press about cases, and interacting with the outside community, such as members of victim advocacy groups, prosecutors, and assistant attorneys general. Each of the two sergeants was responsible for supervising a crew of detectives during his or her designated shift, either 8:00 A.M.–5:00 P.M., the day shift, or 4:30 P.M.–

1:00 A.M., the night shift. Half of the unit's detectives and supervisors were assigned to days, and the other half, nights. The overlap, between 4:30 and 5:00 P.M. allowed day detectives to inform night detectives of new developments that had transpired during the day.

From the very beginning, the ABTF was a diverse group of officers. In its first few years, it had two Black officers and two women officers. Though the exact composition of the unit changed as detectives were transferred in or out, those who had had sustained contact with the unit over its history insisted that it had always had at least one Black officer and at least one female officer. Over its history, slightly more than 60 percent of the detectives assigned to the unit were White. People of color, primarily people of African American, Hispanic, and Asian descent, constituted just over one-third of the unit's detectives. Slightly less than 20 percent of the detectives who had served in the unit were women, including just over 10 percent of the total who were women of color.

The detectives who did most of the work investigating cases were assisted by a variety of civilian and sworn personnel. The detective clerk, usually a former detective, performed administrative tasks: assigning overtime shifts, assembling statistics and logs detailing the unit's investigations, and preparing and filing reports. The secretary was responsible for clerical work: answering the unit's main telephone number, typing transcripts of 911 tapes, and transferring reports to letterhead. The unit's part-time Asian-language interpreters were civilians hired to translate for the unit's Asian-speaking victims. They spoke Chinese, Vietnamese, Laotian, and Hmong.

A Slow Start

Soon after the new law took effect, officers in the unit began to take a more aggressive approach to their job. In part this was because they felt they had a remedy as well as new tools to combat some of the problems they encountered. The unit acquired a surveillance van, one of the first computers in the police department, and several unmarked cruisers. In addition, it was allocated overtime pay to conduct surveillances and to do proactive work in neighborhoods where hate crime was occurring.

Detectives were eager to use the new civil rights law. Their enthusiasm stemmed partially from the difficulties they had had getting convictions for racially motivated crimes under the regular assault and vandalism laws because low-level crimes were rarely taken seriously by courts. Prosecutors, members of the attorney general's office, and judges did not share the detectives' enthusiasm. In spite of the fact that the law appeared to have been so clearly tailored to the problems Center City was experiencing at that time, the district attorney and the attorney general's office, the two offices responsible for bringing prosecution of criminal offenses and for seeking civil injunctions under the new law, appeared reluctant to use it. For example, the attorney general's office sought no civil rights injunctions until 1982, two years after the statute took effect.

Several detectives recounted that those in the two offices insisted that the new civil rights law was to be used only in extreme situations, such as against the Ku Klux Klan. A law used only against extremist groups would have been used very infrequently because in Center City, as in other cities, those responsible for most of the bias-motivated violence did not belong to extremist groups.[22] As one detective recalled, "It was frustrating to deal with the attorney general, who said the law is going to be used only when the KKK comes to town. When's it going to be used, every twenty years?"

ABTF officers began to pressure the AG's office to use the law. Perhaps in response to the unit's urging, the law was first used by the AG's office. The civil injunctions it sought enjoined individuals from further engaging in racially motivated harassment. Assistant attorneys general (AAGs) also accompanied ABTF detectives who were seeking criminal complaints in court. The appearance of the attorney general's office made it harder to dismiss the officers' cases. Accompanying ABTF detectives to court, along with the injunctions that the AG's office had obtained, may have had the effect of shaming the district attorney's office into bringing criminal cases under the statute.

Still, even with the DA's office on board, a formidable obstacle remained in the prosecution of these cases: getting the cases past judges and district court clerk magistrates. Clerk magistrates, or clerks, were employees of the Center City's low-level criminal courts, which had jurisdiction over defendants charged with misdemeanors. They were not required to be lawyers, but were responsible for approving or denying the initial criminal complaint in which the defendant was formally charged with a crime.

In Center City, officers in the ABTF were generally the parties that sought validation of criminal complaints from district court clerk magistrates. The officers in the ABTF filled out the complaint form and appeared on behalf of the victim in front of a clerk magistrate. The clerk magistrate could approve the complaint, deny it outright, continue the case without a finding for a specified period of time, or send it to a hearing in front of a judge. If the complaint is approved, process issues and criminal proceedings against the defendant begin.[23]

At first, both judges and clerk magistrates often denied criminal complaints because they were unaware that the new law had been passed. The absence of publicity surrounding the law's passage meant that even a year after it took effect, some judges did not know that it existed. In the first fifteen months of the law's existence, only two convictions were obtained. Even when the judges did know about the law, many were still reluctant to grant relief. One detective recalled new judges' fears about the law's being overturned by the courts:

> At that time the law was new and no judge wanted to be the judge with the case that went up to the Supreme Court and got the law thrown out. Once that they realized it was okay, it wouldn't hurt them politically and the law wouldn't get thrown out, it was better.

But the new civil rights law did not get thrown out, and though detectives, DAs, and clerk magistrates did not always see eye-to-eye about when the law should be used, the more they invoked the law, the more comfortable all actors in the system became.

Conclusion

Ordinary criminal law did little to confront the type of bias-motivated violence that Mrs. A, her family, and other victims of this type of hate crime face. There are several reasons for this failure. Police officers do not give priority to the type of low-level assaults that many hate crime victims experience. In the case of move-in violence, local police may sympathize with the perpetrators of the harassment and assault or may have incentives not to interfere in what they see as neighborhood struggles. The experience of Center City suggests that a specialized unit located outside the regular unit can, if properly constructed, provide a far better response to victims of this type of crime. Though specialized units may work better than neighborhood precincts, such units are not perfect. Unfortunately, the ABTF was unable to solve Mrs. A's and her family's problems. The unit conducted an ongoing investigation of the harassment she received, but it was never able to stop the harassment. She endured many years of abuse and eventually left the neighborhood.

Though the Center City Police Department did respond to the attacks on minorities, its first actions were tentative. The initial changes it undertook failed because the unit was not responsible for investigating hate crimes. Local police continued to be responsible for investigating hate crimes and responded to victims of hate crimes as they had previously, unhelpfully. The unit was not able to investigate cases when it first started, but it did have a host of activities, including protecting victims and developing plans to prevent future outbreaks of violence. Thus, as a part of policing integration, the unit was engaged in a variety of activities that went beyond the bounds of traditional police work.

In addition to the broad changes in police department policy, the legislature of the state in which Center City is located also passed a civil rights law, with both criminal and civil provisions, aimed at bias-motivated violence. One section of the new law criminalized the willful interference by one person with another person's exercise of state or federal constitutional rights, thereby giving law enforcement a crucial additional tool. Thus, the law's passage was an important step in the struggle against bias-motivated violence. It further provided officers with an additional tool to combat bias-motivated crime. Though the statute's intent—to punish the interference with civil rights and to avoid politically protected speech and "mere" jest—was clear from the definitions section, the elements of the statute were vaguely worded.

4

Investigation
Detectives and the Making of Hate Crime

The victim, perpetrator, detective, mayor, commissioner don't make it civil rights. Only a competent, thorough investigation can do that.   —Center City Detective

For an incident to be identified as a hate crime by police detectives, it must pass through a multilayered process, which begins with a formal investigation of the incident. This chapter focuses on that process. I examine formal procedures the unit developed for investigating civil rights violations and the realities that inevitably arise: detectives' routines and informal practices.

Processing Crime

In many large cities, a citizen's call to 911 sets in motion a process that may include several individuals. The 911 operator contacts a dispatcher in the operations division, describes the incident and its location, and assigns it a code based on its severity. The dispatch goes out over the radio and a police car in the vicinity responds to the call. Generally, the responding officer is a patrol officer, one who works the streets and neighborhoods of the area in which the incident has occurred.

If the incident is simple, for instance, if the caller has contacted the police to get the neighbors to quiet down, the patrol officer who arrives on the scene is likely to be the only officer involved. She or he may write a

ticket or issue a warning and then signal to the dispatcher that police services have been rendered. No report is written, no criminal investigation
is conducted, and the matter is closed. If the incident is more serious,
however, such as an assault or an incident with injuries, the officer is
often required to do more. She or he may assist the victim in obtaining
medical help, arrest suspects, or question those at the scene. After services
are rendered, the officer must write a report with a full description of the
incident. The report is then forwarded to the detectives in the neighborhood precinct for investigation. These detectives handle nearly everything
that happens in their area, including robberies, auto theft, burglaries, assaults, breaking and entering, vandalism, and drug crimes. Some crimes,
though, such as homicide, or crimes involving police officers, sexual assault, prostitution, or gambling, are often investigated by specialized
units—Homicide, Internal Affairs, Sexual Assault, or Vice. These units
handle such crimes irrespective of where in the city they occur. If a victim
reports a crime that falls under the jurisdiction of one of the specialized
units, in most cases the precinct is required to forward the patrol officer's
report to the appropriate specialized unit and the unit conducts an investigation of the crime.

The Anti-Bias Task Force (ABTF), the hate crime unit for the police
department in Center City, was one of these specialized detective units.
ABTF detectives did not respond to calls involving robberies or any of
the other crimes that are broadcast over the police radio. They were responsible only for investigating possible hate crimes and collecting the
evidence required to prosecute hate crime cases for the county district
attorney's office.

All of the cases that the unit investigated were entered into a log of
the cases that listed the race of the victim, race of the perpetrator (if
known), area in which the incident occurred, date the crime occurred,
type of crime—that is, whether it was an assault or vandalism—and for
some cases, the action the unit pursued. Types of action documented in
the log included seeking an injunction under the civil rights law and
pursuing mediation, criminal charges or criminal civil rights charges.
The log also indicated, for some cases, whether the victim refused to
participate in the prosecution. Comparing the log with actual case files
indicates that the log's figures documenting race of perpetrator and the
victim, date of the crime, and crime location, were nearly always accurate; figures on the action taken were not, however, and should be considered approximate.

Figures from the log show that most of the cases the unit investigated were incidents the officer that forwarded the case believed to racially motivated crimes (see Table 4.1). As Table 4.1 shows, 85 percent of the cases the unit investigated between 1990 and 1997 were race-based cases. Though the unit was created to address racially motivated violence, in 1986 the unit began to investigate crimes against gays and lesbians. That same year the unit brought its first case for civil rights charges on behalf of a gay victim. Between 1990 and 1997, 12 percent of the unit's caseload was antigay cases. The unit began to investigate and monitor antireligious violence in the early 1990s. Antireligious cases were 3 percent of the unit's total caseload between 1990 and 1997. "Other" crimes investigated by the unit include politically motivated crimes, one gender-based crime, and disability-based crimes.

In race-based cases, racial minorities were victims in the majority of cases investigated by the unit. Blacks, Asians, and Hispanics constituted roughly 70 percent of the unit's victims (see Table 4.2). In race-based investigations, African Americans were the largest racial group, followed by Whites, Hispanics, and Asians. In the antireligious category, the vast majority of investigations were reports of anti-Semitic crimes. Finally, Whites were victims in the vast majority of the unit's antigay and -lesbian investigations.

The distribution of perpetrators by race was the reverse of the victim configuration. The statistics from the unit's logs indicate that in cases in which a perpetrator was known, Whites were identified as perpetrators in roughly two-thirds of the cases the unit investigated in that time period and minorities in approximately one-third. Between 1990 and 1997, in all three types of crimes, when a perpetrator was identified, he or she was most likely to be White (see Table 4.3). This was especially true in antireligious crime, in which 85 percent of the perpetrators were identified as White. The unit's log indicates that the most common victim/perpetrator configuration was a Black victim and a White perpetrator.

The unit investigated a variety of incidents including arson and attempted arson, assault and battery, vandalism, threats, and harassment. Though all the incidents the unit investigated are not represented, figures from the unit's logs provide a sketch of the distribution of the unit's caseload (see Table 4.4).[1] In race cases, the logs indicate that just under half of the cases that detectives investigated were identified as assault and battery with a deadly weapon. This category

TABLE 4.1
Investigations, by Category, 1990–1997

Category	Number	Percentage
Race	1,683	85.0
Religion	55	3.0
Antigay/Antilesbian	236	12.0
Other	13	0.7
Total	1,987	100.0

Source: ABTF files.

TABLE 4.2
Investigations, by Race of Victim, 1990–1997

Race of Victim	Racial Bias		Antireligious		Antigay/-lesbian	
	N	%	N	%	N	%
Black	605	36.0	0	0	9	4.0
White	476	28.0	52	98.0	220	94.0
Asian	210	13.0	0	0	0	0
Hispanic	358	21.0	0	0	5	2.0
Other	31	2.0	1	2.0	1	0.4
Total	1,680	100.0	53	100.0	235	100.4*

Source: ABTF files.
*Does not equal 100 due to rounding.

TABLE 4.3
Investigations, by Race of Perpetrator, 1990–1997

Race of Victim	Racial Bias		Antireligious		Antigay/-lesbian	
	N	%	N	%	N	%
Black	404	24	3	6	51	22.0
White	1102	66	44	85	136	59.0
Asian	32	2	0	0	1	0.4
Hispanic	113	7	1	2	32	14.0
Other	23	1	4	8	10	4.0
Total	1,676	100	52	101*	230	99.4*

Source: ABTF files.
*Does not equal 100 due to rounding.

TABLE 4.4
Types of Crimes Investigated by ABTF, 1992–1996

Crime Type	Race		Antigay/-lesbian		Religion	
	N	%	N	%	N	%
Arson	25	2	0	0	0	0
Assault and Battery	192	16	41	45	3	9
Assault and Battery with a Deadly Weapon	598	48	37	40	2	6
Vandalism of Motor Vehicles	106	9	*	*	5	15
Willful and Malicious Destruction of Real Property	68	6	*	*	9	27
Threats	171	14	28	30	8	24
Harassment	75	6	19	21	6	18
Total	1,235	100	91	100	33	100

Source: ABTF files.
*Data not collected in this category.

includes assaults with guns, knives, baseball bats or other blunt instruments, and motor vehicles. It also includes cases in which the victim is knocked to the ground and the perpetrator kicks him or her. The logs show that in the race-based cases, in each year a blunt instrument was the most commonly used weapon. A typical example of a case in this category involved a Black woman who passed ten White men on the street. As she passed the men yelled, "Nigger, go home" and "Spook, die." One of them then picked up a rock and threw it at her, hitting her in the back. The logs' figures also indicate that all three types of cases—race, religion, and antigay and -lesbian cases—at least half of the unit's caseload, involved the investigation of low-level crimes, that is, vandalism, threats, simple assaults, and harassment.

Making Crime, Detective Style

In detective slang, the task of investigation is called "making an investigation" or "making a crime." Detectives describe this process of making crime as simply getting to the bottom of what happened. Observers of detectives have found that the process is complex, requiring detectives to "make" crime by constructing aims from the information that

they receive.[2] In this way, crime is not a given but, rather, a social arti-
fact, created by those in the law enforcement community responsible
for enforcing the criminal law. The focus of detectives, who are responsible for investigating crime, then becomes the assembling of information in cases to be presented to prosecutors, judges, the mass media,
and, ultimately, the public.[3]

This process of making crime naturally involves the use of police discretion. Detectives make decisions regarding how their time will be
spent—deciding which cases receive what type of investigation. They
exercise power over information as they decide whether to interview
individuals who have been identified by patrol reports as victims and
witnesses, as well as what to ask such persons if they conduct interviews. Detectives are often also responsible for seeking an initial complaint and have the ability to decide whether to invoke the law and the
circumstances in which to invoke.

Making Hate Crime

In hate crime cases, according to one ABTF detective, you have to investigate the crime, "who the perpetrator was and what was their motivation." He continued:

> In other crimes, you have the first two but evidence of motivation is not
> required. Even though they may say it all the time on TV that you're
> looking for motivation, in an ordinary crime, you aren't.

The requirement under most hate crime law that incidents be motivated by bias makes the process of investigating hate crime more difficult. The reason the perpetrator committed the crime may not be readily apparent when the detective receives the initial crime report. Investigation into the perpetrator's actions before, during, or after the crime
may reveal his or her motivation. Incidents may be prosecuted as bias
crimes or "regular" crimes. Detectives enforcing hate crime laws thus
have discretion to decide not only whether the law will be invoked but
also whether an incident will be labeled bias-motivated. As in other
contexts, the investigation of incidents that may be motivated by bias
involves interpreting the law, deciding whether an incident is worth investigating, interviewing witnesses and crime victims, and assembling a
series of complex events into a case against the perpetrator.

The Primacy and Absence of Investigation

In most cases, without at least some investigation, reading the initial report does not give a detective all the information that he or she needs to discern whether the criminal law should be invoked. The law may not apply in the situation that the patrol officer has described, or the initial account supplied by the responding officer may be missing information that is necessary for the incident to be charged as a crime. Investigation allows detectives to verify that the incident is a crime and to fill gaps and silences in the initial account.

Detectives have the discretion not to investigate all the reports of possible crimes that they receive from patrol. Despite the importance of investigation, many studies of detectives have shown that they choose not to investigate most crimes that are reported to them. Choosing not to investigate incidents that may be crimes is obviously a significant use of police power. If the police have not sought suspects or otherwise investigated a crime, those downstream in the criminal justice system will be less able and far less likely to invoke the law.

Even when detectives do investigate, studies show that they do not spend much time doing so. One study of the investigation of burglary and robbery cases found that, once most cases are referred to detectives for follow-up, they are actively investigated for only one day.[4] In measuring time that detectives spent on cases—including investigative interviews, suspect interviews, accused processing, and report writing—another study found that more than 60 percent of cases received less than one hour of investigative time.[5]

For the detectives in the ABTF, a good measure of the level of investigative activity is length of, or the number of pages in, the case file. Each case file contained all of the documentation that the detective had assembled relating to the incident, including the original report written by the patrol officer (called the "incident report"), photos of the crime scene, a description of the suspect's previous arrests, the criminal complaint if one was filed, court documents relating to the case, and all of the detective's written reports documenting his or her action and interviews associated with the case.

Case file length is comparable to other measures of detective activity, such as minutes or hours detectives spend on each case.[6] Pages are a valid indicator of presumed activity and effort because in the ABTF though files could contain other items, the detectives' reports were the most common item and, in most cases, the item most likely to expand the length of the file. A comparison of case files revealed that the longer the file, the more involved the investigation, and vice versa. The number of detectives' reports represented the activity expended in the case because ABTF detectives were required to document every action taken. As one detective remarked, "If it happened, it went in the report." Frequently interspersed with much longer reports were one-paragraph reports like this:

> Dear Sergeant,
> On 6/7/89, between 6 and 9:30 p.m. I attempted to contact the victim, Mrs. Smith, but no one answered the telephone.
> Respectfully submitted,
> Detective X.

The detectives were conscientious about filing reports because reports were their way of showing a supervisor that they had been working. Showing one's work was important to the detectives, for there was little day-to-day supervision. Frequently, the detectives were out in the field conducting investigations and away from the office for long stretches at a time. Reports in the case file detailing the detectives' activities showed supervisors that they had been working for the entire shift.

Levels of Investigative Activity

At a minimum, each case file contained a cover sheet, a form assigning it to a detective, and a copy of the original incident report, all of which were given to the detective when he or she was assigned the case. Very short case files, three pages or less, contained no detective reports. Because detectives were required to document every call to a victim (even if the victim was not at home) and every investigative action with a report, files with no reports were unlikely to have been investigated at all. As a corollary, long case files were usually cases that had absorbed much of the detectives' work time.

Table 4.5 displays the presumptive level of investigative activity over an eight-year period. Case logs depicting the length of every case the unit investigated were labeled and divided into four groups: no investigation,

TABLE 4.5
Level of Investigation Selected Years, 1987–1996

Level of Investigation	1987		1988		1989		1990		1991		1992		1995		1996	
	N	%	N	%	N	%	N	%	N	%	N	%	N	%	N	%
Substantial Investigation	24	15	32	21	29	14	52	19	43	17.0	56	29.0	50	22.0	77	33.0
Investigation	44	28	47	31	84	42	98	36	141	56.0	72	36.0	117	52.0	120	52.0
Minimal Investigation	77	48	65	43	77	38	106	38	67	27.0	62	32.0	56	25.0	34	16.0
No Investigation	13	8	8	5	12	6	17	6	1	0.03	2	0.01	1	0.05	2	0.08
Total cases	158		152		202		273		252		192		224		233	

Source: ABTF Files.

minimal investigation, investigation, and substantial investigation. Each level was associated with a different degree of investigative activity. Case files labeled "no investigation," contained three or fewer pages and were assumed to contain no investigative reports. Case files of four to seven pages in length fell into the "minimal investigation" category and were sufficiently long to contain one or two investigative reports. Case files in the "investigation" group those between eight and nineteen pages were long enough to have enough reports to support criminal charges. Finally, those marked "substantial investigation," at twenty pages or more, were lengthy enough to signify major investigation and contained several detective reports or other pieces of evidence.

Examining case files and the number of reports filed by detectives suggests that detectives in hate crime units spend more time investigating cases than detectives working in other areas. As Table 4.5 shows, between 1987 and 1997 in Center City the vast majority of cases referred to the bias crime unit (92 percent) received at least minimal investigation. Another study of detectives investigating hate crime as part of a specialized unit produced similar results. That study, of detectives in a hate crime unit in New York City, revealed that they filed three or more reports in 95 percent of their cases.[7]

Controlling Patrol Officers' Discretion

As with detectives' investigations elsewhere, most of the ABTF's investigations were reactive rather than proactive.[8] Patrol officers who respond are supposed to administer the services that are immediately necessary: call for an ambulance, arrest suspects still in the area, and take a police incident report. Except in rare cases, ABTF detectives had no firsthand knowledge of the crime scene. The unit's caseload was generated almost entirely from reports forwarded from patrol officers.

Ideally, the incident report would classify the crime (as an assault, for instance), give the victim's and (if there was one) suspect's name, race, gender, and contact information, as well as the names of witnesses to the incident, and briefly describe the incident. If the patrol officer knew or even suspected that an incident was a hate crime, he or she checked a box on the form for the incident to be forwarded to ABTF for investigation. Either the patrol officer, or the sergeant in charge of the shift, who was supposed to read the report and sign off on it, could send the case to the ABTF.

When a specialized unit investigates but does not respond to 911 calls, getting the initial report forwarded to the unit is crucial. If no mechanism for getting initial crime reports to the unit exists other than the obvious procedure of having patrol officers send reports, the patrol officers, who lack training, may mischaracterize crimes. In the case of hate crimes, there is a danger that patrol officers will fail to categorize particular types of incidents as hate crimes and the unit will not be able to investigate them. A patrol officer could decide that all incidents involving a perpetrator and a victim from two racial groups—for instance Latinos and African Americans—are not hate crimes but, rather, are gang related, and choose not to forward such cases to the detectives who investigate hate crimes. Another worry is that patrol officers will adopt a narrow working definition of hate crime and forward to the unit only cases unambiguously motivated by bias.[9] Patrol officers might decide, for example, that real hate crimes exist only when there is a clear sign of bias motivation, such as a cross burning. Finally, patrol officers unavoidably bring their own biases to bear in response to calls for assistance. Thus, officers who do not believe hate crime laws should be enforced against White perpetrators have the discretion, in the absence of mechanisms that limit discretion, to effectively nullify hate crime law.

In Center City patrol officers proved reluctant to identify and forward to the unit cases in which Whites were accused of committing hate crime. ABTF supervisors discovered this when they learned that one precinct had been minimizing the number of cases that were possible hate crimes. One of the detectives recounted how the unit realized that the precinct officers were covering up incidents:

> Do you remember the 1981 case I told you about, the firebombing in the projects where someone threw a Molotov cocktail in the baby's room? It seemed like that case and the other one came out of nowhere. We'd had no reports of hate crimes. We went back and read all the crime incident reports and found 57 cases of out-and-out hate crime, White on Black and Black on White in the three months leading up to the incident. But they'd been covered up, the name or the race would have been changed. Some of them were violent, too. . . . Out of that same group of incidents a sixteen-year-old White kid stabbed a Black jogger. . . . This was an offshoot of that incident.

After this incident, whenever ABTF supervisors were in the neighborhood, they made a practice of stopping by the neighborhood police precinct and looking through its reports for cases that should be sent to the unit. In addition, the Reports Bureau, a section of the department that gets a copy of every incident report in the city, was required to send every report with a difference in race between the victim and the perpetrator to the ABTF.

Making a Case—Detectives' Initial Screen

As with detectives elsewhere, once a case was forwarded to the unit, the ABTF detectives' investigation involved establishing or making a case.[10] Making a case involved a supervisor screening the case to determine whether the incident was worthy of becoming part of the unit's case files and being at least minimally investigated. For detectives in the unit and elsewhere this initial screen traditionally involves pragmatic considerations such as examining cases for investigative possibilities and probable outcomes.[11] Detectives tend not to investigate unsolvable cases, such as cases that come to the detectives with no leads, cold (that is, no suspects have been identified), and cases in which elements of the crime are lacking. Detectives may inactivate or close cases with these deficiencies. How detectives view their job creates an incentive to get rid of cases that they do not believe to be worth investigating. As another scholar of detectives has written, in detectives' eyes, "monkeying around" with nickel-and-dime cases—trivial crimes with little chance of being solved—was not their job.[12]

Giving Cases "the Broom"

In units in which cases are assigned to detectives, as is so in the ABTF, supervisors do the initial screen. The sergeant who screened cases read each report and in some cases decided after speaking with the victim that the unit would not investigate. Deciding a case was not worth investigating was called giving it "the broom." When a case was screened out at this initial stage, it did not become part of the unit's case files or statistics; rather, it was filed away separately in the "broom drawer."

"Brooming" cases was billed as necessary for efficiency's sake, an attempt to preserve scarce resources by preventing detectives from looking into cases that did not need investigating. This screen required a quick call to the victim and a basic inquiry into the possibility that bias-motivated the incident. By such calls, the sergeant tried to screen out cases that reached the unit by mistake, as well as those that had no hint of bias. If this quick investigation suggested that the case was not bias-motivated or was not a crime, then it would not be assigned to a detective. One sergeant who did the initial screening of cases described how he decided what went into the broom drawer.

> [They were] cases for one reason or another we wouldn't investigate. . . .
> I'd talk to the victim and he'd tell me it wasn't racial or the victim didn't
> want us to investigate. Some people just file a police report because they
> just want to document. They document it and if it happens again. . . .
> The broom drawer was not about trying to keep the numbers down. I'm
> sure there were things that fell through the cracks, but all of it was in
> good faith.

The broom drawer was a kind of purgatory for cases. Cases could make it out of that drawer but rarely did. If another case came to the unit with the same victim and the sergeant remembered that he had given the earlier incident "the broom," the earlier case might be investigated along with the new one. The number of cases that were "broomed" each year was unknown even to ABTF supervisors, for the unit kept no records on the number of cases in the broom drawer.

Investigative Routines and Practices

Adjusting the Initial Frame

Studies of detectives have highlighted the importance of their everyday routines as well as procedure.[13] Procedure consists of a set of formal rules of decision created by an institution of which members are a part. Routines, by contrast, consist of the everyday practices individuals have developed to negotiate vagueness, and to deal with contradictions and complex situations to which procedures do not speak. Police use routines to classify what is socially constructed and contextually situated as a type of incident that the law can appreciate—a "racial" or an "antireligious" incident. Mystery novels, television shows, and movies suggest that detectives spend most of their time looking for the bad guy or trying to figure out "who dunnit." Framed this way, investigations are an unmediated search for truth. This myth strongly conflicts with reality. The incident described in the incident report that the detective first receives is not yet a crime but, rather, a loosely structured account assembled by the patrol officers.

Previous research has shown that patrol officers mold the victim's accounts in at least two ways: first, by labeling an occurrence as a type of crime; and second, by writing a description to fit the label.[14] In Center City, the very first box on the incident report requires the patrol officer to fix the incident into a legal category—an assault and battery, harassment, threat, and so on. Thus, a patrol officer must first decide what type of crime has occurred. After that, he can get the victim's name and identifying details. The narrative description of the incident, which is most important to the detectives in the hate crime unit, is at the bottom of the form.

The initial report had the patrol officer's frame, which attempted to fix meaning to the events in question. One person was labeled as the victim, another as the suspect, and the incident was categorized criminally, for example, as an assault. In the CCPD, patrol officers were not allowed to decide that an incident was a hate crime and to seek criminal civil rights charges. In spite of this, sending a case to the unit created some suggestion that the incident was a hate crime. Regardless of patrol officers' labeling, the detectives were *very* suspicious of the way incidents were constructed on incident reports because, they insisted, the quality of reports varied so widely.

ABTF detectives often protested that initial reports were usually not accurate. Their principal complaint in this regard was that slurs or epithets used in the crime and reported to the officer were left out of the incident report. Another common missing item was evidence of previous contact between the victim and the suspect. Both of these factors, the use of slurs or epithets and previous harassment by the suspect—for reasons that will be explained in more detail later—signaled the possibility of bias. In addition to being incomplete, patrol officers' accounts were often confusing, contradictory, and sometimes just plain wrong.

Given the inaccuracy of many patrol officers' reports, detectives in Center City, like detectives elsewhere, often treated the description of the event and the "facts" the initial report contained as a tentative, preliminary account.[15] In Center City, their first task became getting to the bottom of what happened or clarifying the details of the story. Though they interviewed victims and witnesses to do this, ABTF detectives did not embark on an unmediated search for truth. Instead, they filtered the initial account contained in the incident report through a series of "stock stories" created based on what had happened in previous cases. These were scenarios that they considered likely to recur. A sergeant pulled out an incident report that he had not yet investigated, describing an altercation between a White victim and a Black suspect. He showed me how he read incident reports:

> See this report? [He reads] "The victim is walking down the street with another man and out of nowhere a Black man sucker punches him." This is very unusual. First, one man walks up to two people and punches one of them? That doesn't usually happen. Hate is cowardly. Perpetrators usually outnumber victims. I think what will happen is that the victim is gay and was walking with another man. Maybe they were holding hands, I don't know, and the Black guy thought they were gay and punched them because of that. Still this is unusual because it's not in front of a gay club. In fact, it's around the corner from a station. Maybe the guy is a street person or a deinstitutionalized person and is just wacko.

Interpreting the account on the incident report before calling the victim, this officer generated a series of possibilities that frame the event. He assumed that the crime was not an anti-White crime but an antigay crime, that the victim was gay, and that he was acting in such a way that the perpetrator would know that. The sergeant left room for an alternative—that the suspect was mentally disturbed—but identified the first scenario as the more likely of the two.

If there were gaps in the story, the detectives often assumed, based on their experience with patrol officers, that these silences stemmed from the fact that the patrol officer had constructed the account incorrectly. They assumed that patrol inadvertence had caused the inconsistency. The detective quoted above continues his discussion of the report:

> There's no indication that he [the victim] said anything. It's not written on the incident report. That doesn't mean that the victim didn't say it though. In the gay and lesbian cases, the victim may be very clear about this and that words were said and the patrol officer just doesn't write it down. We had a case with two lesbians who were assaulted and we found out about it and we went in and nothing happened for another six months. Later they were assaulted again and reported it to the district and said that they wanted the words used by the perpetrator noted on the

form and wanted it sent to the ABTF. The officers at first said you don't want it said like that. Later, when they pressed him, he said that he was in charge of writing the form and that he would decide whether or not to contact the ABTF. We never heard about it and, rather than put up with the harassment, the women moved out of the neighborhood.

The detectives had partners—largely for safety when conducting investigations—but one's cases were one's own responsibility. Nonetheless, there was some interaction on cases, particularly when first reading the account and generating a story about what happened. Sitting around the office, one detective reads the incident report in one of his cases to the others and his supervisor:

> *Detective 1:* The incident report says a Hispanic man in the crosswalk has called a White woman a "mother fucking White cunt" and spit on her car. The court officers suggested she seek complaints in court.
>
> *Detective 2:* I'll bet what you'll find is that something happened and she called him a "spic" and he called her a "White c" and spit on her car.
>
> *Detective 1:* Nothing he has done qualifies as a crime. [Flipping through the criminal code] I'm looking for a crime.

This example illustrates the process of labeling before investigation and the great discretion the detectives have in assigning meaning to events. In this case the victim felt this was an incident that deserved police attention. From the patrol officers' submitting the report to the unit and advising the victim to seek a complaint, we can infer the patrol officer believed the incident was a crime as well. The ABTF detectives disagreed and freely rejected the patrol officer's construction of the event in the incident report, as well as that of the victim. The detectives filled in the facts based on their experience with previous cases. More important, because they, not the officer in the district, had the power to seek charges in these cases, their interpretation mattered most.

The detectives' interpretation was important from a practical rather than a legal perspective. In the case above, the woman did not need the police to seek a misdemeanor criminal complaint against the man who spit on her car. The law of the jurisdiction allowed the woman to seek a complaint before a clerk magistrate herself. Citizens rarely did this, however, and, according to detectives, clerk magistrates rarely approved complaints sought by citizens.

The detectives, as a group, discussed the case above and quickly rejected it. Group discussion of cases was aided by technological advancements and the organization of the office. In the days before fax machines, detectives were sent to pick up the reports from the districts. When new reports came in, they were delivered directly to a supervisor. Later, incident reports came off the fax machine, located in the center of the open office. In order for incidents to be processed as quickly as possible, all detectives were charged with the responsibility of taking incident reports off the machine, logging them in, and delivering them to the appropriate sergeant for assignment. Hearing the fax machine ringing, the detectives would often walk over and look at the report and then read it to any detectives who happened to be standing around.

Assessing Victim Credibility—Investigating Victims

As part of getting to the bottom of an incident, ABTF detectives, like detectives elsewhere, must assess victim credibility.[16] This process began right after the detectives read the initial account that they received from patrol. The detectives assessed the legitimacy of the accounts of victims, witnesses, and suspects in the same way—by checking each person's criminal record. This was done before the detectives spoke with the victim or witnesses. Criminal records, therefore had the power to frame the detectives' view of victims' stories.

The detectives referred to checking a criminal history as "doing a BOP" (for Bureau of Prisons) on someone. A BOP gave a detailed criminal history of arrests, the disposition and type of criminal charges, and the current status of any warrants. It was easy to check a BOP, for the records were collected in an on-line database. In the office, the BOP computer terminal was located just to the left of the fax machine, and detectives often pulled a fax off the machine and walked over and checked the victim's or suspect's criminal record immediately. In the following example a White detective pulled an incident report describing an encounter between a White man and a Black woman off the fax machine and read it aloud to the office:

> Threats to kill. She says he called her a nigger bitch and threatened her with a gun. This isn't racially motivated. Maybe we should send this over

to sexual assault. [Does a BOP.] This *is* a record! [Reading from the incident report] He admitted to calling her a nigger, but says he didn't threaten her with a gun. This is just part of living in *that* neighborhood.

The case illuminates several routine practices and illustrates quite clearly the power the detectives had to characterize the incident. First, the detective encounters the case, hot off the presses. Second, he reads it to the office, submitting the question to the other detectives of what happened. Third, the detective did a BOP—in this case of a suspect. The detective also frames the account. After reading the initial report, the detective decides that what happened was not racially motivated. He characterizes the threat as normal, given the neighborhood—a poorer section of town.

The detective's comments suggest that he decided the incident was probably not racially motivated because this type of behavior—using slurs and threatening with a gun—is normal among the poor. In deciding that this was a case in which the law should not be enforced because the conduct was normal for a subgroup of the population, the detective's behavior was similar to that of patrol officers in another study who believed that assault laws should not be enforced in the Black community because Blacks normally settle disputes violently.[17] In that study, as with this ABTF detective, police discretion not to enforce the law leads to a situation in which the law is enforced differently in different neighborhoods based on the officer's stereotype of how the group behaves.

The incident also reveals how a category of motivation the law does not proscribe can "pollute" an incident. Officers liked pure cases, cases in which only one of the categories of animus that the unit investigated motivated the incident. Though the unit had brought one gender case in the past, it was an extraordinary one that involved a man who had had four abusive relationships in which all four women had filed orders of protection. Gender-based violence was not normally investigated by the unit. The use of the slur "bitch" suggested to the detective above that the crime might have been motivated by gender, as opposed to race. Gender thus "polluted" the case, leading the detective to discount the racial slur and the difference in race between the victim and the suspect.

Criminal History and Victim Credibility

Though some of the detectives did a BOP in order to investigate how potentially dangerous their interviewee was, its primary investigative use was to evaluate the credibility of those one was interviewing, including the victim. Checking the criminal history of a victim frequently told the detectives about the victim's previous encounters with the law in a way that allowed the detectives to view the circumstances surrounding the incident in a different light. The ABTF detectives' behavior in one case illustrates this. In the office one evening, several detectives learned of incident in which a gay man had been called a faggot and was then assaulted while walking his dog. Instead of writing a report and making sure the victim had received medical attention, the patrol officers who reported to the scene gave the victim the option to "go home or get arrested." Because the responding patrol officers never issued an incident report describing the event, the unit learned of the incident only from a letter forwarded to the unit by the police commissioner's office. The letter, which had also been sent to several newspapers, denounced the police department's treatment of several antigay hate crimes and detailed police action in each of the incidents.

As the detectives listened to their supervisor read the letter, all were highly critical of the patrol officers' actions. One even suggested that the police may have been responsible for the attack.

> *Supervisor:* Six officers from Precinct [X] responded and they said to the victim you have two choices, you can either get arrested or you can go home. Those are the choices they give you in "[X]."
>
> *Detective 1:* Are they sure the police didn't do it? Maybe we should let Internal Affairs know about this.
>
> *Detective 2:* So they make a mess and we clean it up? So we clean up their mess?
>
> *Supervisor:* We clean up everybody's shit. I've let the lieutenant know about this. [To Detective 2] Generate an incident report and talk to the victim. There were no reports. His [the victim's] mouth is all messed up.

Detective 2 immediately walked over to the BOP machine and put in the victim's name and date of birth in order to get his criminal history.

> *Detective 1:* [Reading from terminal.] "Drunk and disorderly." "Drunk and disorderly." "Drunk and disorderly." He's a drunk.

Detective 2: That's probably why the cops told him to go home or go to jail.

Detective 1: He's not a bad guy, just a sick one.

Here, reading that the victim had been charged with being drunk and disorderly—in this case, *ten years* earlier—dramatically changed the detectives' perspective about the incident. Before they knew of the victim's criminal history, they were ready to assume that a hate crime had occurred and that the patrol officers had not recognized this. The criminal charges delegitimized the victim and transformed the person who, they had previously assumed, was assaulted into someone unworthy of the special treatment normally accorded to hate crime victims.

The detectives were especially wary of victims with drunk and disorderly charges, drug charges, or who were previously convicted on hate crime charges. These charges frame incidents in ways the detectives found difficult to discard later, even after they learned more about the incidents surrounding the case from the victim. The following conversation took place several days after detectives learned of the incident described above. One detective said to several others:

> After 12 A.M. only the crooks and the drunks are out. I can sympathize with the cops that time of night. The only people out are drunk. Something happens and a few weeks later they scream bias. Again, you weren't there, you only get one side of the story.

Even though here the victim was seriously injured in the attack and the investigating officers acted improperly, the victim's previous charges made the detectives, who had been sympathetic, skeptical of the victim's story. Instead of siding with the victim, they questioned whether the victim was telling the truth and sympathized with the officers of whom they had been quite critical.

Having drunk and disorderly and drug-related charges on their record damaged victims' credibility for two reasons. Drunk and disorderly charges were suspect because the detectives particularly despised alcohol abuse, perhaps in part because a large number of the unit's suspects used alcohol as an excuse for committing hate crimes. The officers were also suspicious of drug users after having had experiences in which drug deals gone bad were first reported as hate crimes.

The high rate of recidivism among perpetrators of hate crime made the detectives suspicious of reports in which the purported victim had been arrested for or even charged with civil rights violations. If victims did have such charges on their record, detectives considered one or two other scenarios far more likely. First, that the incident was truly a hate crime but the "victim" was really the *perpetrator* or, alternatively, that the incident was not a hate crime but, rather, retaliation for the victim's earlier actions.

The detectives asserted that the victim's criminal history was a signal of the victim's credibility because it gave them information about the incident that was not available in the initial report. This told some of the detectives how to read the situation and whether the victim should be believed. They assumed trustworthy victims would not have long criminal histories. Hence, such a history suggested that the reported incident was not really a hate crime. One detective described what makes a victim believable: "Personal credibility. Someone who has been to jail six or seven times doesn't have as much credibility as someone who hasn't."

In a similar case, another detective described his use of a criminal-history check to interpret the report of a hate crime that he had been assigned to investigate. Here, a routine check of the victim revealed drug charges, which, combined with the detective's partner's knowledge of the witnesses' activities, cast doubt on the victim's story that he had been assaulted because of his race. When asked what BOP told him, one officer responded:

> It tells me their knowledge of the system. For example, you have a victim who has been assaulted with a board. When he was a minor, he had a drug charge. The witness has a long history of drug trafficking. My partner knew who the kid was instantly. Could it have been something else? Sounds like a drug deal.

A Victim-Centered Approach

The practice of checking victims' criminal histories reveals a conflict between the primacy unit procedures placed on victims' unmediated stories and the detectives' training in the academy. Here, suspicious of the victim's story, the detective behaved like the model interviewer imagined in the main Center City Police Department procedures. The model detective patterned for all police officers in the academy was Sergeant Joe Friday of the late-1960s television show *Dragnet*. Friday reminded women he was interviewing that he wanted, "Just the facts, Ma'am." These procedures restricted the purpose of interviewing victims to the "gather[ing of] pertinent data and relevant facts concerning a particular incident or to substantiate or corroborate information already obtained from other sources."[18] Witness testimony is seen as highly suspect, and police officers are cautioned at length that witnesses might lie, give inaccurate, inconsistent, or incomplete descriptions of events, or be uncooperative.[19]

Because ABTF detectives were interviewing individuals who had been traumatized by hate crime, the unit's interview procedures diverged sharply from those taught in the police academy. The unit's guidelines and procedures focused the investigation on the story told by the victim of the crime. In the unit a distinction was made between "witnesses" who happened to have seen the crime or otherwise have information about it and "the victim" or victims who were the object of the perpetrator's assault. The unit's logbooks, screening classification forms, and statistics all used "victim" as opposed to *complainant*, the term used on the police department incident report form and in the police department generally.

The unit's investigation procedures manifest this victim-centered approach. As soon as a case was assigned a detective, he or she was required to telephone the victim and set up an appointment to review the case at the victim's home—a place where the victim could feel comfortable. Interviews were not to be conducted over the telephone.

The types of questions asked also differed from those asked in the interrogation of other crimes. Unlike Sergeant Friday of *Dragnet*, ABTF detectives were not supposed to get "just the facts" of the crime. This policy stemmed in part from the law the detectives were enforcing. Center City's hate crime law required proof of motivation to support criminal civil rights charges. Thus, in addition to recording victims' vital statistics and collecting physical evidence, the unit's procedure required detectives to ask victims broad questions about the circumstances and events in their lives that might have led to the crime. In direct contrast to investigations that downplay the importance of the victim's perception of why the incident occurred, ABTF procedures emphasized it. One of the unit's "bias indicators," for instance, was the victim's perception of the incident. Thus, what the victim thinks becomes important. Detectives were told to ask, "Why do you think this happened to you?" As detectives wrote up their interviews, the victim's account, though not dispositive of what happened, later became part of the official record.

The routine of first checking a victim's criminal history was fundamentally at odds with unit procedures, which required that the victim's account be unmediated. Most of the detectives had not left behind the suspiciousness they had been taught in the academy and on the streets and referred to their training as police officers as one of the reasons for checking the criminal history of all involved. "We *should* do it all the time," one supervisor noted. The detectives' responses suggested they believed that in order to be good *police officers*, they needed to be suspicious of everything—of all stories told, even those told by individuals identified as victims.

Interviewing Victims, Searching for Bias

After reading the initial report and checking the victim's criminal history, the detective usually contacted the victim and set up an interview. The primary focus of the initial investigation was the victim's interview. This was particularly true when the detectives dealt with cases in which suspects had not been identified by patrol. Most crimes did not come to the unit solved, and the victims were generally viewed as an important source for information. Victims could provide information regarding incidents that had transpired, and the individual or individuals who committed them. One detective said when he investigated cases he talked to the victim because the victim's perception was the only evidence he may get that the incident was a hate crime. The victim may also be able to provide information regarding the perpetrator's identity. Many of the cases involved multiple incidents in which the victim had had several encounters with the perpetrator. In such cases, it was likely that the victim might be able to provide a description. In cases involving vandalism, the victim was not likely to have seen the perpetrator but may have been able to suggest why the crime was committed, something that would be relevant to whether it was a hate crime.

Despite the practice of checking the victim's criminal record before the interview, the detectives' behavior toward victims was generally quite sympathetic. ABTF detectives called the individual victimized by the crime the "victim" even before they determined that that individual had been victimized by a crime; in this they were unlike other detectives, who use legal terms like "complaining witness" or "complainant" to refer to crime victims.[20] Often, detectives in the unit went so far as to personalize cases, referring to the victim in the cases they were assigned as "my victim."

Part of the reason that detectives personalized cases was that in doing their job, they were thrown into contact with victims whom they got to know and discovered to be grateful for their help. Getting circumstances of the crime from the victims often required that the detectives conduct in-depth interviews that touched on personal issues, including the victim's health, parentage, and how well the victim got along with his or her family. If a victim's case was adjudicated, the detective might have sustained contact with the victim, taking the victim back and forth to court for a number of months. If a second incident happened to a victim a few years later, it would be assigned to the officer who had had the victim previously. Sometimes officers developed personal relationships with victims. Several officers told me that they maintained a close relationship with some victims over the years, checking up on them once a year and handling problems for them occasionally.

Allowing the Victim to Tell Her or His Story

The detectives' interviews did not place limits on the victim's telling of her or his story. Surprisingly, most detectives in the ABTF rejected their earlier training and did not, like Sergeant Friday, demand, "Just the facts." Interviews were conducted at the victim's home. Some lasted as long as three hours. Although several of the detectives insisted that all they wanted to know was who, what, when, where, and why, observations and reports reveal that detectives conducted the victim interview in such a way as to allow the victim to report much more. The detectives allowed the victim to tell his or her story, first, by asking for a description of what happened in his or her own words. When the victim acquiesced, the story emerged sporadically, with relevant factors that might have legal significance emerging later in the telling.

In questioning victims, the detectives tried to draw a wide net over the victim's narrative to catch as many details as possible. They took copious notes during the interview and occasionally interrupted to ask more questions. I watched them interview one mixed-race victim who had been harassed by Whites after moving into an all-White neighborhood.

The victim described having his house stoned. The detectives asked, "Where were you when the pebbles hit? How many pebbles were there? Did you hear the sound of them hitting the glass? Did you hear anyone say anything?" The victim was asked to describe the suspect and to recall any previous encounters with that suspect or any other suspect. Similarly, his roommates were asked about previous encounters between the victim and suspect.

The focus on interviews as a primary method of making one's case in the hate crime unit is distinct from the practices of detectives previously studied. In his study of detectives in Toronto, Richard V. Ericson reports that they did not use interviews to generate suspects but, rather, to confirm identifications because most interviews occurred after a suspect had been identified.[21] In asking for more rather than less context, ABTF detectives' practices are oriented toward doing what hate crime law requires. The hate crime law in Center City required that the suspect's actions be motivated by bias. Designed around the law, the unit's procedures listed several bias indicators or, "objective facts, circumstances, or patterns attending a criminal(s) which, standing alone or in conjunction with other facts or circumstances, suggest that the offender's actions were motivated in whole or in part by any form of bias."[22] The list of bias crime indicators is a detailed one, reflecting several possible locations for evidence of bias (see Table 4.6). Though the bias crime indicators were primarily to help the detectives to classify crimes, they served an investigative purpose, too. They gave detectives guidelines for the type of evidence to pay attention to in the field.

ABTF detectives' practices suggest that they did not use the list of bias crime indicators as a checklist when they questioned victims. Some of the questions the list suggested were relevant—for example, whether the incident occurred on a day of significance; whether the victim was a member of an advocacy group that supports a targeted group; and whether the victim was engaged in activities promoting his or her group—were almost never asked by detectives. In general, such questions are useful when the interviewer has no idea why the victim was targeted. The detectives may not have asked these questions because, in the vast majority of cases, they thought they knew why the victim had been targeted.

The issue of differences between the victim and the perpetrator group was one of the most important bias indicators. Frequently, the first question the detectives asked was whether a victim was a racial, religious, or other "minority" in the area in which the attack occurred. In later questions designed to elicit information about the perpetrator's motivation, detectives also asked about comments, drawings, or symbols made by the suspect, and the previous contact between the suspect and the victim. Rather than serving as a way of verifying that an incident was bias-motivated, the list of bias indicators primarily served to remind the detectives to look widely for indications of bias.

Trying to discern the roots of the conflict, the detectives questioned victims closely about any contact she or he had with the suspect and what had transpired. Detectives also asked about the victim's and the suspect's prior relationship, if one existed. Were they neighbors? Friends? Strangers? The detectives were trying to find clues as to whether the victim had been selected because of his or her race, religion, or sexual orientation. The ABTF detectives, like detectives investigating hate crime elsewhere, consider bias motivation inconsistent with a relationship between the victim and perpetrator.[23] Recall, for example, the discussion in chapter 1 describing the decision by the sheriff in Grayson County, Virginia, that the beheading of G. P. Johnson was not a hate crime because the murderer and victim were friends. For ABTF detectives, preexisting relationships, such as neighbors, friends (or enemies), schoolmates, or coworkers, between a victim and a suspect were important because they suggested a range of explanations for the crime—a dispute, jealousy, anger—other than bias.

Because of the absence of any prior conflict's polluting evidence of bias, strangers made good suspects. One victim advocate commented on this practice of discounting hate crime because of a prior relationship, "People like crimes that happen on sidewalks, not in homes, [done] by people who are strangers. They have no problem with [identifying crime done by] skinheads."

Listening to the victims often required the detectives to listen for information the victims *left out* of the account, and sometimes to reinterpret events for the victim. In the early 1980s, Southeast Asians immigrating to Center City were frequently victimized by hate crime. The immigrants' language difficulties, fear of the police, and other cultural differences served as barriers to the full reporting of incidents and investigation of crimes. The unit's supervisors attempted to mitigate this situation by having brochures about the unit translated into several Asian languages, hiring Asian-language interpreters, and even by taking classes in conversational Vietnamese. One sergeant responsible for hate crime

TABLE 4.6
Bias Crime Indicators

Racial, Ethnic, Gender, and Cultural Differences
- Racial, religious, ethnic/national origin, handicap, or sexual orientation group of victim differs from that of offender.
- Victim is a member of a group that is overwhelmingly outnumbered by members of another group in the area in which the incident occurred.
- Victim was engaged in activities promoting his or her group.
- Incident coincided with a holiday or date of particular significance to the victim's group.
- Victim, although not a member of the targeted group, is a member of an advocacy group that supports the victim group, or the victim was in the company of a member of the targeted group.
- Historically, animosity exists between the victim's group and the suspect's group.

Comments, Written Statements, Gestures
- Bias-related comments, written statements, or gestures were made by the offender.

Drawings, Markings, Symbols, and Graffiti
- Bias-related drawings, markings, symbols, or graffiti were left at the scene of the incident.

Representations of Organized Hate Groups
- Objects or items that represent the work of organized hate groups were left (for example, hoods, burning crosses) or an organized hate group claimed responsibility for the incident.
- Previous existence of bias crime incidents
- Victim was visiting the location where previous bias crimes had been committed against members of the victim's group.
- Several incidents occurred in the same area, and the victims were members of the same group.
- Victim has received previous harassing mail or phone calls or has been the victim of verbal abuse based on his/her affiliation with a targeted group.

Victim/Witness Perception
- Victims or witnesses perceive that the incident was motivated by bias.
- Suspect was previously involved in a similar incident or is a member of, or associates with members of an organized hate group.

Lack of Other Motives
- No clear economic or other motive for the incident exists.

Source: ABTF files.

training in the unit and at the police academy stressed the importance of listening closely to the victim and making sure the victim fully understood the questions asked. He described an experience his sergeant had many years before when he was questioning Asian victims.

Some of the Asian victims might not even know what the language is. My sergeant had a case where he was using this nine-year-old kid as an interpreter for his grandfather, who'd been attacked. He asked the kid whether his grandfather had been called any names. The kid asked his grandfather and said yes, but only animal names. "Animal names?" asked the sergeant. "Yes," said the kid, "duck and goose." They'd been calling him a fucking gook.

Marshaling Evidence of Motivation

In order to seek charges for civil rights violations, the detectives needed to do more than just identify bias; they needed evidence of the perpetrator's motivation. In gathering evidence of motivation in preparation for seeking a civil rights complaint, they often looked to the suspect's language—the use of slurs or epithets before, during, or after the attack. Slurs or epithets used in a context that suggested the crime was bias-motivated were important to the detectives because it was a vivid, clear signal of the perpetrator's motivation. When asked what was needed for a civil rights violation, one detective replied,

> You obviously want language. If not, now you have to prove what is in the mind of the perpetrator. That's a tough charge to prove. The most perfect case for civil rights violations was "Main" Street, the "Smith" case. The guy ran down the street yelling, "I'm a redneck motherfucker and I hate niggers," right before he hit Mr. Smith.

From bringing cases to court, from following cases through the legal system, and from prosecutors, the importance of language-based evidence to strong hate crime cases had been drilled into the detectives. When I asked how important language was, another detective responded, "Without language, lots of times you don't have a case." It was not enough that the perpetrator had used slurs and epithets; for a civil rights case to succeed, language had to convey bias motivation. The converse was true as well. Even if the motivation were there, without slurs or epithets, one might not have a viable case. In remarks that were typical of the comments of the other detectives, one remarked, "Lots of times, there's a civil rights case but not enough to bring charges, to go to court. You may have an assault but not enough language. You had to have language and incidents over a consistent time."

Recording evidence of the language used prior to, during, or after the crime was so important to civil rights prosecutions that the department stressed this to officers who did not investigate hate crimes. In a

departmental memorandum, all officers were reminded of the importance of recording the language used by perpetrators.

> When assessing the situation at the scene of any incident, the Patrol Super-
> visor must keep in mind that it is often the language used in a verbal or
> physical assault that is the key to determining whether or not an incident
> constitutes a civil rights violation. It is critical in each case that the Patrol
> Supervisor ensures the police officer(s) request and capture, in the 1.1 inci-
> dent report, the exact language used by the alleged offender(s) during the
> offense. In such situations, any verbal or physical evidence, including such
> things as letters, derogatory graffiti, etc. should be treated as evidence.

Evidence of the suspect's language came from victims, witnesses, or the
suspects themselves. After the victim had told his or her story, often the
first thing detectives asked the victim concerned the language used by
the suspect before, during, or after the crime. Victims were asked about
language at different times and in different ways. Their responses to the
questions regarding language were noted in reports, sometimes in bold,
sometimes in all capital letters, and sometimes in highlighted text.

The Treatment of Suspects

Finding Suspects

In many of the initial reports the unit received, no one was identified
as a suspect, or the role of the person who had been named as a suspect
in the hate crime was unclear. Sometimes the victim provided information that assisted the detectives in identifying suspects. In cases with
several suspects, supervisors directed detectives in the unit to canvass
the area to search for information. This meant that the detectives went
to the crime scene, literally knocked on every door in the vicinity, and
asked if any individuals had information regarding the incident.

Knocking on all the doors in a several-block vicinity, interviewing
residents, and writing up the reports of their investigation required a
significant time investment. The detectives believed that hate crimes as
a genre, and the difficulty that solving them presented, necessitated
such time-intensive investigations. One detective who pioneered the
unit's investigation procedures discussed why the unit developed these
investigative practices.

Haters realize how to get their message across. They attack what is sacred—where people live, where they worship, where they bury their dead. I realized that I had less likelihood of finding the perpetrator unless I investigate more than other crimes. . . . I just got involved in investigation as a good police officer and I proved that this is solvable crime. People thought that these weren't solvable. When perpetrators commit hate crimes they don't get money, they don't get to settle something with someone, they get bragging rights. They have to tell someone.

The process of finely combing the neighborhood developed early in the unit's history. Many cases then involved finding out who was responsible for breaking the windows of minorities in the middle of the night. Hence, supervisors in the unit developed many investigative procedures for cases that had few leads. One longtime investigator, a sergeant who had been in the unit many years and trained several detectives, described how he investigated cases:

First, I go and look at the exact location of the incident. Second, I do a door-to-door canvass. I stand up and look up at the building. If you do that you may see the little old lady who sees everything and may have seen the incident.

Other circumstances also made knocking on doors a valuable show of force, if not always a way to solve crimes. Many of the hate crimes took place in small, tightly knit, largely White communities, and residents of such communities were often reluctant to cooperate. Some of the witnesses to the crime supported the perpetrators' actions or felt loyalty to the Whites who commit hate crimes. Others, who may have wanted to help, were often afraid to speak for fear of retaliation by the perpetrators, their friends, neighbors, or relatives. Witnesses feared ostracism by the community, too. Given the reluctance of witnesses, sometimes knocking on doors did not yield suspects, but it did put the perpetrators on notice that the unit was aware of their activities. One detective said:

Even if I can't take it to court, I investigate it until I'm up against the wall so the next time it does become a winner and maybe it won't happen again. It sends a message to the perp that you're watching him. I saw investigation as a way to send a message. When I do an investigation, I want to know all about him, who his girlfriend is, what he drinks. I talk to his neighbors.

Interrogating Suspects

When suspects were found, if they agreed to talk to the police, they were brought to the unit's office in police headquarters and interrogated. Though suspects were "Mirandized," the atmosphere was designed to be coercive—both physically and emotionally. Interrogations were conducted in the sergeant's office, a room that was roughly eight feet by ten feet and crowded with three large desks. The supervisors in the unit liked to do separate interrogations of suspects for a single incident, in order to ferret out conflicting or inconsistent stories. The detectives used aggressive body language to intimidate suspects into confessing. One veteran of many interrogations discussed the physically confining and oppressive manner in which interrogations were conducted:

> One may give a story; another may give a different story. They will say stuff that couldn't have occurred. If they're minors they're interrogated in the presence of an uninterested adult. Usually, it's their parent. Sometimes the parent can be a help. We interview suspects here. We don't do it at home. There's all sorts of techniques you can use. Put their back to the door. Make sure you're using those chairs that can roll so you can get in close.

One head of the unit, a tall, stout supervisor, "Parker,"[24] was famous for his ability to extract confessions. They named the ability after him, calling it "Parkerizing." Suspects were clearly intimidated. "After the interrogation," Parker told me, "you could look at one of them and tell they'd been Parkerized. Police biz and show biz are so much alike." In a dramatic, physically tense environment suspects confessed. One respondent asserted that 90 percent of the unit's cases were solved by using confessions. She described a suspect's being "Parkerized," one night.

> It was one of those hot August nights. They offered [the suspect] cigarettes and candy. Everyone was smoking. There was a cloud of smoke and it was hot—100°—in the office. The guy finally starts to cry, and he says, "Turn the tape off because I'm crying," and the sergeant says, "No, it'll make you more sympathetic."

Interrogations were not restricted to the primary suspect. The detectives had been known to embark on "fishing expeditions"—interviewing witnesses whom they had no reason to believe knew anything about the crime—on the off chance that being brought in would make them "give up" vital information. One sergeant discussed a case for which they had no lead except the name "Stewart," so they called a family with the same name who lived in the neighborhood in which the crime occurred and had one of the Stewarts come down to the unit.

> One case, we asked around and poked around and all we could come up with was the name "Stewart," so I said, "Bring him down here." "But all we got is Stewart," one of my detectives said. We called him down here and the father came in here and said, "You don't want us, you want the other Stewart."

In this case their hunch that bringing in a random "Stewart" from the neighborhood would yield information paid off.

During interrogations detectives were searching not only for the identity of the person who committed the crime and an admission of guilt but also *why* the crime was committed. For civil rights violations or hate crime charges, the detectives needed to present evidence showing why the victim had been selected. Because the detectives needed to show why the crime was committed, even after the perpetrator had confessed, they often spent a large amount of time clarifying the perpetrator's motivation. In the interrogation below, the detectives are trying to find out why a Puerto Rican man was maced at a bus stop by two young White men.

> *Detective:* I think . . . he was sprayed because he was a Puerto Rican, right?
>
> *Suspect:* Because he bothered my friend.
>
> *Detective:* You don't even know for sure whether he was the one who bothered your friend. So there were two reasons, he was Puerto Rican and he bothered your friend?
>
> *Suspect:* MMM.
>
> *Detective:* Is that a yes?
>
> *Suspect:* Yes.
>
> *Detective:* And he was a Puerto Rican and he was in Gertown. Is that a yes?
>
> *Suspect:* Yes.
>
> *Detective:* And neither Puerto Ricans or Blacks should be in Gertown at night, is that a golden rule? If he was Black and he was walking down that street and that girl yelled, "Hey nigger," he would have got the same treatment as the Puerto Rican?

Suspect: So wouldn't have a White walking through [a Black neighborhood]?

Detective: I'm not saying, but he would have got the same treatment, right?

Suspect: I don't know.

Detective: And you went over and you sprayed him like you said for two reasons. He was a Puerto Rican in Gertown and he beat up your friend?

Suspect: He was a Puerto Rican and he beat up my friend.

Part of examining the suspect's motivation involved questions about the language he or she had used. Suspects were repeatedly questioned about their language before and during the incident. Below is a brief portion of the transcript of an interrogation. The suspect being questioned by the detective was accused of being involved in an attack by a gang of Whites on a White man, his son, and their Black passenger as they were driving through Hillsdale, a predominately White neighborhood in which the unit had investigated many cases. During this interrogation, the detective is trying to verify another statement, which had asserted that just before the attack someone had yelled, "Get that van; get the nigger and the nigger lovers." Notice how during the interrogation the detective not only tries to pin down the suspect's involvement and others' involvement in the crime (as is typical of police interrogations) but also focuses closely on the language used during the attack.

Detective: Who else was with you that started running? You're saying three were running with you, X and Y?

Suspect: Yeah, and all the little kids.

Detective: Anybody else?

Suspect: That's about it. That's the only people that ran with us, plus all the people that were witnesses there.

Detective: And you're saying the language was the niggers did this, the niggers did that?

Suspect: Yeah.

Detective: Those were the words. Were there any words as far as getting the niggers?

Suspect: No. Just get them, get the van, get that van. Get that van.

Detective: But you said the word niggers?

Suspect: Yes, the word niggers was involved.

Detective: The words nigger lover?
Suspect: No, nothing about a nigger lover.
Detective: Was there anything about no niggers in Hillsdale?
Suspect: Huh?
Detective: No niggers in Hillsdale.

Conclusion—Enforcing the Law through Investigation

Investigation is the first step in the process of transforming criminal behavior into hate crime. Investigating hate crime, similar to investigating other criminal behavior, requires the detectives to first establish that the incident report they received from patrol is worthy of investigation by the hate crime unit. As part of the prescreening process, cases that were either not crimes or were clearly not bias-motivated were excluded from the unit's case file. The unit's investigative procedures differ from the narrow fact-finding quests or investigations where the victim's story serves only to lend credibility to the arrest of a suspect already in custody. ABTF procedures required the investigation to begin with the victim interview; the victim was to be asked a series of questions regarding the events and why they transpired. If the investigations yielded suspects who agreed to be questioned, officers worked to elicit confessions from the suspects.

Detectives' everyday routines are crucial to investigation. Some routines like checking victims' criminal records to evaluate their credibility were at odds with other unit procedures. This situation suggests an important implication for changing police procedures. When creating new procedures, officials must take into account prior training, which can lead detectives to adopt routines that substantially undercut the procedural changes.

Detectives clearly have discretionary control over information. They can and often do disregard the initial frame placed on the story by a patrol officer and substitute their own. They are free to solicit information from whomever they wish and have control of the use of the information that an individual provides. Despite practices that allowed the victim to speak, victims' accounts were not necessarily automatically accepted as truth.

One way of evaluating whether police officers are enforcing the law is to look to whether they follow up on cases through investigation.

Most studies of police officers suggest that they only minimally fulfill their duty to investigate. Most cases fall through the cracks. Evaluating this empirically, the ABTF fares better than other investigative units at carrying out its duties. The bottom line is that once a case is referred to a particular detective in this unit, it is likely to be at least minimally investigated. Detectives in the unit were required to document everything, and for fear of incurring the wrath of a supervisor, they did. One supervisor kicked those who were not working out of the unit. This particularly tough sergeant recounted how he dealt with lazy detectives:

> Some we brought up [to the unit] and let go immediately. They thought they were on a ride and they get here and find me breathing down their neck. One thing that I did is to put the bar way up high. Document everything. If it's not in writing, it didn't happen.

In this way, unit procedures facilitated ABTF detectives' investigative practices. Discretion allows detectives to make crime by mediating victims' stories through the detective's previous experience. Ultimately, how they treat hate crime victims depends on their orientation to their job, how they see the unit's mission, and whether they have an agenda that prevents them from interacting with victims.

5

The Difficulty of Hate Crime
Investigation

As the previous chapter suggests, for detectives, the initial part of constructing hate crime requires assembling basic information regarding who committed the incident in question and why. Investigation is the process through which detectives acquire this information about crimes. The previous chapter emphasized detective control over the initial process of making crime. Detectives may decide which crimes they will investigate based on their judgment regarding what has happened. Once they decide to investigate, however, there is a potential for a shift in the balance of power because when investigating a crime, detectives have limited control over access to the types of information they need to identify suspects and discover the crime's origin. This is of course true for all detectives—witnesses may lie, have faulty memories, or just not wish to come forward. Witnesses' and crime victims' control over information limits detectives' access to information and serves as a barrier to the investigation of incidents, and thus has the potential to prevent even the most committed detective from getting to the bottom of the crimes of which he or she undertakes investigation.

This chapter shifts the focus from the general problem of enforcement to the problem of the enforcement of hate crime law in an impacted community. As the chapter shows, detectives trying to enforce laws in a community that is resistant face particularly difficult access to information.

The Politics of Resistance: Enforcing Hate Crime Law

Public attitudes regarding whether a law is going to be enforced are said to be an important determinant of police action. One prevailing assumption, long recognized, is that police officers choose not to enforce the law when its noninvocation protects public respect and support.[1] Noninvocation of the law is thought to be the norm in situations in which the law is applied against a subgroup that deviates from the community, and also when the community as a whole does not feel a law should be enforced.[2]

If police officers are supposed to be hesitant to enforce unpopular laws, then the behavior of the ABTF requires explaining. From 1987 through 1996, the unit spent a significant amount of time and energy enforcing an unpopular hate crime law in one particular neighborhood. During that period more than a quarter of the incidents that the ABTF investigated came from Gertown, an all-White working-class neighborhood that contained less than 10 percent of the city's population. Despite its small size, each year from 1989 until 1996, the highest number of incidents reported to the unit occurred in Gertown. In order to decrease the number of incidents in Gertown, the unit began to conduct proactive surveillances of the housing projects in Gertown and Hillsdale, another area of the city with a high number of incidents. These surveillances or "proactive patrols" occurred from 6:00 P.M. until 1:00 A.M. every Thursday, Friday, and Saturday evening. Between the surveillances and the inevitable investigations that flowed from such a large number of incidents, the unit spent a lot of time in Gertown.

Hate crime law was more than just unpopular in Gertown; residents were mobilized against its enforcement. They blocked investigations and created few incentives for detectives to enforce the law. Many of the hate crimes that occurred in Gertown could be directly attributed to residents' reaction to the integration of formerly all-White housing developments. Like individuals in other neighborhoods in Center City had done earlier, some of those who wanted Gertown to remain all White greeted the newcomers with violence. The unit faced greater difficulties enforcing the law in Gertown than in other neighborhoods because leaders in the community could organize and control the area. In this way they were able to mount sustained opposition to ABTF efforts to enforce hate crime law against White perpetrators.

Gertown's Struggle to Prevent Integration

Throughout the 1970s and 1980s, Gertown remained a predominately White neighborhood, even as other parts of the city slowly began to integrate. In 1980, for instance, only fifteen Blacks lived in Gertown.[3] This was true despite the fact that three public housing units, 15 percent of the units in Center City, were located in Gertown. The city's first attempts to integrate one development in the 1970s failed; Blacks moved in only to be quickly moved out.

Gertown's struggle against school desgregration in the early 1970s served to further unite an already strong community against invasion by outsiders. For many residents, their biggest interest became to preserve their community intact; they were deeply resistant to any change. For instance, in the early 1960s the Center City zoning board proposed a new development in Gertown to ease some of the housing shortages. Residents recalled how a similar project had led to working-class peoples being displaced by the wealthy in another Center City neighborhood, and they protested so loudly that the mayor withdrew the proposal.

Keeping outsiders—especially minorities—out became the focus of a new political movement in the late 1970s in Gertown. Gertown was for them and many wanted to keep it that way. Drawing on the neighborhood's earlier struggles over school desegregation, they argued that outsiders wished to break up their community. Leaders of residents' organizations called on everyone in the neighborhood to band together to preserve life as they knew it.

The Integration of Gertown Public Housing

Changes in the rest of Center City ultimately forced the integration of Gertown. Increased Asian and Hispanic immigration had led to an increase in the number of minorities living in the city. At the same time, rising prices had led to a severe housing shortage. Gertown public housing, which was almost exclusively White, was set to be integrated after a federal government review of the Center City Housing Office's (CHO)—the public agency that administered low-income housing—practice of assigning public housing found that it blatantly discriminated against minorities.

In Gertown several practices led to segregated housing. First, CHO maintained separate lists for housing developments in different areas of the city. Applicants were allowed to choose the list on which they wanted their names. Second, the agency failed to comply with a previous compliance agreement, which stipulated that minorities were to be given priority in developments that had few people of their race. Despite waiting lists that were more than 80 percent minority, Whites received more than half of the open public housing. Minorities waited an average of nine months longer than Whites for housing. CHO agents also discouraged minorities from living in White areas. The CHO director, who was Black, blamed Center City's ugly racial history. A longtime resident of housing developments, she asserted that she had delayed desegregation because of her fear for the safety of Black tenants.[4]

Though several housing developments in the city were mentioned, the federal government's report focused on the developments in Gertown, where a handful of Asian Americans, Indians, and Hispanics but no Blacks lived. To rectify the racial imbalance, CHO agreed to use one housing list for the whole city. Those who had been denied housing because of race under the old system were to be moved to the top of the list. After that, prospective tenants were given priority based on the date they had been placed on the list.

The implications of the new system on Gertown were significant. Under it, tenants could no longer be assured of going to the housing development of their choice. If they did not take the placement offered, they would be moved to the end of the list. With minorities making up the vast majority of the list, Gertown's housing developments could no longer remain all White.

Gertown's Reaction to Integration

As CHO made plans for minorities to move into the Gertown housing developments, reaction among Gertown residents was swift. At community meetings, tenants fiercely opposed to integration denounced the mayor—who had been one of Gertown's favored sons. Poorer White residents of Gertown who needed public housing, because of rising rents in the private sector, complained they would not be able to choose housing units around their friends and family because units were to be allocated on a first-available basis. Drawing on their early struggles to prevent school integration, residents insisted that not allowing poor White Gertown residents their choice of housing development was "forced housing." Voicing the concerns of many, the president of one of the neighborhood organizations declared, "I equate it with busing. People will say we have homeless here. Why not let them move into public housing?"[5] Opponents argued that those who had lived in Gertown for generations were being forced out by their high rents. The president of the residents' group maintained, "It isn't an issue of minorities coming in—it's Gertown people being forced out."[6] Gertowners took some of their anger to the polls. Although the mayor won the election, he lost Gertown, receiving only 500 votes out of the more than 9,000 cast in Gertown precincts.

For some residents, it was more than just Gertowners being forced out. They had problems with minorities moving in. A common complaint among them was that introducing Blacks would bring crime and, ultimately, the ruin of the neighborhood. Residents discussed the possibility of anticrime patrols.

Violence was a widely predicted response to integrating the developments. One Center City City Council member from Gertown who was opposed to the integration said, "The vast majority of Gertown people don't want to jeopardize the safety of black people. That's not to say there wouldn't be some people who might take things into their own hands."[7] One resident pointed to a strip of painted-over graffiti, remarking, "It used to say, 'niggers go home.' If they move in, it's going to be war."[8] A spokesman for a tenants' organization threatened, "It's forced housing. It shouldn't be happening. If you force people, they're going to rebel. It may be all right for the winter but it's going to be a hot summer."[9] Mindful of the violence that had occurred in Gertown during the late 1970s and the threats and predictions, the mayor called on the ABTF and CHO to develop a plan to move residents in safely.

Policing Integration

Most of the ABTF's activities during the first two years of the move-ins were oriented toward helping new tenants move into their apartments. In advance of the move-ins, CHO would send a list of the minority tenants' names to the ABTF, indicating when and where they were moving in. The unit would watch the family during the actual process of moving into their apartment and stay until 1:00 A.M. in order to catch perpetrators or prevent any incidents from taking place. The unit also began to patrol the streets of Gertown for signs of trouble three nights each week.

Though the explosive, extremely violent incidents that were expected never happened, the number of reported hate crime cases in Gertown housing developments increased rather dramatically. In 1989, twenty cases were reported, up from four cases the previous year. In 1990, the number of cases more than doubled, jumping to forty-two. In 1991, the number of cases increased 40 percent, to 59 cases. Other housing developments showed increases over this time, but none were as dramatic as in Gertown's. In his annual report to the police commissioner, the head of the ABTF attributed the increases in Gertown directly to the move-ins.

As the unit followed up on the new cases that were occurring in Gertown, the detectives encountered a new phenomenon: organized resistance to the enforcement of hate crime law. Though White residents in other neighborhoods had opposed their actions, this was different, primarily because Gertown's opposition to the unit's investigations was organized. Earlier struggles had created a legacy of resistance on which the residents leading the opposition were able to draw. Residents who had first organized to resist school desegregation led the new resistance. One of the community organizations formed during the school desegregation era, the "Gertown Resource Committee" (GRC), served as a mouthpiece for those opposed to the unit's activities. It also had resources to publicize the resistance. Three members of GRC had columns in the *Gertown Voice*, and they used this space to publicize their opposition to the unit and mobilize others to resist the unit's investigations.

Residents opposed to the unit's investigation of the growing numbers of hate crimes committed by Whites complained that the wrong people were being investigated. The *real* hate crimes in Gertown, they insisted, were committed by Blacks and other minorities against Whites. They also insisted that minorities were causing drug-related crime in the area. When confronted with the assertion that such statements were racist or that the community was racist for opposing housing integration, residents in Gertown protested. They countered that their statements were legitimate and pointed to the crime rate in the city's minority neighborhoods as evidence of the truth of the statements. Residents argued that by focusing on the actions of Whites, the media and the ABTF were ignoring "dozens and dozens" of assaults on local Whites by Blacks. [10] The liberal media, the head of GRC declared, frequently got it wrong.

> Last week saw our neighborhood make the daily news—again. "Three black women attacked by Whites in Gertown," the headlines screams. It

was the lead story on radio and TV news too. Editorials demanded an investigation as cries of racism echoed from indignant liberal voices and fraudulent civil rights windbags. . . .

But, a little bit of investigation found that it didn't happen like that at all. . . . Then all of a sudden the story died real quick. Embarrassed, the news media slinked back to their O. J. Simpson coverage—while even so quietly acknowledging that—oops, they may have made a mistake. Aren't they special, these media guardians of justice and truth?[11]

Though the media's coverage of hate crime was regularly criticized, residents and members of the community opposed to the enforcement of hate crime law saved most of their fire for the ABTF. In a weekly newspaper column, the head of GRC often described the ABTF in vitriolic terms. He wrote that ABTF officers had been caught sleeping on the job and were terrible when they did investigate. Sometimes he decried their incompetence, calling them, among other things, "Center City's answer to the F-troop," "stiffs," "wanna-be cops," "punks," the "Keystone Cops," and the "Stumble Bums of Law Enforcement." In addition, the head of GRC severely criticized the unit for what he identified as a failure to follow up on hate crimes in which the attackers were minorities. In the column below, he wrote of visiting the victim of an anti-White hate crime:

> [M]yself and Councilman [X] went to the home of 16-year-old "Joe" last Monday night. Joe, as most know, was attacked and beaten unconscious by a group of minorities. Groups of residents who came out of their homes heard the Hispanic males screaming anti-White slurs as they beat Joe. Witnesses have come forward to testify to what they saw and heard. But, you guessed it, the Anti-Bias Task Force, at least as of Monday morning, said they weren't going to classify this as a racial incident this [*sic*] of course came as no surprise to anyone—the victim was White.
>
> Every time the ABTF opens their mouths they prove us right. They are incompetent bigots, stitched, swollen and bruised.[12]

GRC continually publicized the actions of the unit, criticizing them as racist and biased against Whites. In a later column the GRC head wrote:

> [T]he Anti-Bias Task Force, ABTF, is back to their old racist ways again. They are back in the projects using their trademark when dealing with racial incidents.

Last week a confrontation occurred during which witnesses say assaults and racial insults were being committed by groups of Hispanic and White youths resulted in, as always, only Whites being arrested even though the Hispanics were seen carrying bats, only Whites were charged.[13]

GRC's most frequent complaints about the unit were that it was biased against Whites and used "Gestapo-like" tactics against the Whites they investigated for hate crime violations. One of the tactics complained about included the stopping of Whites on the street and asking them their names. The head of GRC told the *Center City Daily News*, "If the victim is black and attacked by Whites, the Anti-Bias Task Force pounces on them like the Gestapo."[14] Activists in the community had a variety of names for the unit, the favorite being the "Caucasian Detaining Unit." This nickname, frequently used in the *Gertown Voice*, was printed on T-shirts and sold around the neighborhood. The profits, GRC leaders said, were to go to the "Gertown Legal Defense Fund" to hire investigators to uncover fictitious charges against Whites.[15]

Gertowners' Criticism and Unit Morale

The detectives were well aware that they were disliked, even hated, by some in the community. They read the *Gertown Voice* and the *Center City Daily News* voraciously. One of the detectives purchased the *Voice*, which was distributed only in Gertown, every week to see if the unit had been mentioned. Frequently, a copy of the paper was left around the office. Several detectives saved copies of any articles that mentioned the unit in either their personal files or the unit's files.

The bitter tone of the criticism and the personal nature of some of the attacks Gertown residents leveled at the members of the unit suggested that part of the community's strategy was to make the ABTF officers' job so distasteful that the unit would stop enforcing the law in Gertown. The unit did not stop enforcing the law, but the criticism definitely affected the detectives' morale and made it harder to do their jobs. One of the detectives who had been viciously criticized for a number of years in the *Voice* acknowledged that what was written about him was hurtful: "Reading the *Voice*, I know it was written by a Nazi, but it still hurts because I'm human and I want people to like me." One Black officer discussed what it was like to enforce crime in the community where many of the citizens hated the officers:

In the developments, they hated us. The only time I was ever called a "nigger" as a police officer, it was by a White teen. I was chasing him. They said we were there to protect the niggers, spics, and gooks. "Arresting our good kids." I'd tell people it was about everybody's rights.

Several detectives maintained that enforcing the law in a community mobilized against their presence did not bother them, but their supervisors insisted that the community's negative opinion of the unit really affected the unit's morale. It was difficult, one sergeant insisted, for officers not to become depressed about the community's active dislike of their actions. As one detective said:

> I had issues with it. How do you keep the guys here, when they say this? . . . It's very hard on the guys. . . . People form an opinion about you, you take it all in.

White officers, particularly White ethnics, found themselves enforcing the law against others of their own racial and class background, working-class Whites. Some found the conflict between home and job too difficult to manage and left the unit. The difficulty was particularly pronounced for the officers who were from Gertown or other neighborhoods in which the unit frequently had cases. These officers were caught between doing the job and loyalty to longtime friends and family. Mindful of the stress placed on officers caught between the unit and home, supervisors had one officer in the unit who was from Gertown stay behind in the office while the rest of the unit was in Gertown protecting gays and lesbians marching in a parade. Another detective recalled his duties that day.

> Detective Y had a problem with how we handled the Gertown cases. He was from Gertown. His mother lived in Gertown and his friends were there. It really became a problem at St. Patrick's Day. Finally, we had to tell the supervisor, "You can't put him out there with us. His mother lives in Gertown. You can't have her getting harassed because someone sees her son with gays and lesbians." So we didn't put him out there. He stayed in the office and answered phones.

A Call to Resist

The weekly editorials in the *Gertown Voice* served not just to criticize the actions of the ABTF but also to call for action. The real battle,

GRC argued, was between "them"—the minorities—and "us"—the White residents of Gertown. Because the ABTF would not protect White residents, the youth of Gertown needed to band together to resist beatings by the outsiders. Invoking community ownership and pride as the justification for resistance, the head of GRC wrote in an editorial in the *Voice*:

> [W]e as a community must come together. We must unite to defend ourselves. Let all locals, especially the youth who seem to be the main targets, forget about territories. Remember, whether you come from [names various housing developments], wherever, you are all Gertowners, who must come to each other's aid—at least until the last imported drug dealer and gang member has been removed from this neighborhood.[16]

Residents' Obstructionist Activities

The opposition of Gertowners to the enforcement of hate crime law made it harder to investigate crimes. Gertown was small and insular. Many of the assaults and much of the vandalism in the developments happened in the summer when residents were outdoors—in a yard, on sidewalks or streets in front of large apartments with many windows, and on playgrounds and basketball courts. Normally, this would have been the perfect situation for a detective investigating a crime. In most cases with *that* many people in *that* small a place, one could almost be sure that *someone* would have had to see *something*.

For residents mobilized against the law, the key to subverting investigations was to prevent the detectives in the unit from discovering who the suspects were, finding out that an incident was a crime (as opposed to, say, a gesture of self-defense during a fight, or a person hurt accidentally), or uncovering why the incident occurred. Residents used a variety of mechanisms to hinder the unit's investigation. A number of residents had police scanners and would listen for the police dispatcher sending cars to the developments. When an incident was going on, they would run out to try to break it up, take physical evidence, and caution witnesses not to speak to the police. In one case, a fight between a few Blacks, Whites, and Hispanics that degenerated into a huge brawl preceded the stabbing of two White youths. According to a witness, during the fight a Gertown resident, a woman in her sixties, came out of her house and said to the crowd, "You don't want no civil suit! Kids from the Rocks go this way and kids from the Heights go this way."

The crowd dispersed. Women from the neighborhood began carting away the sticks and bottles before the police arrived. In another case, a detective told me that as he was investigating a crime, a member of GRC tried to prevent a boy in the community from identifying himself by yelling out, "Don't say a fucking thing! You don't have to tell them anything."

The leaders of the resistance also informed residents of the unit's investigations in the *Gertown Voice*, and on a popular weekly radio program, *The Gertown Show*. Those opposed to the enforcement of the law tried to limit the information the unit received about incidents by warning residents not to cooperate with the unit because it was biased against the community. One *Gertown Voice* column suggested that these warnings had been effective. White witnesses in Gertown were not talking:

> The ABTF wants to know why the White kids won't talk to them. Haven't they gotten the message yet? We don't like or trust them! We will talk to our regular Center City Police Detectives that will treat us fairly and not make us the criminal every time. Again Do Not talk to the ABTF Without A Lawyer Present! They're telling the kids not to listen to us. Easy question. Who do you trust—us or them?

In this column, written by the head of the tenant's council in one of the housing developments, the unit was a threat not only to the community but also to the witness's own child.

The column also suggested that in order to protect one's rights, one needed a lawyer when talking to detectives in the unit. It cautioned that if one did not have a lawyer present, one might get into trouble. This was a wise move on the part of those who wished to restrict the flow of information. Though the parents of underage suspects frequently attended interrogations, the detectives' preference was not to have anyone other than the suspect at the interrogation. If the suspect were accompanied by anyone, especially a lawyer, he or she might be less vulnerable to the detectives' coercion.

This strategy worked in preventing information from getting to the unit. It made people not want to talk to the detectives because what they said would not be fairly interpreted. Witnesses were reluctant to talk; they worried that regardless of what they said, it would be used against the community because the ABTF hated Gertown. Several detectives reported great reluctance among residents in the community to indicate that they had seen anything. Their reticence meant that detectives had to work carefully, using informants who called the detectives only at the unit, as opposed to the detectives' showing up at the person's house, as was typical for interviewing victims and witnesses. In one case the unit investigated in Gertown, Whites verbally harassed a Black person who had moved into a private home and threw two large rocks through his windows. Later the detective investigating the incident reported on his canvass of the area:

> No one saw or heard either incident. . . . We could put out the word and say we're looking for X. There's another person who may have seen something so I told our contact who knows him to have him get in touch with us. Some people hear "ABTF" and they don't want to have anything to do with it.

Ironically, residents' reluctance to talk with members of the ABTF hindered investigations of Black-on-White bias crimes that the community might have supported. In one case, the unit was investigating the case of two White youths who had been stabbed late at night by two Blacks in Gertown. No suspects were identified and the officers in the unit had little insight into how the conflict originated or, more important, why. The only information they had was that there had been several 911 calls the same evening indicating that two Black boys were being chased by White kids with sticks and bicycle rims. Two detectives who were new to the unit were sent to gather more information and encountered a White woman who spoke with them about the incident. After more than an hour, she found out that they were with the ABTF and exclaimed, "You people are from the Mean Machine!" Frustrated, one detective replied, "What do *you* think? You've been talking to us." The woman replied, "Do you read the *Voice*? Do you know what they say about you?"

The detectives investigating the above case were lucky that their identity remained hidden for so long. Some residents recognized by sight detectives who had investigated several cases in the neighborhood. Several detectives who had been involved in investigations in Gertown indicated that Gertown residents with whom they wished to speak had refused point blank. Their reluctance held, even if the unit were investigating cases in which *victims* were White and the minorities were believed to be the *perpetrators*. One White detective who had previously investigated hate crimes was investigating a case and the victim declared that she did not want to talk to him without a lawyer. "Ma'am," he said, "You're a *victim*, in this case." In another case, the same detective contacted the mother of a White victim to reschedule an appointment. She indicated that she did not wish to meet with the detective at all. When the detective asked why, the woman stated that she had learned that the detective had been involved in the earlier investigation in the neighborhood and she did not feel the detective would handle the case fairly.

The insularity of the housing developments in Gertown also made it easier for those mobilized against the enforcement of the law to coerce other White residents into not cooperating. Many residents in the developments had few contacts outside the community. Loyalty to the community was prized, and residents feared ostracism. The leaders of GRC had substantial contacts in the community. One community organizer active with GRC was the supervisor of the neighborhood's teen center. Another was the head of the tenants' council. With substantial ties throughout the community, they could ostracize certain residents either by spreading the word that they were traitors or by writing about them in an anonymous column in the *Gertown Voice*. Persons who were ostracized in the developments were forced to suffer in silence, because many had to live there; they were too poor to afford private housing.

The fear of being ostracized was palpable. Frequently, those who agreed to give information told officers that they would not testify in court or that they did not want officers from the ABTF coming to their homes. For example, in one case a woman who called 911 and gave the full details of the crime, told the 911 operator that she did not want to give her name. When detectives contacted her, she said she would not testify in court, because she had to live in the developments.

Hillsdale's Code of Silence

In Hillsdale, another small ethnic neighborhood in Center City, resistance to the enforcement of the law was not organized, but the detectives still faced opposition to bias crime investigations. Hillsdale was just a few square miles yet had a disproportionate number of bias-motivated incidents. In 1990, CHO released figures indicating that though only 6 percent of the public housing population lived in Hillsdale, in the two previous years, roughly a quarter of the verified racial incidents had occurred there.[17] Similar to Gertown residents, residents of

Hillsdale had fought school integration tooth and nail. Given its history of violent resistance, officials in Center City were pleasantly surprised when the integration of the all-White housing developments in Hillsdale—several years before Gertown's—proceeded without serious incident. This did not mean that the White residents in Hillsdale were happy that the developments had been integrated. In fact, some had many of the same complaints about Blacks, that they brought crime to the neighborhood and did not belong in Hillsdale. "This is a conflict over how we want to live," said a twenty-year-old White resident who had grown up in a Hillsdale housing project. "We don't want their ways—their loud music and drugs. Hillsdale is for us, always has been, and it always should be."[18]

Though detectives in the unit never mentioned the existence of community leaders in Hillsdale who were mobilized against the unit, their requests for information were met with a stubborn silence. After a number of racial incidents, an eight-foot-tall cross was set on fire early one fall evening in a courtyard of an apartment building. The ABTF assumed the target to be minorities living in the area. Investigating the incident, officers in the unit conducted a canvass of the area immediately around the cross. The result of their neighborhood canvass is almost comical. The selection below is taken from detective reports of the investigation.

BUILDING 1

Apartment #8: Resident smelled smoke and heard the voices of boys and men, but did not see anyone near the cross.

Apartment #10: Resident reports that she did not hear or see anything.

Apartment #11: Resident reports that she did not hear or see anything.

Apartment #12: Resident reports she was sleeping during the incident.

Apartment #13: Resident reports that she did not hear or see anything.

Apartment #15: Resident reports that she did not hear or see anything.

Apartment #16: Resident reports that she did not hear or see anything.

BUILDING 2

Apartment #5: Resident states that she heard screams but did not see anything.

Apartment #10: Resident states he knows nothing and saw nothing.

In their canvass of more than thirty apartments, detectives reported that no one had seen anything. Even in apartments immediately overlooking the courtyard, several residents insisted they were asleep or noticed nothing until the fire department came. Some residents were so afraid to speak that even though they told the detectives they neither saw nor heard anything, they wished to remain anonymous about *that*. Frustrated, the head of the unit complained that residents' lack of cooperation and reluctance to break the silence hindered investigation. In the end, the crime was solved, but with the help of an outsider, who naturally wished to remain anonymous.

Pressuring the Unit through Departmental Channels

Residents of Gertown who were mobilized against the enforcement of the law were not content with limiting the flow of information the unit received. They also contacted their elected officials, who put pressure on the mayor and the police commissioner, who in turn pressured the unit to justify the high number of White perpetrators and low number of White victims. When residents of Gertown complained to the commissioner's office, they did not argue that hate crime law should not be enforced in the neighborhood but, rather, that the unit failed to label crimes against Whites as race related and thus the unit was biased against the community.

City police departments are especially vulnerable to pressure from politically powerful communities like Gertown. In Center City, the police commissioner was appointed by the mayor and held his position at the mayor's pleasure. The commissioner's office had two reasons to keep the investigations in Gertown as low key as possible. First, the commissioner was charged with keeping the peace—which came to be defined as keeping the overall crime rate as low as possible. Second, two of three police commissioners during the unit's history were from Gertown, and the failure to keep peace in their own "backyard" would have reflected poorly on the effectiveness of their administration.

Complaints from Gertown residents led the mayor to call on the commissioner's office, which in turn requested that the unit justify the fact the White victims were a minority of the unit's case load. The commissioner's office put pressure on the unit subtly. For instance, on at least one occasion the commissioner's office called the unit and asked only for the number of cases with White victims the unit was investigating. The unit understood the message that the commissioner was sending. One longtime member of the unit recalled:

> There's always pressure of some type to make a case. It may not be expressed. If the assistant to the commissioner calls about a White defendant, it's pressure not to solve. If it's about a White person who was assaulted in another part of the city, it doesn't have to be said they want us to solve it.

The pressure on the police department to reduce crime in all areas of the city created tension between enforcing the civil rights law and doing what the department defined as a good job. This stems in part from the nature of hate crime and is true for all police officers enforcing hate crime law. Researchers believe that hate crime is underreported.[19] Investigating underreported crimes is likely to yield increasingly larger numbers of crime. In addition to being blamed for driving the overall crime rate up, hate crime units or other police officers responsible for enforcing hate crime law are not likely to be lauded for their enforcement efforts when they identify a large number of "hate crimes"; a high hate crime rate makes a city look more bigoted rather than more tolerant or progressive.

In its annual report to the commissioner's office, the unit released figures detailing the number of cases it investigated. Often the unit's surveillance and outreach to the minority community led to more, rather than fewer, cases. For instance, in the late 1980s, three years in which the number of cases investigated remained fairly static were followed by several years in which the number of cases the unit investigated increased (see Table 5.1).

The commissioner's office asked the leaders of the unit to justify its rising caseload. Detectives in the ABTF viewed these inquiries as "pressure to keep the numbers down." Pressure also came from the captains who ran the neighborhood precincts. They were concerned about the number of cases the unit investigated in each area of the city because the unit's annual reports, in addition to giving the total number of

TABLE 5.1
Investigations, 1986–1993

Year	Number of Cases Investigated
1986	157
1987	158
1988	152
1989	202
1990	273
1991	218
1992	252
1993	276

Source: ABTF files.

cases investigated, also provided a neighborhood-by-neighborhood comparison of each year's incidents. Those responsible for controlling crime in particular precincts wanted to keep the numbers of cases in the unit's reports low to avoid looking as if they were not controlling crime. One detective reported that in addition to pressuring the unit not to classify incidents as hate crime, captains would call the unit before the annual report was released, asking, "What are my figures from last year?"

Increases and decreases in the number of cases investigated by the unit each year were reported in the press. The detectives indicated that a high number of hate crimes was embarrassing to the mayor. The mayor worried that the city looked racist, for the city frequently reported the highest numbers in the state.

The mayor brought his concerns to the police commissioner, whom he had appointed. In response to queries from the commissioner's office, ABTF supervisors tried to explain the increases in the number of cases the unit investigated each year. The supervisors offered a variety of explanations for the increases so as to shift blame from the unit. A section of one annual report read:

Precinct 1—Shows a dramatic increase in the number of incidents, from four (4) to sixteen incidents. An analysis of the victim statistics for these incidents shows a significantly higher number of White victims. This may be related to increasing gang activity in the downtown area.

Precinct 2—This increase is directly attributable to improved outreach to the Asian community by ABTF and district personnel resulting in better reporting of incidents.

Precinct 3—This increase is directly attributable to the increase of minority families within the Hillsdale development.

Another annual report attempted to explain an increase of twenty-four cases over the previous year:

> The increase [of twenty-four cases], although lower than figures reported in other major cities, is clearly not acceptable. The primary reason for the increase can be directly attributed to one incident that caused a series of other incidents. That incident was the racial altercation at Gertown Senior High in May. This altercation and the "pay back" or follow-up incidents resulted in May and June having much higher numbers of cases. This officer estimates that, had the school incident not occurred, the total number of cases handled by the Unit would have been in the 235–240 range, which would have been a decrease from the previous year.

Effects of Community Pressure—Treatment of White Victims

Residents in Gertown wanted the unit to do more than just explain the number of cases it was investigating; instead, residents focused on decreasing the number of victims of color in Gertown. It would have been easy for the ABTF to reduce its caseload. As the previous chapter suggests, the unit could reduce its caseload by giving cases "the broom," preventing them from being investigated and thus being part of the unit's caseload. Accordingly, one objective measure of the effect of pressure on the unit would be a decrease in the number of cases the unit investigated in Hillsdale and Gertown. The supervisors could simply have accomplished a decrease by giving many more cases that occurred in Gertown and Hillsdale "the broom."

Because records were not kept on the number of cases given "the broom," it is impossible to discern whether pressure placed on the unit by the department led it to reduce its caseload in this manner. There are two other measures, however, that can be used to evaluate the effect of pressure on the unit: changes in the number of cases investigated with White perpetrators and minority victims, and changes in the number of White perpetrators criminally charged or charged with criminal civil rights violations. Decreases in either could be indicative of the success of the community's efforts.

Data from the unit's logbook suggest that the pressure put on the unit by the rest of the department did not lead to a drastic drop in the number of cases investigated annually. Between 1987 and 1996, the number of cases the unit investigated in all neighborhoods in the city increased during six of the ten years. Moreover, in three of the four years during which the number of cases investigated in neighborhoods other than Gertown or Hillsdale *decreased*, the number in those two neighborhoods *increased*.

Data from the logbooks also suggest that the unit did not decrease the overall number of White perpetrators and victims of color in Gertown in response to pressure from members of GRC and the rest of the department. Table 5.2 depicts the perpetrator-victim configuration in race-based investigations for incidents occurring in Gertown between 1990 and 1996. As the table shows, investigations of White perpetrators who targeted victims of color significantly outnumbered those involving perpetrators of color who targeted White victims. In addition, in four of six of those years, the number of investigations of crimes involving White perpetrators and minority victims increased over the number the previous year. The unit's data on the criminal and civil rights charges for hate crimes also reveals constancy in charging. Between 1990 and 1997, five years showed an increase in the number of charges brought against White perpetrators.

The foregoing does not mean that pressure from the community had no effect. As stated above, the unit's reports to the police commissioner

TABLE 5.2
Gertown Perpetrators and Victims in Race-Based Investigations, 1990–1996

Perpetrator and Victim	1990	1991	1992	1993	1994	1995	1996
White Perpetrator, Asian, Black, Latino* Victim	48	51	36	60	63	59	84
Asian, Black, Latino* Perpetrator, White Victim	15	12	23	37	29	24	24
Asian, Black, Latino* Perpetrator, Asian, Black, Latino* Victim	1	0	0	0	2	1	0
White Perpetrator, White Victim	1	0	0	1	1	0	1
Total	65	63	59	98	95	84	109

Source: ABTF files.
*Includes mixed race, other victims of color.

reflected the unit's supervisors' desire to justify the unit's practices. There was another effect as well. Pressure from the community and the resulting pressure from the department may have affected officers' behavior toward White victims. The department's pressure and *Gertown Voice* columns criticizing the unit served the purpose of putting the officers on notice that they were being watched. Observation of the units' detectives suggested that because they felt the department and the community were watching them, they needed to be sure that they could not be accused of being unfair to White victims. When investigating cases in which Whites were the victims of hate crimes, some detectives appeared to overcompensate in order to show the unit was not biased against Whites. In several Gertown cases with White victims, detectives bent over backwards to leave no stone unturned. In one such case, an ABTF detective generated a one-inch-thick case file of reports of third-party threats, a crime for which the ABTF normally would not have brought charges at all.

The Media Spotlight on Hate Crimes

The Center City news media closely followed Gertown's resistance to integration and the hate crimes committed in Gertown after the integration of the housing developments. Center City's newspapers followed the developments from differing angles. The *Gertown Voice*, Gertown's community newspaper, sided with those in the community opposed to the unit's investigations. Between the *Daily News* and the *Tribune*, the two largest papers in town, the *Daily News* was considered more liberal than the *Tribune*. One member of the unit recalled what he considered the media's "playing up" of the situation in Gertown: "We have two newspapers in this town. The *Daily News* is more a leader in support of racial healing. The *Tribune* has been responsible for fanning the flames of racial hatred."

The mayor's decision to allow integration of Gertown developments, the agreement between CHO and HUD, the changes in CHO, and the resulting response from tenants in Gertown were all covered in great detail in the *Daily News*. The number of stories reported in the newspaper was disproportionate to the percentage of the unit's cases that were occurring in Gertown. To quantify how much the unit was mentioned in connection with particular neighborhoods, an online computer search was done of the full text of the *Daily News*, using "Anti-Bias Task Force" as the key word. From 1979 until 1999 the unit's name was mentioned 568 times, though not all the references concerned the unit's investigations. Although the *Daily News* covered incidents that were possibly bias-motivated in other neighborhoods too, the ABTF was mentioned much more frequently in connection with Gertown than other neighborhoods.

In comparing the coverage of incidents across the city, the *Daily News* gave much more attention to the unit's investigations in Gertown than in other neighborhoods. In the first year of the move-ins, 1988, the number of articles linking the unit to Gertown was roughly on par with that of other neighborhoods (see Table 5.3). The next year, there were more than twice as many articles linking the unit to incidents in Gertown as there were in any other neighborhoods. In the following three years, the *Daily News* exploded with stories detailing the unit's investigations in Gertown. In 1992, for example, there were seventeen stories mentioning the unit and Gertown, with at most three mentioning other neighborhoods. An assault arising out of a single incident might be given one story in Hillsdale; in Gertown it was given two or three.

It was not just the disproportionate number of stories that the *Daily News* did on Gertown investigations that was so inflammatory, it was the sensationalistic manner in which many of the stories were written. In a fashion uncharacteristic of the prize-winning newspaper, headlines of articles describing violence that occurred in Gertown screamed: "Beating Stirs Racial Fears," "Violence Stark against Recent Gains,"

TABLE 5.3
Center City Daily News *Articles Referencing the ABTF, by Neighborhood, 1988–1994*

Neighborhood	1988	1989	1990	1991	1992	1993	1994
Gertown	5	5	8	7	17	15	22
Hillsdale	0	0	6	0	2	9	2
Hillside	4	2	2	0	0	0	0
Tarrytown	0	0	0	0	1	0	0
All Other Neighborhoods	2	4	3	1	5	4	1
Total	11	11	19	8	25	28	25

Source: Center City Daily News Archives.

"Racial Data Given by CHO; Most Complaints in Gertown," "Hatred in the Mayor's Backyard." Though the texts were generally more moderate than the headlines, *Daily News* stories often described the situation in Gertown as if the residents were involved in a racial war. Stories concerning a single incident often rehashed the details of previous incidents—some of them years old—or listed the running total of racial incidents in Gertown for that year.

The *Daily News* even made Gertown look as if the neighborhood were steeped in racism when it reported positive stories about the neighborhood. One story, attempting to end stereotypes about the neighborhood, failed to dispel the idea that the media had misrepresented Gertown in the past. The article begins well enough by quoting a Black woman who was one of the first to move into an all-White housing project and did not face violence or any problems. The story quickly devolved, however, into a description of the reputation for "militant bigotry" that had stuck to the neighborhood. Three times the neighborhood's troubled history was gone into. The testimony of one dubious-sounding White victim, who asserted he had not received the attention that Blacks got, was followed immediately by a quote from the ABTF saying that Whites in Gertown had attempted to hide behind stereotypes and to "play the race card."

Racial conflict attracted attention from other newspapers and the radio, too. When several White families, whose sons had been involved in a hate crime committed against a Hispanic family, were evicted from the development, Center City's tabloid, the *Tribune*, placed the news of the eviction in massive letters on its front page. A local AM radio station broadcast its morning show live from the developments on the day the family was to be evicted. A flyer advertising the broadcast, advised residents of the neighborhood, "Drop in and be heard!"

The media scrutinized the unit's investigations in Gertown closely, not only because a majority of the incidents occurred in Gertown in the late 1980s and early 1990s, but also incidents in Gertown were good stories. This was true for two reasons. Gertown's violent racist and hate crimes or "racial assaults"—as they were more often referred to in Gertown—conjured up vivid images from the 70s of anti-integration protestors shouting racist slogans. Hate crimes in Gertown were also "news" because the city's mayor was from Gertown. Having been elected by one of the widest margins in Center City's history, the mayor was obviously popular, and anything associated with him attracted attention. In addition, if the story or issue was provocative enough, it had the potential to elicit a response from the mayor's office. This was especially true of cases involving race and the mayor's neighborhood, a lively drama in which the community cast out a favored son.

The papers reported Gertowners' shunning of the mayor for what they regarded as his capitulation on the integration issue. For one of the mayor's tours of Gertown, a banner had been hung across the streets that read, "'Mickey,' Shame on you, look what you did to Gertown." The mayor was hurt by the community's rejection. He told a reporter,

> Not a week goes by that I don't get some hate mail, telephone calls. . . . I was in [X] housing project last week when they had some trouble there. We got telephone calls at home, "This wouldn't happen if you didn't let the Blacks in the projects." That kind of thing. I'll be honest. As much as I love Gertown, those little negative things, those stabs in the back, they hurt.[20]

Sometimes the media coverage of bias-motivated violence in Gertown generated more coverage. In one instance, after the *Daily News* heavily covered the shooting of a Black man by a White Gertown resident, the mayor revived his civil rights panel and took a very firm stand against the hate crimes being committed in Gertown. In another case, a *Daily News* story indicated that most of the verified racial complaints in CHO housing developments since integration of the developments had occurred in Gertown. The mayor responded by calling the story another cheap shot at the people of Gertown, in a press release sent only to *other* newspapers in the city, not the *Daily News*. He maintained that the *Daily News* had misstated the situation in an attempt to stereotype the community.[21]

The residents in Gertown who objected to media coverage of the unit's activities had reactions similar to those in other areas in which highly publicized hate crimes have occurred. Residents of a neighborhood or town in which a hate crime occurs often object when the town is mentioned in media reports of the crime. Residents feel they must defend the town's reputation. For instance in both Elk County, Virginia, the town in which G. P. Johnson was killed, and Jasper, Texas, the site of the killing of James Byrd, town residents were anxious that their towns not be labeled racist.[22] In Gertown, residents objected to having the unit mentioned in conjunction with incidents in Gertown more often than other neighborhoods. As in other places, mentioning the unit in conjunction with incidents that occurred in Gertown suggested that the *neighborhood* and not just the perpetrator was racist. More-over, the label "racist" had heightened salience in Center City since the school desegregation crisis of the mid-seventies, when the city had earned the dubious distinction of being termed the most racist town in the state. Recalling these times, Center City residents were hypersensi-tive to an allegation that their neighborhood was racist.

Investigating Crimes in the Media Spotlight

Media coverage of the unit's investigations was a double-edged sword. In its early days the unit instigated the media coverage. One de-tective stated that in order to decrease incidents in the community, unit members had told the media about arrests the unit had made. "We re-ally publicized our arrests. Within a year after the integration of the developments, every Gertown kid knew about civil rights violations." In later years the media spotlight made it harder to investigate crimes.

Detectives came to resent the intrusion of the media while cases were under investigation for several reasons. The media's stories about an investigation often appeared the day after the incident, and the prompt reportage immediately put the community on the defensive and ended any chance of surprise in investigating the crime. Witnesses knew the type of incident they were being questioned about and were thus "primed" and better able to self-censor. Their answers, if they were willing to give any, would be based on loyalty to the neighborhood or fear of being labeled a traitor. The press could chase away victims as well as suspects and witnesses. After one incident was reported in the news, the investigating detective complained, "They scared my victim. Channel [X] showed up this morning knocking on her door and now she's disappeared. She won't return my calls. Sometimes the media just doesn't get it."

Media attention could also increase tension generally and retaliation by the side that felt it had been wronged. Detectives juggled the con-cerns of the two communities—the White community, which was vocal in its opposition to the enforcement of the law against Whites, and the minority community, which favored hate crime classification when mi-norities were attacked. When stories were published right after an incident occurred, the unit was often called upon to identify the incident as racial or not before the time for a full investigation elapsed.

The unit was cautious in how it characterized the crime to reporters. If there was an incident involving a White and a minority, and the unit said that it was a bias-motivated attack against the minority, the White community reacted with outrage. If the unit said it was still investigating the incident in question, or indicated that the incident was a bias-motivated attack by a minority, the minority community might react negatively. Though the minority community in Gertown was small, its plight moved other minorities in the other neighborhoods in Center City, particularly in the Black section of the city. The minorities were politically active in grassroots activity in the city in the 1970s but had never been seen as a population whose support was critical. The Black community's lack of political power could be attributed to its low numbers, its limited location (one voting district), and to poor minority turnout at the polls.

The Influence of Victim Advocacy Groups

The Black community's interests in the issue of hate crime were most often represented by organizations. The local NAACP chapter, while not a powerful force in the city, had been successful in bringing court suits that led to the desegregation of schools and public housing and its officers often spoke with the unit and the press on behalf of Black victims of hate crime in Gertown. Minority victims of hate crime in Gertown—Asians, Hispanics, and Blacks—also found advocates in victim advocacy groups.

Center City's victim advocacy community at the time was composed of five main organizations that served the victims of hate crime. One of the organizations, LEGAL, was primarily a civil rights organization that brought suits on behalf of victims of hate crime as well as the other types of civil rights suits. LEGAL primarily served the African American, Asian American, and Hispanic communities. Another of the organizations, STAAV (Stop Anti-Asian Violence), was a small community-based nonprofit organization dedicated to helping victims of anti-Asian violence. Center City's chapter of the NAACP spoke on behalf of Black victims when necessary. GLAP (Gay and Lesbian Anti-Violence Project) was an advocacy organization that addressed the needs of Center City's gay and lesbian victims of hate crime. Finally, Center City also had a branch of the Anti-Defamation League (ADL), a private nonprofit organization dedicated to stopping the defamation of Jews and increasing tolerance.

With the exception of the ADL, all of the organizations were quite small and had just one staff member apiece, the director. They spent the vast majority of their time and resources dispensing aid to victims, especially in helping them negotiate the complex law enforcement system and telling them about the remedies available. The director of STAAV explained the organization's need to tell some of her clients, many of whom were immigrants, about the criminal justice system.

> Often they don't understand that they can go forward when a hate crime occurs. They may be afraid of the legal system. They may view their government as oppressive or have had experiences with police brutality. Or they think that they need a lawyer and a lawyer would cost money.

An activity important for all of the organizations was to make calls to the police or the prosecutor's office in order to advise the unit of cases or to follow up on victim's cases. Occasionally, especially in the gay and lesbian community, the unit would learn of cases of bias-motivated violence from an advocacy group. Sometimes these cases had not been reported to the police, or they had been reported to the police and not been forwarded to the unit. The detectives were sometimes sensitive to calls to check on the status of cases the unit was investigating. The head of one organization felt the need to tread carefully while making inquiries of detectives in the unit:

> I just call the ABTF to check in on what's going on. I have to do that carefully. When I call, it's so threatening. It gets people worried. I just want information. The detective who is taking the call may be very suspicious of outsiders. Their response depends on the day of the week.

Though all of the organizations expressed confidence in the unit's current commander, there was some disparity in how receptive each group found the ABTF to be to their concerns. For instance, STAAV, GLAP, and the ADL indicated that they had never had problems with the unit; the representative of the ADL described the officers in the unit as "fine officers." The NAACP and LEGAL, the two organizations that served the Black community, indicated that they were less than happy with the way the unit had behaved in the past. The head of LEGAL described the difficulty she had in getting the police to take seriously her less-than-perfect victims:

> My experience with the ABTF officers varies a lot. . . . They [the police] want random acts with Mother Teresa as a victim. I have a lot of mouthy victims. Police say you know what she said. It's as if there's a subconscious need to put a different spin on it. Why is there a need to say that it wasn't that ugly?

As supporters and promoters of victims, victim advocates accepted victims' stories much more readily than the detectives did. For instance, none of the victim advocates interviewed made regular attempts to corroborate victims' stories before providing assistance or before contacting the ABTF. Instead, many relied on their intuitive sense in their approaches to victims. When asked how she could tell whether an incident was significant or not, one victim advocate replied, "I was trained as a social worker. You get to know when it's a real case." While not wholly uncritical, victim advocates, who claimed to have had few encounters with victims who were lying or making exaggerated claims, were much more accepting of victims' stories. Given their approach to victims, sometimes the searching inquiry and procedures in place in the unit to weigh victims' credibility irritated victim advocates. One victim advocate complained about the use of bias indicators and one detective's use of past cases to evaluate present cases:

> I don't use "bias indicators." I don't dissect the human drama into little tiny pieces I can brush off my desk. I use it to build up a big picture. I don't need bias indicators when a cup of urine is thrown through my client's window. My clients know it when they see it. Victims know what is going on.
>
> One ABTF detective thinks that you can smell a hate crime. He thinks that he knows the story, thinks he can size up the situation without investigation. That's dangerous to do here. It means he's sizing up people not because of what happened to them, but because of what happened to someone else.

Though ABTF detectives responded quickly to advocacy groups' requests for investigation of cases brought to the unit's attention, they did not always charge such cases as hate crimes. In making the decision to so charge a case, detectives cared more about the outcome of their investigation than whether a group was exerting pressure on the unit. In one highly publicized case, a young Jewish man was seriously beaten by an Arab man at a college party. The ADL learned about the case and a highly unusual meeting involving the advocacy group, the victim's lawyer, the ABTF, the victim, and members of the AG's office and the DA's office called to discuss the investigation. The ADL and the victim maintained the incident was anti-Semitic. According to the detective reports, the incident was investigated aggressively because of the victim's injuries. In the course of the investigation, witnesses indicated that the attack was retaliation for an attack earlier that evening, and criminal rather than hate crime charges were eventually filed against the perpetrator.

Though they knew advocacy groups often desired classification of incidents as bias-motivated, detectives in the ABTF denied that they had ever been inclined to classify a crime as bias-motivated because of an advocacy group's pressure. One supervisor in the unit responded to the questions about pressure casually: "Advocacy groups, that's what they do. Just focus on that issue. . . . I never had any problems with the groups. I respect what they're doing. I can beg to differ on certain cases." The same supervisor cautioned the detectives in the unit to hold firm in their determinations of bias, especially in the number of cases identified as bias-motivated:

> The stats for this year will be different. The advocacy groups are going to be saying . . . they weren't down that much. I want to be able to say yes, say we've reviewed it. I don't want to kowtow to any groups. . . . It's a more legitimate picture. Definitely people will be upset.

Conclusion

Public support for invoking a particular law makes the process of investigation easier. If witnesses are needed to provide evidence about suspects or the circumstances of a crime, they are more likely to come forward if there is public support for invoking the laws; they need not fear reprisal from the rest of the community for helping the police. Similarly, public opinion in support of particular criminal laws may increase the likelihood that such crimes will be reported to the police and that victims will come forward. Given these barriers, and the fact that police generally have discretion over which laws they enforce, it is not surprising that often officers choose not to enforce unpopular laws.

In Center City, hate crime law was very unpopular among many of the residents of all-White neighborhoods. Residents in Gertown and Hillsdale viewed minorities who were relocating to their neighborhoods as intruders and fought the enforcement of civil rights laws designed to punish those trying to drive the minorities out. Community support for violence aimed at minorities has been noted in other close-knit, all-White neighborhoods.[23] If the community supports driving minorities out, then perpetrators may see themselves as defending their neighborhood.

Though Gertown residents used a variety of obstructionist tactics to block investigations and had a measure of political power on their side, they were unable to achieve their goal of stopping detectives from enforcing the law. Residents were not able to prevent the enforcement of hate crime laws primarily for two reasons. First, the residents were unsuccessful because they failed to make an argument that fit into the political climate of the 1980s and 1990s. They were White working-class ethnics who wanted to keep minorities out of the public housing in their neighborhood. Much of their rhetoric was openly racist, and they defended the tactics of those who resorted to violence. The liberal media in Center City did not support the views of the residents and increased the visibility of hate crime in the neighborhoods allied against the enforcement of law. Though minorities were not a strong voting force in the city, there were a number of victim advocacy organizations willing to increase the visibility of investigations. Though Gertown had significant political power, the mayor and police commissioner could not afford to stop enforcement of the hate crime law, especially in light of the city's past. Two decades earlier, the city had been embarrassed by the openly racist attitudes of Gertown and Hillsdale. Higher-ups chose the middle ground and put the unit on notice that it was being watched.

Second, ABTF practice and procedures created structures that were able to block Gertowners' efforts to prevent hate crimes from being investigated. Through their work in the unit, detectives developed a personal desire to help victims of bias-motivated crime. This desire to help victims was bolstered by the unit's institutional culture, which provided an incentive to thoroughly investigate cases. In this way, the detectives in the ABTF differ from those described in other studies of detective work as primarily motivated by case clearance. There are costs to making clearance the focus of detective work. An emphasis on clearance with no other prevailing pressures creates an incentive for detectives not to investigate as they strive to process as many cases as possible. By substituting victim service for case clearance, as ABTF supervisors did, fewer detectives will look for the easy way out provided by their nonenforcement power.

Even though Gertown residents failed, the investigation of incidents in Gertown serves as an example of the difficulty of enforcing hate crime laws. Hate crimes are likely to occur if residents of all-White neighborhoods see hate crimes if a different way, as legitimate efforts to control the face of their neighborhoods. The experience in Gertown shows that they have obstructionist potential to prevent the enforcement of law. It also suggests that residents in neighborhoods allied against the law may succeed if they can tell a story that will be successful in the political environment in which they are telling it.

The influence of victim advocacy groups in Center City was limited to their ability to get the unit to investigate cases that it had not yet investigated. The unit was open to group input regarding notification but not regarding charging individuals with civil rights violations. With respect to the decision to proceed in a particular way, the unit remained firmly committed to its internal procedures and determined to protect itself against any fallout that might result from groups' displeasure with declining statistics.

6

Police Culture and Hate Crime

In police departments, organizational norms constitute a powerful force in shaping police behavior. Organizational norms set standards of behavior for patrol officers, detectives, and members of the command staff. In a job that is quite generally unstructured, norms provide guidance regarding the treatment of witnesses and suspects, guidance on how to prioritize cases, and guidance as to which charges should be sought.[1] When courts, policy makers, or higher-ups in the police department change legal rules or procedures, they must take into account organizational norms that predate the changes. As Skolnick writes, "[N]orms located within police organization are more powerful than court decisions in shaping behavior."[2] Changes in procedure, such as increasing the priority of hate crime, similar to changes in legal rules regarding police interrogation, must confront officers' preexisting behaviors and attitudes. This chapter describes some of the challenges of implementing hate crime law, given departmental organization, structure, and norms.

The Districts

Detectives must rely on others in the organization for information. Patrol officers are responsible for forwarding crime reports to detectives, and thus their approach to bias-motivated crime becomes important. The patrol officer, as the first individual responding to the scene, plays a pivotal role in the gathering of evidence.[3] Immediately after the crime, witnesses and evidence may still be at the crime scene; everyone's recollection may be at its best. A good report written by the patrol officer, with a clear description of the incident, including any slurs used during the attack, could prove very useful to the detectives investigating the crime. At the same time, if the patrol officer fails to collect a piece of physical evidence and it is destroyed, this cannot be rectified by the investigating detective.[4]

In the Center City Police Department (CPD), patrol officers were attached to each neighborhood police district. Each district had a police station, detectives to investigate the crimes that were not sent to the specialized unit, and supervisors. Patrol officers were responsible for responding to citizen requests for services and maintaining order in the neighborhoods; district detectives were responsible for investigating crimes that occurred within the district. Similar to other research, which has found that officers enforce the law differently in different communities,[5] officers who worked in the neighborhood precincts in Center City policed the neighborhood in a way that manifested a close, almost clientelist, relationship with neighborhood residents. The enforcement of laws against public drinking and drunk driving serve as good examples. In Gertown, one of the neighborhoods served by two stations, alcoholism was a tremendous problem. In order to keep the peace and cut down on their workload, officers in the district did not enforce laws prohibiting public drinking or drunken driving. One Black detective in the ABTF who had formerly been assigned to Gertown recalled being criticized by superiors for stopping cars and writing citations for drunk driving:

> I worked nights back then. They used to send one car, and they'd send me out. . . . I was working nights, what I am gonna do all night? I had to stay awake. What else am I going to do? I'd stop cars. Every car I stopped, the driver was drunk. They called me a racist because I stopped cars for OUIs [operating under the influence]. They said I was locking up White people. Why are you stopping people? They're just drunk.

From its beginning, the ABTF was unpopular in the districts. When it was first started, part of its unpopularity may have stemmed from its low status in the department. As chapter 3 describes, the unit was given little power, and no detectives were assigned to the unit to investigate incidents. Because the unit was assigned to the commissioner's office, located at police headquarters, and investigated "civil rights," officers outside the unit assumed that its real mission was to investigate police officers. Moreover, being supervised by a civilian instead of a police officer made the unit the object of scorn.

Worse than the disrespect the unit faced was the open dislike of many district officers. Several officers said that the ABTF was the most unpopular unit in the police department. Some of the officers outside the unit disliked the ABTF because its mission was to enforce the civil rights law. These officers sympathized with the perpetrators and believed that the unit should not have been investigating crimes against minorities. One detective talked about how these officers felt about the unit:

> Some just thought that we went too far. Cops believe that certain people should stay in their neighborhoods. "What the hell are they doing there?" They weren't too enthused about us. If it was something serious though, they'd help. Some cops agree with ideas of the kids, that minorities shouldn't live in Gertown.

Another Black detective recalled how unpopular the members of the unit were with other officers, "I found graffiti in my locker and in the bathroom, with my name, not just the unit. I was thrown down a flight of stairs in the station. During the time I was in ABTF, all this happened."

Officers in the districts who sympathized with persons in the community did little to hide their derision for members of the unit. One evening one of the unit's supervisors found a poster, ostensibly created by Gertown residents who disliked the unit's activities, hanging on the bulletin board in the Gertown precinct. The poster, whose message was printed in all capital letters, broadcast loathing of the unit and disdain for its activities:

> ABTF. These are the intials for the Anti-Bias Task Force of the Center City Police Dept. This unit is made up of the dregs of the Central City Police Department. Most normal cops don't want anything to do with this unit, and we don't blame them. They must have been trained in [area of the city], because all they do is follow young White boys around and then pick them up every chance that they get. Their former boss used to be called "Ben-Dover" in [an area of the city with a large gay and lesbian population] for obvious reasons. Not one member of this unit has any balls, and instead of preying on young White boys in Gertown, they should be guarding a harem for some rich sheik, where they couldn't get into any trouble.

Some district officers characterized the unit's activities as not real "police work." Some believed the members of the unit were policing name calling. Others in the districts did not believe that individuals' civil rights were ever violated. One police officer who worked in the Gertown precinct asserted that minority residents were falsely crying race. In response to a question about the problems with civil rights in Gertown at a bias-crime training session, he replied:

> They're using race to exaggerate claims of civil rights. More people are getting good at alleging race when it's something else. For example, last week I had a Black family suspected of dealing using the eight-year-old to deliver drugs. They claimed they'd been a victim of a hate crime.

Some of the district officers' feelings toward the unit may have stemmed from jealousy. As chapter 4 describes, the detectives spent a significant amount of time investigating each case. Part of the reason that so much time could be spent on cases is that detectives in the ABTF had an incredibly low caseload relative to other police officers. For example, one detective who had been in another specialized unit, Sexual Assault, estimated that her previous unit had ten times as many cases as the ABTF. In addition, detectives in the ABTF each had his or her own car and regularly received overtime assignments. Those outside the unit may have thought that ABTF detectives were being incredibly well rewarded for doing something that was not even police work.

Another reason district officers may not have helped the ABTF in its investigations was that they viewed the ABTF as intruding on their turf. This was in some ways true. By investigating assaults, harassment, and vandalism, it was investigating crimes that would have been the responsibility of the neighborhood detectives had they not been hate crimes. The unit and districts had very different approaches to investigating hate crime. Before the unit had the power to investigate crimes, the districts conducted investigations and, as chapter 3 describes, patrol officers frequently denied services to victims and neighborhood detectives were reluctant to investigate bias-motivated violence. As was the case with drunk driving, officers in Gertown were socialized to turn a blind eye to hate crimes in order to protect their relationship with the community. One detective told the story of a young White officer who was assigned to Gertown and began to report bias-motivated crime against minorities. After a few residents complained, the patrolman was assigned elsewhere.

Effects on Investigation

District officers' dislike of the unit hindered the unit's investigations when it was manifested in officers refusing to come to the unit's assistance or in the form of deliberate attempts to block the unit's activities. One detective in the unit recalled members of the district trying to undermine the unit by letting those who were being investigated know the ABTF was investigating bias-motivated conduct. This detective recalled an operation that he assumed was foiled by police officers from the districts:

> Early on, it was horrendous. They thought of the ABTF as Mickey Mouse do-gooders. We learned to eliminate the districts from what we were doing. They'd tip off the haters.

> We had this case where Blacks were being kept out of the bar. Blacks and Whites who were dressed the same, they'd ask them [the Blacks] for a second piece of ID. And if they had that, they'd ask them for $10. We closed the place down. Soon there was another one set up near headquarters. It was a high-class place. We were going to go in there. . . . When we went in the place there was a Black sitting at every table. They were paid to sit there. They probably didn't even know why. Somebody tipped them [the club] off.

Another ABTF detective also recalled the lack of cooperation from officers in the districts:

> It was awful. We had no support. They'd talk out of both sides of their mouth. They'd mix no cooperation with weak cooperation. We'd call and ask for help and they'd say "we have only two people we can assign." A couple of districts were supportive. There was a Black commander in Precinct [X]. And [officer's name] in Precinct [Y] was supportive. It was off the wall. Like working for another city asking for cooperation.

Tension between the unit and the officers in the neighborhood was also caused by the fact that detectives in the ABTF sometimes exposed the district officers' poor performance. Department procedure required that officers responding to 911 calls write a police report in all situations that they believed to be actual crimes. Patrol officers were not required to write a report when supplying basic police services—telling someone to turn down music, for example. Instead of writing a report after the service has been provided, the patrol officers could "missile" the call, meaning no report is given. Instead, the officer just tells the dispatcher that she or he has rendered police services. Patrol officers had complete discretion to "missile" a call, though if done in cases when it was not warranted, their doing so could come back to haunt them.

Allowing patrol officers not to write reports in cases that did not need follow-up was designed to increase efficiency. Failing to write a report in actual bias crime cases, though, could substantially diminish the unit's efforts to address such cases. If a patrol officer "missiles" a call, he or she eliminates the paper trail. Because the two mechanisms that the unit used to prevent patrol officers from acting as the sole filter of hate crimes depended on an officer's filling out a paper report, the unit was unable to find out about cases that the officer "missiled," except in those rare cases when the victim or an advocate called the unit directly.

Not writing a report that could have led to an investigation could have effects far beyond the individual case. Detectives in the ABTF accused the neighborhood officers in Gertown of ignoring incidents that later led to serious problems. Sometimes small incidents snowballed into larger ones, either as a result of retaliation or because perpetrators assumed that the police tolerated their criminal behavior. The detectives in the unit insisted that responding to the initial incident signaled to those in the community that retaliation and escalation had consequences. In the midst of a large-scale investigation, one detective complained bitterly:

> The police officers in Gertown don't give a shit. Minorities get no social services over there, not from CHO [Center City Housing Office], not from anyone. Something happens, people call the police, they come and say, "You were called a nigger, what's the big deal?" No wonder people don't call the police. Sometimes this happens time and time again to people. It usually starts out small with their tires slashed, then their windows [are] broken, then someone calls their kid a nigger. If they have a good kid who'll turn the other cheek, then maybe we won't have an incident like this. Some kids will stand up for themselves, though, and we'll have a violent incident.

The detective continued:

> They don't do anything over there [in the Gertown precinct]. You'll never see a file that big [pointing to the file on one of the unit's cases,

which, two days after the incident, was an inch thick] in the district. . . . They won't do anything there. They finally took away their [the district officers'] television. If they are assigned a walking beat, they won't do it. If you put one of them in a car, nine times out of ten he's not patrolling, he's at home. Oh, they'll give a walking beat to the rookie—they'll [rookies] do anything, because they want to keep their job.

From advocacy group calls and sometimes through the investigation of other incidents, detectives often discovered that patrol officers failed to respond to bias crime victims' calls in a timely fashion. In other cases, when they did respond, they often treated the victim badly and "missiled" the call without making a report. Detectives also criticized the reports written by patrol officers with missing or incomplete information. Coming behind the officers in the districts, the unit could (and occasionally did) expose the neighborhood precinct's mistakes. A detective described one incident in which he ensured that an officer was disciplined for refusing to provide services for a hate crime victim:

> We had a case with two lesbians who were assaulted, and we found out about it and went in and nothing happened for another six months. Later they were assaulted again and reported it to the district and said that they wanted the words used by the perpetrator noted on the form and wanted it sent to the ABTF. The officer at first said, "You don't want it said like that." Later, when they pressed him he said that he was in charge of writing the form and that he would decide whether or not to contact the ABTF. We never heard about it, and rather than put up with the harassment, the women moved out of the neighborhood. I later heard about it at a press conference. . . . I'd never heard of the incident. The funny thing is the women were praising the ABTF, who'd come to their aid in the first incident but were saying the CCPD had failed them. Can you believe that? They [the press] stuck a microphone in my face and I said, "No, the Center City Police Department failed you." They didn't like that upstairs. I talked to his [the original officer's] captain, and that guy was eventually removed to a position where he doesn't deal with the public anymore.

This detective's statements also illuminate why the unit's approach sometimes put it at odds with the rest of the department, both in the districts and with the command staff. Here, the two victims praised the unit for its good work, and condemned others in the department for their neglect. Rather than silently accepting the praise, the officer added his own voice in criticism of the police department, angering those in charge of public relations. Back in the neighborhood district, the ABTF detective got the officer who had brushed off the victims transferred.

Personal and Professional Costs

The rancor between the districts, the rest of the department, and the unit affected detectives' personal and professional lives. Officers who spent time in the unit cited personal and sometimes professional costs associated with enforcing law with which their fellow officers did not agree. One detective insisted that the job came with built-in enemies, in the department and outside. He remarked, "No matter what I do it's not right; people are always there to kick my brains in. Most people wish I would go away." For many detectives, it was hard to be so disliked. One supervisor explained that though the detectives tried to just do their job, laugh and make jokes about it, the criticism of other police officers still hurt the members of the unit. "It didn't make them feel good about their job," the supervisor said. Officers in the unit who had once had cordial relations with other police officers lost friends after they were transferred to the unit. The constant criticism distressed some of the detectives. One White detective who had spent several years in the unit, fighting the community and bureaucracy, began to cry as he recounted how he had been personally affected by the department and the community's dislike of him. As tears welled up, he said, "There's a lot of pain here. It's very painful."

Detectives also asserted that professional costs came from their outspoken support of victims, particularly in the form of failing to advance in their careers. One detective complained that as a result of his leading the unit, his career was at a dead end. Though no one associated with the unit was fired, members frequently used as examples two committed, award-winning detectives who had been very aggressive victim advocates. The absence of promotions for the pair served as evidence to the members of the unit that the job had professional costs.

Part of the reason that the disapproval of other officers so bothered the detectives in the unit is that one of the departmental norms was brotherhood, a code that demanded police officers stick together no matter what. "Breaking the code" was a serious transgression, an explicit violation of organizational norm. The dislike shown by officers in the district was a sign that they believed that detectives in the ABTF would break the code and betray brother officers. One detective explained, "It's hard to be a cop and walk into the station and know that they despise you, that they think that just because you're in the ABTF, you'd break the code."

Detectives' Differential Orientation to Victims

The nature and context of bias-motivated crime mean that detectives are responsible for unusual tasks; they must reorient their priorities. Center City detectives, like detectives investigating hate crime in other cities,[6] shifted their perspective. In order to present clear evidence of the perpetrator's motivation, supervisors created a set of investigative procedures centered on allowing the victim to tell an unmediated story. Because most of the bias-motivated crimes in Center City involved vandalism and low-level assaults, officers in the ABTF were expected to investigate crimes that normally would not be investigated and were required to show concern to the victims of this type of crime. Finally, the detectives were primarily involved in investigating crime and providing protective service to gays and lesbians, and to people of color—Asians, Hispanics and Blacks—who had been attacked by Whites.

The differences between what those in the ABTF and what other detectives were required to do had an important, though intended, impact on the ABTF detectives' socialization. Unlike detectives who spend little time with crime victims, ABTF detectives' contact with victims was sustained. The unit first began to spend lots of time with victims in its early days when problems with the clerk magistrates' approving of charges meant that cases had to be well investigated and scrupulously documented. To create rock-solid cases, sometimes ABTF detectives interviewed victims more than once. Interviews took place in the victim's home and could last for several hours. If a court case developed as a result of the detective's investigation, then the detective provided a ride for the victim, who often was not able to afford to own an automobile. The detectives also frequently provided protective services to the victims, including helping a victim move into his or her residence; providing surveillance outside the residence; and if the harassment was severe, spending nights inside the residence. Thus, ABTF detectives had repeated contact with some victims. This distinguished the ABTF detectives' role from the traditional detective role, which involves neither the provision of protective services nor significant investigation.

Though the unit had specific procedures for the treatment of victims that differed substantially from those of the districts, its officers did not all carry out the procedures in the same way. An unusual degree of sensitivity was expected of all the detectives, whose interactions with victims could not be easily observed by their supervisors, but each had a significant degree of discretion in regard to treatment of victims, especially whether he or she treated them respectfully and took their cases seriously. Individual detectives also had discretion in deciding the cases' fates, for example, whether criminal action was taken or whether anything happened at all. Though supervisors had to approve charges, the individual detective was the expert on the facts because he or she had talked with the victim, had seen the crime scene, and had interviewed witnesses and assessed their credibility. When considering approving charges, supervisors generally based their decisions on facts given to them by the detective who had investigated the case. If a detective insisted that a witness was not credible or that an incident reported as an assault was really a fight, the supervisor was likely to tell the detective to inactivate the case.

Supervisors selected detectives for the unit based on evaluations of their ability to investigate crime and their desire to work hard, and largely without regard to their stance on hate crimes or hate crime victims. At any given time the unit represented a broad spectrum of identities and perspectives. Most of the officers were straight, but the unit had at least one gay officer. From the first crew, the unit had women officers, including more than one female supervisor. Though the unit, like the force itself, was majority White, several officers of color—Asians, Hispanics, and Blacks—served in the unit. Officers held a variety of religious and political orientations as well. Some of the officers were conservative Republicans, others staunch Democrats.

Diverse as the unit was, those in the unit denied that a detective's race or politics were important criteria for their membership in it. The police commissioner selected the head of the unit from a group of available lieutenants who applied for the position. The lieutenant selected the sergeants. The detectives were selected from outside the unit by the sergeants; the focus, they insisted, was on choosing good detectives. One officer who supervised the unit for a number of years described what he was looking for: "I wanted the toughest, meanest cops. They say I shouldn't use the word mean. I wanted them tough and mean enough to fight bias in the community, in the department, and yes, in homes." This sergeant found that officers often were trained by the department in a way that ill-suited them for listening to victims. The typical skeptical cop, he maintained, was not suitable for dealing with victims of bias crime; officers in the unit needed to have good listening skills. More than anything, detectives were selected for their ability to write well and work hard.

By not selecting officers who were oriented to enforcing civil rights law, the supervisors virtually guaranteed that the detectives in the unit did not all see the world, or their jobs, in the same way. The mission of the unit, and its culture, was to protect all victims of bias. The unit had a hard time socializing detectives who came into the unit with agendas that conflicted with the unit's mission. A White detective, whom I call "Angelo,"[7] served as a good example of the failure of the unit to socialize detectives. Angelo expressed great skepticism that people of color were the primary targets of racism in Center City. Many of his beliefs were similar to those expressed in Gertown and in other communities that mobilized against the enforcement of hate crime law. For instance, Angelo acted as if he believed that the unit really protected only people of color, that Center City's White neighborhoods had been ruined by school desegregation and integration, and that the city's Black neighborhoods were drug-ridden and filled with women who spent their lives on welfare. He spoke of his desire to protect White victims to one of his supervisors as the two were patrolling Gertown one evening.

> *Angelo:* You know, I go to all these seminars and I'm a White male cop, the person that these people hate. They hate us because they've been victimized. Any minority is free to be a victim of racism but a White person can never be a victim of racism. But I know that's not true because I'm a White person and I've been a victim of racism.
>
> *Supervisor:* When were you a victim of racism?
>
> *Angelo:* Center City was a city of neighborhoods that was totally destroyed. If there was really different schools, why didn't they bus the teachers around? No, because some guy from the suburbs had the idea to bus the kids, a great city was ruined. My wife was a victim of racism too. She was forced out because of racism. The Black girls would beat her up because she wouldn't let them play with her hair. They wanted to play with White hair and she wouldn't let them. . . . No one asks us why we left the city and

why we're scared to come back. It's not right. That's why I'm here. I want both sides of the issue represented.

During the same surveillance patrol, the car passed a private club in a predominately White area. Angelo expressed views on bias-motivated violence against gay men that directly contradicted his supervisor's views and the unit's norms.

Angelo: [Referring to the club] Anybody can join for twenty-five a year. No Blacks, no Spanish, no Jews, though. Gays, yeah, plenty of them. Doing stuff they shouldn't have been. Looking and stuff at the young guys. And they got beat up. They deserved it. You know who did it? The fourteen-year-old boys! That's not the place to be doing that. They shouldn't have been doing that.

Supervisor: So it's ok they got beat up because they were looking at the bodies of men?

Angelo: They shouldn't have been looking at teenagers. What if you were fourteen and you were in the shower and this old person is looking at you like they're interested in you?

Supervisor: So if I'm naked and this woman is looking at me and she may be desiring me or she may be admiring me, if I'm uncomfortable, I should cover up.

Angelo: What if you're young and you're not like that?

Supervisor: You don't beat them up; you put some clothes on. It's ok to use violence if someone is looking at you in a way that you don't like when you're naked?

Angelo: They shouldn't be looking at you in the sauna. There's a time and a place for everything.

Supervisor: When is a time and place to pick someone up?

Angelo: At home. In your own home.

Angelo later asserted that he had chosen to go to the unit to "set the record straight." In a similar vein, another White detective, who was from Gertown, a community that resisted the enforcement of hate crime law, declared that the Gertown perspective had been underrepresented in the unit and he was there to make sure that it would be represented.

Angelo's perspective clearly affected how he did his job. For him, cases that came to the unit did not have victims but, rather, "complainants." He treated victims of color summarily on the telephone. One of the detectives said that one of Angelo's Black victims, a local celebrity, was never notified of the outcome of the case against the person who had assaulted him, even though it was the unit's custom to do so. The treatment of victims had exceedingly low visibility, so the vast majority of Angelo's conduct went unobserved by the unit's supervisors. When it was observed, however, he was sharply rebuked. This happened once when he was evaluating a new case and happened to tell his supervisor, "I know what this is about." The supervisor seemed skeptical, and Angelo responded, "It's a drug case." The supervisor asked, "How do you know?" He replied, "Do you see where it happened?" Angelo then named a street in a Black neighborhood. "I worked there," said Angelo. "Really," said the supervisor. "I used to live on that street. Am I dealing drugs?"

Soft on Hate Crime

Angelo was one of a handful of White officers who had served in the unit who were "soft" on bias crime. Those with that perspective often minimized bias-motivated violence, characterizing it as "kid stuff," "drunk talk," "name calling," or "disputes." They tended to minimize the nature of the unit's caseload. In the words of one detective, "I've had lots of cases with gays where they've been assaulted and attributed it to their sexual orientation when it was really because they did something that caused the perpetrator to lash out. . . . People scream a lot about civil rights. I think this legal system abuses civil rights law." Unsurprisingly, officers who shared this perspective did not think that perpetrators of bias-motivated violence should receive serious punishment. They were dismissive of victims because they believed the incidents presented were not worthy of their attention. One such detective asked when he first came to the unit whether the unit's job was to investigate cross burnings. When the detective he was questioning replied, "No, nothing like that," the new detective responded, "So it's just bullshit, then?" In a response that was typical of a soft approach to bias crime, the same detective later explained to me the types of cases the unit handled:

> Most crimes are not necessarily bias-motivated. They are neighbor disputes, improper actions. . . . So far a lot of incidents, school kids are

sarcastic, other nonsense on cars. I think heavy metal is an inspiration. They did it to a car; they didn't know whose it was. You could mediate that in the home, school-age kids, could be mediated. Or a dispute over services, a shouting match, inflammatory language, racial, sexual, et cetera. Other incidents, like the [X case], when the victim made herself look like a victim. I tell officers, go slowly before you start to push the panic buttons, getting everyone all upset.

The perspective that the incidents the unit investigated were minor and could be mediated rather than criminally prosecuted was mirrored in the actions of another White detective who was investigating a swastika that had been painted on a garage. This story was related by his investigating partner:

We had a case in [X area,] a White man had a swastika written on his garage. "What's the problem?" the person I was with from the unit asked. Just imagine how that guy felt. Then we went inside his house. The guy from the unit said that some barbed wire from one of the concentration camps was one of his greatest treasures. The victim was looking at him and looking at me. The guy was Jewish. Can you imagine how he felt? I told [my partner] to get the fuck out of here. I'll take care of this. He asked me what the problem was. This same guy, in an argument with a member of the AG's office, he asked, "How the hell did you escape the ovens?" This was over a *case*.

Detectives who believed that the incidents the unit investigated were minor were also more likely to say that incidents were not hate crimes and not to file charges. When the unit's practices changed such that cases could be more easily returned to the district if they were not hate crimes, they also returned more cases to the district without investigating them. When they did investigate them, such detectives tended to favor mediation or warning suspects as opposed to seeking charges. The absence of oversight by supervisors meant that victims assigned to these officers received fewer services.

Detectives who were soft on hate crime, while noteworthy, were the exception rather than the rule. Most ABTF detectives behaved in a manner consistent with the unit's norms. The case record and interviews suggest that the vast majority of the White detectives who served in the unit were sensitive to victims' needs, experiences, and difficulties. Though the worst examples of poor treatment of victims came from White detectives, many of the unit's White detectives distinguished themselves in service to victims. One such detective commented on detectives who were soft on hate crime and preferred mediation to seeking criminal charges. His statements regarding the seriousness of hate crime contrast sharply with the comments of the White detectives quoted above:

> When you have hate crime and you are arresting people that are the constituents . . . from a politically powerful population, what do you do? Decriminalize the act. If you're raped do you want to hear we a have a great little mediation for you? For years, I fought to make this a major crime and now it's being mediated.
>
> Victims are powerless; they arrive in that position and you convince them not to go to court! That's the opposite of what I did. The victim had no one on his side. I want to say I'm going to take this injunction and wrap this piece of paper around you. My protection will be with you. I bring my police power to the table to protect victims.
>
> The commissioner wanted to keep the numbers down. . . . I wanted to see the numbers go up because if people can't go to the cops, they go to the streets. Look at L.A. Cops in L.A. tell someone to stop and assume the position; they did it instantly. It happened to a whole lot of people. That's dangerous, their dignity was gone. It's not about one individual; it's about everyone in the victim's group. The swastika is a message to every Jew, everywhere, though cops may call it graffiti, or vandalism.

"Conversion" and the Making of Victim Advocates

How well officers treated victims and investigated cases had perhaps less to do with their race or gender than with their desire to do their job well. Officers of color often came to the unit with more sensitivity toward victims of bias crime, born of their own experiences with racism, but many White officers developed sensitivity and a commitment to victims. Officers termed the socialization process through which they developed empathy for victims and a heightened desire to help "conversion." Conversion occurred as officers worked closely with victims and saw in detail their genuine fright and terror. The process transformed them from ordinary cops into advocates for victims. One of the first detectives in the unit described his conversion experience as occurring when he connected with a father in a Black family. Vandals had shattered seventeen windows of the family's house simultaneously. The detective was deeply touched by this man's feeling of devastation and powerlessness. "I like to think that as a detective, I should be doing something here. I also got to know these people. It got to be hard to walk away. I thought I should be able to *do* something."

Conversion required seeing victims' pain in its entirety. Seeing victims' pain in great detail allowed detectives to empathize with victims. Detectives insisted that this was required do the job well. Conversion allowed the detectives to believe what was happening to people was both real and important. The connection between *seeing* what victims had gone through and developing an understanding and commitment to the job was expressed by one detective:

> You can read all the case reports you want but you never get what's really happening out there until you see what the victims are going through. You have to go out there and see what is happening and see what effect it has on them. "David," he's a really nice guy, but he hasn't seen that. "Mike" has seen it. He's seen what hate can do.

In the same vein, another detective insisted that not everyone came to the unit equally committed to civil rights issues:

> We shouldn't expect that. I don't care about their attitudes on race. Just be a good cop. If a person came to the unit . . . and he started to investigate these cases, you'll be converted. They got to go in there and talk to families.

Doing the work, investigating cases, helped convert detectives and helped them to understand the victim's perspective. One detective explained the value of learning the victim's perspective:

> Coming home finding a rock thrown through your window, to some people that's a small thing; but coming home and finding the tires on your car slashed, windows broken, or "nigger" written somewhere, again and again. Some people have twenty or thirty incidents. And if you're in public housing, you don't have the resources to move. What you can do is you can go to court, maybe. And what'll happen? . . .
>
> You have to see what these victims are going through. Like the gay man who knows he was attacked because he was gay and reports it to the police and the cop who takes the reports doesn't like gays—some of them you can tell because as he's taking the report and he's like "And this really happened to you?" You think that victim is going to the police again? No way.

Conversion changed the officers' worldview—how they saw victims and how they defined their job. As such, it was an emotional metamorphosis for the detectives who experienced it. One Black detective described her conversion:

> Seeing stuff happen, a cross burning bigger than I am, dumpsters on fire, brought out things inside of me I never even knew existed. In my first year I thought I'd leave.

Officers in the unit repeatedly contended that one did not need to be politically or socially liberal to do the job well. All one needed was to be converted. If fact, sometimes even liberals needed conversion. A White cop in the unit, who as a rookie was known as the "liberal" in the precinct, talked about his conversion on the issue of sexuality.

> A gay conversion has been an education of mine. When I came here I was a civil rights guy except for the gay issue. I thought we should take the first gay case strictly as a provable civil rights violation. Civil rights are not a big mystery.
>
> No working cops get involved and aren't converted. No cops leave the unit saying they couldn't do that racial BS; [it's] more like they couldn't do police work.

For most detectives, the unit created a unique space and time for interaction with victims of hate crime that allowed for conversion. Ultimately, the difference between cops who had been "converted" and those who had not was that those who had believed that what was happening to victims was real, and they worked their hardest to do something about it because they believed it was unfair. Officers whose personal agenda or laziness kept them out of the trenches with victims were never converted.

Though the time detectives spent with victims was a significant factor in bringing about conversion, the two most important variables that led to conversion may have been the culture in the unit that suggested what the unit was doing was important and that the phenomena with which the detectives were dealing were important. Detectives were dealing with people who were very vulnerable and terribly scared; many were reaching out to the detectives in the unit as a last resort. Many of the crimes to which victims had been subjected were violent and vicious. It may have been easier for detectives to believe that what was happening was wrong when they saw these brutal, graphic manifestations of hate.

Explaining Detectives' Commitment

So why did the officers risk the disdain of fellow officers, and in some cases advancement, to work in the unit? It is important to note that not all of them did. Some asked for transfers and left the unit. Two who had left cited the politics of the job as a reason for leaving. Still, there were many officers who spent ten years or more in the unit; and for them, a number of reasons for staying made sense. One was the resources. As explained in chapter 3, after the initial period of underfunding, the unit was allocated an abundance of resources. Every detective in the unit had an unmarked car and the chance to work overtime shifts. Driving an unmarked police cruiser to work, with gas and maintenance paid for by the city, meant that a detective did not have to use his or her personal car. Overtime was important because regular overtime shifts—not the norm in other parts of the department—significantly increased the detectives' income; to leave would effectively be taking a pay cut. All of these reasons and the relatively unsupervised nature of the job created incentives to stay put. The comments of one detective show that there were things to be appreciated about investigating hate crimes:

> This is the only unit where everyone has their own car, [he or she] can come and go as they please, no log sheet. The freedom alone will keep people. Answering calls, we don't have to do that. We do one type of crime as opposed to fifty others. In the district, you do robberies, handbag snaps.

Though resources may have played a part in why officers stayed in the unit, the fact some officers did choose to leave and others paid a very high price for being in the unit implies that another factor was probably operative as well. Officers' statements about the value of their work indicate that they deemed it important, regardless of what others in the department thought. The construction of their work as valuable stemmed in part from their "conversion"; converted officers wanted to do something to alleviate the suffering of individuals they found in need of help.

Handling Criticism

Being in a unit where the culture is victim-oriented provided institutional support for a detective's choice to value service to victims. Criticism from the outside just made the unit tighter and more cohesive and increased the desire to be insulated from outside detractors. Within the unit, detectives believed that they were right and that those outside the unit were wrong:

> We knew in our hearts and minds that we were doing what we were trained to do in a fair, objective way. We were confident that we were objective in going after the right people. . . . The leaders say that we only targeted Whites; we were only after them because they were White. They won't focus on the fact that someone was being called a nigger while they were being beaten up.

It was not just that the members of the unit believed that they were doing the right thing; it was also that the other detectives in the unit provided support. In the same vein another detective described how, with the support of the unit, he was able to withstand the criticism from outsiders:

> I guess I knew I was right. Sometimes it works. It was them against us, those who stayed really cemented. Like the old Special Forces unit. It was like family, even guys that weren't the greatest never let anyone criticize the unit on the outside. All the criticism was on the inside. . . . The bottom line is that you're doing the right thing; you're doing God's work.

Conclusion

The experience of the ABTF illustrates a number of important implications regarding the investigation of hate crime. First, as other research has shown, police officers may not consider the investigation of bias-motivated violence real police work.[8] In Center City, officers in the districts had additional reasons to be dismissive of the unit: their disdain for the type of work in which the unit was engaged, the unit's ability to expose the districts' poor police work, and the unit's resources. Given the importance of organizational norms to police behavior, in order to investigate hate crimes, units that face the above difficulties must create norms that reject the construction of bias-motivated violence as not real police work. In addition, detectives who face ostracism from peers may require internal support.

Police departments investigate hate crime in a variety of ways. In some cities, hate crimes are referred to detectives who investigate all other types of crime. In others, like Seattle, one officer may be designated as responsible for investigating all of the city's possible hate crime. In Atlanta, hate crimes are referred to "Special Investigations"— detectives who investigate several specialized crimes, for example, drug crimes, homicide, and sexual assault. Finally, as was the case in the city that Boyd and associates studied, a single detective located in each precinct may be responsible for investigating all possible hate crimes that occurred in the precinct.[9]

In Center City, the department chose to create a separate centralized unit devoted entirely to the investigation of bias-motivated crime. Research on police has indicated that the organization of investigation— whether specialized detective units or generalist patrol officers—makes little difference in how productive the officers are.[10] One study of detectives investigating robberies found few differences in arrest rates between agencies that assigned initial responsibility for investigation to patrol officers, and those that assigned detectives to conduct initial investigations.[11]

The experiences of the ABTF suggest that hate crime may be an area in which specialized units are more effective. The approach of most ABTF detectives differed quite dramatically from the detectives profiled by Boyd and associates in their study of detectives who investigate hate crime. In part, this was structural. As a separate unit, the ABTF was able to create norms that were distinct from those in the rest of the department. The unit's low caseload also gave the detectives an opportunity to have much more interaction with victims, thereby allowing conversion to take place.

In addition, police have difficulty giving full attention to bias crimes when they must investigate low-level bias crimes and violent crimes at the same time. Because the unit focused entirely on one type of crime, bias crimes were not mixed with other violent crimes, forcing officers to juggle their investigation with crime that department norms indicated should have more priority.

With its own separate space, the unit was able to create norms that rejected the idea, common among police in the districts and elsewhere, that hate crime was not important or should not be investigated. Because the unit investigated a unique type of crime, it was easier for detectives transferred to the unit to accept its special procedures, some of which differed dramatically from those in the rest of the department.

Finally, the centralized unit provided clear experiential advantages over locating a few officers in each district. The city had, at most, only a few hundred reported hate crimes, spread throughout the city, each year; all were divided among the ABTF detectives. Because they investigated such widespread cases, rather than just the incidents that occurred in their area, over time the detectives developed a wealth of investigative experience. That experience and the investigative innovations developed were passed along as more seasoned detectives advised new ones. In addition, as a separate unit, the ABTF provided support for officers who faced the rejection and derision of colleagues.

7

The Decision to Seek Charges

In cases in which a suspect was identified, once the investigation was completed, ABTF detectives had to decide how the incident was going to be handled. This chapter explores the wide range of options available to detectives and how they decide among them. The chapter also describes the detectives' perspective regarding the kinds of cases appropriate for criminal civil rights violations or bias crime charges, and the kinds in which the detectives are reluctant to invoke the law. At the chapter's close, I present a model showing how detectives make decisions in hate crime cases.

The Detectives' Decision-Making Options

If a suspect is identified, detectives have five options as to how they may proceed. The first three do not involve an invocation of the hate crime law or other criminal law. Detectives may (1) do nothing; (2) send the case back to the district detectives; or (3) monitor the situation, warning any possible perpetrators encountered. The fourth option requires either an invocation of the law or the use of formal procedures; that is, detectives may seek regular criminal charges or pursue mediation or a civil injunction under the civil rights law. The fifth option, to seek charges for criminal civil rights violations against the perpetrator, is the focus of most of this chapter and is described in detail below.

Option 1. Do Nothing

If the detective elects to do nothing, the case is closed or moved to inactive status. In a case in which a suspect was identified, the most frequent reason for the detective to close it without action was the victim's refusal to participate in the prosecution of the crime. For a detective to seek any type of charges, the victim had to be willing to participate in the prosecution of the crime. Research has shown that police use their discretion not to invoke the law when the victim refuses to participate in prosecution.[1] Perhaps for strategic reasons having to do with the probable success of a "victimless" prosecution, unit protocol prevented ABTF detectives from seeking charges if the crime victim was unwilling to testify against the defendant. The detective inferred a victim's lack of desire from the failure to return phone calls at any stage of the investigation. The refusal to cooperate or a declaration that the victim was not going to take part in the prosecution ended the detective's activity on the case. The detective immediately moved the case to inactive status.

In interviews, detectives insisted that victims' refusal to cooperate was a very large problem for the unit. The data from the unit's logs supports this assertion. Between 1991 and 1997, detectives noted that an average of 13 percent of victims refused to go forward with prosecution. Victims, who usually had been terrified by their experiences, had a disincentive to go forward. Perpetrators, who often lived in the same housing development or neighborhood as their victims, frequently threatened retaliation after they were charged with a crime.

The cost of the criminal process to victims served as a disincentive as well. For victims, invoking the process was a punishment.[2] Seeing a case through until trial or even until a plea agreement was reached required a number of court appearances at which the victim's attendance was required. If the victim did not appear, the charges against the defendant were likely to be dismissed. Because the victim was not given an exact time when the case would be called, appearing in court could mean that the victim had to miss an entire workday. Many of the unit's victims were poor and simply could not afford to be absent from their jobs. One detective discussed how central the victim was to the decision to go to court and how difficult court appearance was for the victim:

> The real court factor is the victim. If the victim says no, then there's no case. If the victim doesn't come, then there's a continuance. After he or she doesn't show again, finally it's thrown out.

> People sit there from 9:00 A.M. to 4:30 P.M. Their job doesn't pay for that. They [victims] say, just tell them [the perpetrator] to leave me alone; it'll be fine. This happens especially when they [the prosecutor] tell you that if it goes to court it may drag on a year.

Given the hardship of prosecution, it is surprising that many more victims did not refuse to participate.

Option 2: Sending It Back

Crimes not motivated by bias were the responsibility of the neighborhood detectives. Therefore, if after a brief investigation the ABTF detective determined that a case was not bias-motivated he or she had the option of sending it back to the district for investigation. Once a case was returned to the district, the detective removed it from the unit's active case files. Upon receiving the case, the district was supposed to investigate, search for suspects, and pursue criminal charges if the case warranted. Most ABTF detectives rarely pursued this option. Sending a case back to the district was generally reserved for nuisance cases that ABTF detectives believed the district was trying to pass off to them. The unit did not keep records on how often it returned cases to the district, but those in charge of the unit insisted that the number was relatively small.

The Implications of Sending Cases Back. The detectives readily accepted that sending cases back ended any chances that the crimes would be investigated. Detectives in the ABTF often commented on the failure of district detectives, as research had documented is commonly the case, to investigate crimes. That district detectives gave low priority to low-level crime was only part of the reason that so few crimes were investigated. Several of the detectives asserted that residents of Gertown did not receive adequate police services for "regular" crimes because the officers in their neighborhood precinct were so unresponsive. When I asked one officer why he was not sending a hate crime that he believed to have been faked back to the district, he said that the district "would not know what to do with it."

According to the ABTF detectives, victims whose cases were under the jurisdiction of the district detectives frequently did not understand that their cases were not going to be investigated. In one case, an ABTF detective spoke with a gay man who contacted the unit because he believed he was a victim of a hate crime. After a brief interview, the detective concluded that the man was not a victim of a hate crime. The victim's case had not been referred to the unit, and it was under the jurisdiction of the district detectives, whom the victim had assumed were investigating his case. The ABTF detective called the district and found that the case had not been assigned to a particular officer at the district. "It would probably never be investigated," commented the detective.

The concern that the crimes be fully investigated meant that even if an ABTF detective were fairly certain that a case was not bias-motivated, once an investigation had been undertaken, he or she would rarely pass the investigation back to the neighborhood detectives. Rather than returning a case, not technically the province of the unit, the unit usually continued with the investigation anyway. In a case in which two Black men had stabbed two young White men, the detectives joked about sending the case back to the detectives in the neighborhood for investigation. Their comments suggested that if they did, the neighborhood detectives, rather than expend any effort themselves, despite the victim's serious injuries, would insist that the victim seek his own criminal complaint. "Going to court and seeking a complaint" refers to a process used for misdemeanors and simple assaults; the victim obtains a police report and goes into the district court to file a complaint. The victim then appears at the probable cause hearing. In the Center City Police Department this option was reserved for cases that the police considered unimportant.

> *Detective 1* [to *Detectives 2* and *3*]: I deem this "not racial." I'm
> sending it back to the precinct. (Laughs)
> *Detective 2:* (Laughs) Where d'you think they would get with it?
> *Detective 3:* They'd tell them to go to court and seek a complaint!
> (All detectives laugh.)

Despite the fact that this case was deemed "not racially motivated" by the investigating ABTF detective, it was *not* sent back to the district for investigation. On the contrary, the ABTF detectives continued to investigate the case because they believed that the district detectives would not investigate it. ABTF detectives continued to investigate many cases they felt were not really their responsibility, primarily for three reasons. First, they believed the victim should get some type of police attention and they knew he or she would not get it if the case were referred back to the district. Second, if a detective had invested time in a case, he may have wanted to see a particular criminal justice outcome. Third, even if the incident were not bias-motivated, if it had occurred in Gertown, Hillsdale, or another explosive neighborhood, the detective often wanted to catch the perpetrator to prevent a retaliation that could lead to bias-motivated incidents later.

Option 3: Monitoring the Situation, Warning the Perpetrators

Another option, short of filing charges, involved monitoring the situation and, if the perpetrator were discovered, warning the perpetrator about his or her conduct. Monitoring a situation often involved driving by the victim's house, and periodically checking in with the victim to see if the incidents were continuing. If suspects were found, especially in cases involving behavior that was not criminal, the ABTF's monitoring detectives warned that it must cease. In recounting a story about a warning, one detective explains why the unit did not return a case to the district:

> We had a case with a seven-year-old kid who had gone to the corner store and [from] a group of White kids standing outside, one had said to him, "Run, nigger, run" and stamped his boot. The kid was terrified and took off.
>
> We took that and investigated it because the district wouldn't have done anything. We found the kids who did it and told them not to do it again, that if they did, they'd be in trouble. They can't go around scaring little kids like that. The boy was really terrified. Can you imagine? A seven-year-old kid.

Sometimes the monitoring or warning worked; several files were marked "case inactivated when no further incidents." Above is a good example of the type of case that would receive no services if referred back to the district for investigation. The conduct was arguably non-criminal, and if criminal, consisted only of threats, a low-level crime. There is little chance that the district, which prioritized cases according to severity, would have followed up on the incident.

Option 4: "Regular" Criminal Charges, Civil Rights Injunctions, and Mediation

Criminal charges were sought by the ABTF in three types of situations: (1) when the investigating detective believed the crime to be bias-motivated but did not have enough evidence to seek criminal civil rights violations; (2) when the crime was not bias-motivated, but the detective believed the perpetrator should be sanctioned; and (3) when the detective was seeking criminal civil rights violations. In bias crime cases, the detectives often sought criminal charges in addition to criminal civil rights charges in the event the perpetrator was found not guilty of committing civil rights violations. Filing both types of charges helped ensure that the perpetrator was punished.

The unit's log gives an approximate figure for the number of criminal charges officers filed. Between 1990 and 1997, they filed criminal charges in approximately 20 percent of the cases the unit investigated (see Table 7.1). Though the largest percentage of all criminal charges filed were in race-based cases, detectives were slightly more likely to file criminal charges in antigay cases.

The small percentage of criminal charges overall may have been due to the fact that there were other ways to dispose of cases. Cases in which a single perpetrator or a group of perpetrators engaged in a pattern of harassment might be settled by civil rights injunction. The attorney general's office sought injunctions using the civil portion of the civil rights law. Injunctions prohibited the perpetrator, under penalty of arrest, from engaging in further bias-motivated conduct. According to unit logs, this was a rare choice for detectives. Fewer than thirty injunctions were brought between 1990 and 1997.

Crimes committed by residents of Center City public housing developments against other residents were sometimes settled by mediation. The criminal courts, schools, and sometimes even the detectives themselves conducted mediation. It was used in cases involving few if any injuries, and in cases in which both parties were likely to remain in contact with each other—especially students and residents of the developments.

Though the number of cases marked as "mediated" in the case logs tripled during the 1990s, informal dispute resolution was not new. The ABTF detectives had always engaged in some form of informal dispute resolution. In the mid-to-late 1990s, however, as part of a drive to teach many city workers mediation techniques, the detectives acquired formal training in mediation. The training legitimized informal dispute resolution practices. After detectives were trained, their statistics began to reflect their use of mediation to resolve disputes. In 1997, the unit's log reflects that thirty-one cases, 13 percent of cases investigated that year, were settled by mediation.

Option 5: Criminal Civil Rights Violations

The final option, seeking civil rights violations, was the most important option from the unit's perspective. If the detectives believed a case to be bias-motivated and an appropriate vehicle for such charges, they could elect to seek criminal civil rights violations or hate crime charges. Table 7.1 shows the detectives' records from the unit's logs, depicting the percentage of cases in which they sought criminal civil rights charges. The figures do not represent the total number of cases that the detectives believed to be hate crimes. My evaluation of these logs suggests that the data they contain are incomplete.

Questions concerning the accuracy of the logs aside, any measure of the cases in which police end up requesting bias crime charges is scarcely a measure of the cases that they believe to be bias crimes. Several things must converge before a detective can request charges for civil rights violations. In addition to identifying a suspect, the detective must gather sufficient evidence of motivation to request charges. Detectives in the unit said they often thought cases were hate crimes but were unable to prove it, and therefore did not seek charges. They also reported sometimes being unable to find a suspect in cases that they believed to be hate crimes.

Criminal civil rights violations required proof not only that the perpetrator had committed a crime but also that in doing so, he or she had intended to deprive the victim of his or her civil rights. As the remainder of this chapter and the next will argue, assembling evidence of this intent that prosecutors, clerk magistrates, and judges would accept presented unique challenges for the detectives. Perhaps because of the motivational requirement, the unit's logs show that between 1990 and 1997 charges for criminal civil rights violations were even more infrequent than regular criminal charges and were filed in just 9 percent of cases that the unit investigated (see Table 7.1). The figures reported are for all requests for civil rights charges, including those that were later denied by the district attorney's office. The highest number of requests came in 1993, thirty-three cases, some 11 percent of the cases the unit investigated that year.

Deciding to Seek Criminal Civil Rights Charges

Deciding that a case warranted criminal civil rights charges was a complicated process in which the ABTF detective weighed the facts and cir-

TABLE 7.1
Action Sought, by Type of Crime, 1990–1997

Type of Crime	Criminal Charges		Civil Rights Violations	
	N	%	N	%
Race	344	83.0	142	80.0
Antigay/ -lesbian	59	14.0	30	3.0
Religion	7	2.0	5	16.0
Other	2	0.4	1	0.5
Total Charges	412	99*	178	100*
Total Investigations	1,989	21.0	1,989	9.0

Source: ABTF files.
*Does not equal 100 due to rounding.

cumstances of the crime, as well as the characteristics of the case, against his or her experience. The decision that the officer had to make was twofold: it required (1) that the officer first identify the bias motivation, and then (2) that he or she make a strategic decision as to whether to actually seek charges. Below are the rules of thumb that officers used to identify and then select cases appropriate for hate crime charges.

ABTF detectives developed filtering mechanisms and employed informal guidelines to isolate bias motivation, in part because many of the cases referred to the unit were not bias-motivated; the unit received many such cases because it encouraged patrol officers to send any cases they deemed appropriate. The unit did this to ensure that it was notified of all bias-motivated conduct. It also, as a check on patrol, had the Reports Bureau forward cases with a possibility of bias, as discussed earlier. When the Reports Bureau forwarded all reports that had slurs or epithets and a difference in race between victim and perpetrator, the unit's case numbers drastically increased, because vulgarities, especially slurs and epithets, were commonplace in acts of violence. One officer estimated that slurs and epithets were used in 70 percent of incidents with injuries and 90 percent of traffic accidents.

Basic Requirements for Hate Crimes

Detectives' practices reveal that hate crimes had two basic requirements. The perpetrator and victim had to have different identities— race, gender, sexual orientation, and so on—and the context in which the crime occurred must be one that suggested that it was motivated by bias rather than some other emotion—anger, revenge, jealousy, or the like.

1. Different Identities. The first requirement, and the more important, was that the victim and perpetrator have different identities or backgrounds. If the victim had been attacked because of, say, his or her race, the race of the perpetrator had to be different. Detectives did not believe that bias-motivated incidents happened within the same identity group; any incident in which the victim and the perpetrator shared the same race were routinely dismissed as having other origins.

The heavy presumption against bias motivation among individuals of the same race applied to cases having to do with antigay bias as well: gays could not commit hate crimes against other gays. In one case involving a Black gay man who had been attacked by another gay man and called a "faggot," two detectives called the former "a victim of no crime" because both men were gay.

There were two important exceptions to the practice of dismissing same-group attacks. The first concerned heterosexual men who were attacked by other heterosexuals because they were thought to be gay. The unit had investigated several cases that fit this scenario. For example, in one, the victims, who were not gay, were in a taxicab and were approached by a group of men who said, "Get out of the car, faggots." After one man exited the cab and ran, the perpetrator gave chase. When he caught the victim, he began to kick him, screaming, "Fucking homos." The unit sought civil rights violations: the victim had been attacked because he was *presumed* to be gay. Two defendants pled guilty to both criminal charges and civil rights charges.

The second important exception to the practice of dismissing same-group attacks concerned attacks against one or the other party in an interracial couple. ABTF detectives accepted that such attacks were frequently bias-motivated. They had seen particularly dramatic examples of this, especially involving Whites attacked by other Whites for dating minorities.

The practice of dismissing cases when individuals had similar identities meant that detectives were often unable to appreciate the fact that victims and perpetrators had multiple identities and myriad perspectives on their identities. In the case described above involving the gay victim who the detectives decided was not a victim of hate crime, the detectives did not even explore the possibility that the hate crime could be a race-based crime or that the perpetrator was a "self-hating gay" and the attack occurred because of the victim's sexual orientation.

Automatic dismissal of all cases in which both the perpetrator and the victim are gay means that detectives may miss cases that should be treated as hate crimes. There have been cases of so-called self-hating gays targeting and killing other gay men. In Center City, detectives told of several homicides that occurred in a public area where many gay men had sex. The killer selected sex partners and clubbed each to death while the two were engaged in intercourse. The detectives said that when they caught the man, he declared that he had committed the crimes because he hated gays. A similar case occurred in Minneapolis in 1991: a gay man committed two antigay murders on the banks of the Mississippi in a secluded area frequented by gay men. The perpetrator discussed his self-hatred and hatred of other gay men in Arthur Dong's documentary film *Licensed to Kill* (1997).

2. *Looking to the Crime's Context.* Examining a crime's context required that detectives examine its setting and other situational aspects in order to shed light on why the incident occurred. Setting included the crime's precise location, whether it occurred indoors or out, and what the perpetrator and victim were doing immediately before the crime. In exploring these situational aspects the detectives were looking for evidence that the crime was motivated *not* by bias but, rather, by anger, jealousy, or revenge, to name a few of the motivations that ABTF detectives wished to rule out. If a crime were motivated by jealousy over a woman, to use an example that detectives sometimes mentioned, it was not a hate crime. Discussing cases around the office, one detective highlighted the importance of context:

> We've had some problems in Precinct [X] . . . some things that may have had bias indicators but eventually were referred back. These are cases in which language may have been used but in the context of something like a traffic accident.

Detectives were trained to ask, as part of evaluating context, whether the incident could have happened or would have escalated if the perpetrator and the victim had been of the same race or other background. If the incident still would have happened and would have unfolded in the same way, then the detectives assumed that the incident was not a hate crime.

Detectives did not examine the setting of every crime and weigh whether the perpetrator had been motivated by anger, jealousy, and revenge. Instead, they used shortcuts to filter out non-bias-motivated cases. These shortcuts, the "typical non-hate crime" and the use of bias indicators, were based on incidents that were repeatedly referred to the unit but were not bias-motivated.

"The Typical Non-Hate Crime"

The first shortcut was based on how detectives behaved, perhaps without intending to. I call it the "typical non-hate crime." The typical non-hate crime involved five scenarios—cases involving drugs, fights, retaliation for earlier fights, traffic accidents, and neighbor disputes. Though detectives were frequently not able to determine what motivated an incident (and no civil rights charges were sought), typical non-hate crimes were the examples offered when they decided that a case was not motivated by bias. One detective explained that this type of incident was "less than 51 percent bias-motivated." When asked for an example, he replied, "A traffic accident between someone Asian and someone White. Racial epithets, slurs are exchanged."

There were no particular circumstances attached to the typical non-hate crime. As long as incidents that were really about "traffic" involved cars, and neighbor disputes involved individuals who lived near each other, a non-hate crime could occur in many ways. Any and every case involving a car could really be over traffic. Any situation involving young White and Black men, like the story in chapter 2 involving a White man shot in the buttocks during a meeting with a drug dealer, could really be about drugs.

For the detectives, deciding that something is bias-motivated began with the ruling out of alternate explanations. Because every incident that had a basic fact situation could be one of the typical non-hate crime cases, incidents were first evaluated against the typical non-hate crime. Real hate crimes then became defined, in part, in opposition to the typical non-hate crime. In this way, ABTF detectives' practices were distinct from those of other detectives investigating hate crime. Instead of creating archetypal hate crimes with particular characteristics—cases with extreme violence, those involving members of organized hate groups, and other significant outward manifestations of bias—and calling these the "normal hate crimes,"[3] ABTF detectives identified classes of crimes frequently referred to the unit that should *not* be considered hate crimes.

Weeding Out False Reports

In trying to discern whether an incident was a typical non-hate crime, the detective's initial task was ordinary detective work: trying to "figure out what happened." Part of figuring out what happened required sorting the conflicting stories that emerged from interviewing suspects and victims, and trying to ascertain who was telling the truth and who was lying. Though a sample of the case files revealed less than one manufactured hate crime a year, the specter of false reports—incidents individuals manufactured to extract some type of benefit—loomed large. Nearly every detective mentioned that sometimes individuals made things up to manipulate the system. When asked for examples, they generally provided the same ones: prominent cases in which an individual had deliberately claimed to be a victim when he or she was not, either for the attention or in order to receive some tangible benefit.

The detectives were well aware that some individuals might be lying so as to attract attention or sympathy. One such incident involved a Jewish college student who reported that swastikas and anti-Semitic threats had appeared on her door. After several such reportings, the college installed a hidden camera that captured the student calmly stepping over a sheet of paper with a note and swastika on it that had been slid under the door. The note was not reported to the police until the next day, when her roommate discovered it. The victim's cavalier attitude toward the note when she believed herself unobserved signaled to the police that she was the person who had left the note. The detectives surmised that her reporting of the earlier messages had been a plea for attention.

Another situation that detectives in the unit encountered on several occasions involved individuals living in public housing who faked hate crimes so that the housing office would move them to another housing development or give them a Section 8 certificate allowing them to move into private housing. One detective explained:

> There is money to be made in false civil rights reports. If someone wants a Section 8 certificate, right now they are not taking applications unless one is a victim of a hate crime. We had an incident when a guy who was

gay knew that he could get a Section 8 certificate if he said that his civil rights were violated. He said that he was being harassed and that he had no entrance to certain courtyards and that he could not park his car in certain areas. Sometimes people will say they are being harassed and that they want a transfer to a certain housing development. Then you find out they have a mother or sister in that development.

One downside of providing an unusual degree of service was that it attracted the attention of those who want the police to investigate a crime that had happened to them. A variation on the false report was the victim who deliberately misrepresented what happened to him or her in order to get the system to pay attention to the crime. Officers were forced to weed out cases in which the victim had added slurs and epithets in order to get the police—any police—to investigate the crime. One detective remarked:

> People realized that they were getting more attention. They were aware of our success rate, also aware of other steps. Other things were done to protect you. People started wising up, if you say it's racial you get personal attention—round-the-clock protection, nail the guy to the wall [when we catch him]: high bail or no bail. That's what we started asking for in civil rights cases. They started to think, "I want to really slam this guy who hurt me so I'm going to say it's racial and I'm going to get attention." Like when people want someone to come right away and they report an OT, officer in trouble.

Bias Indicators

Bias indicators, described in chapter 4, were sometimes used by the detectives as a shortcut to help them decide that a crime was bias-motivated. The most important bias indicators were (1) differences in race, religion, sexual orientation, and ethnicity; (2) words, writing, or gestures used during the crime; (3) problem location; (4) the victim's group significantly outnumbered in the area; and (5) suspect has a history of bias-motivated attacks.

The detectives' use of bias indicators was much more self-conscious than their use of the typical non-hate crime. New detectives who were just learning how to investigate hate crime used them as a starting point when they began their investigation. More established detectives tended to use them as a justification for cases they believed to be bias-motivated. Although the list did not suggest that some indicators carried less weight than others, officers in the unit learned to ascribe less weight to particular indicators. For example, "problem location," a place in which a number of bias-motivated incidents had happened in the past, while not dispositive, was something to which the detectives gave significant weight in their determination of bias. By contrast, often patrol officers referred cases in which the only indication that the incident was motivated by bias was that the victim and suspect were of different races. Detectives knew that such cases were not necessarily bias-motivated.

Policing Crime, Not Speech

One of critics' primary worries about enforcers of hate crime legislation is that the use of slurs and epithets or other similar language by the perpetrator automatically signifies bias. None of the evidence from Center City supports the contention that ABTF detectives invoked bias crime laws solely because perpetrators used slurs or epithets, despite the importance of language to cases in which they sought civil rights violations. Civil rights violations needed much more than language. The detectives emphasized that the suspect had to have committed a crime, that is, there had to have been action, not just language. When asked how the detectives decided that a case is a civil rights violation, one detective clarified the relationship between language and action:

> It's not language alone. You investigate actions. Words are the secondary buttress of actions. They prove the history of the action; prove that they went after someone because of race. You have to put the blinders on. Is this something the perpetrator would have done if the victim were Black or White? You have to consider both sides, walk the line.

Another explained:

> We look to the totality of the circumstances, criminal action and the words and also at the incident. . . . Language alerts us to the possibility of bias, but it's just the possibility.
> . . . It's not clear-cut. It's easier for us when you have, as we've . . . had, the same defendant for two crimes. It's hard because of the totality of the circumstances. None of us are in the minds of the perpetrators. They may have acted because they're ticked off because someone is hitting on their girlfriend or because the person is of a different race and is hitting on the girlfriend.

As their above comments show, the detectives were very receptive to the possibility that bias had not motivated the incident when slurs or epithets were used. They were wary of using language as evidence of motivation when there was any indication that language was used for a reason other than bias.

Relationship and Bias

Further evidence that language was not dispositive of bias was that detectives identified the relationship between people as an important part of the context of the crime. Language was discounted as a factor indicating motivation in exchanges between people who knew each other. As other research has found,[4] a preexisting relationship, good or bad, between the victim and the suspect is a sign to the police that an incident is not bias-motivated. One former detective complained about a case the unit investigated: "[I]t was . . . a gay guy complaining about his boyfriend. It was not a legitimate case." In another case, a gay man repeatedly tried to get civil rights charges against someone with whom he had had consensual sex in the past. Like prosecutors who refuse to bring charges in rape cases in which the victim may have had previous consensual sex with the perpetrator,[5] the ABTF detectives refused to consider the gay victim's case for civil rights charges. They insisted that because the victim and the perpetrator had had consensual sex on a previous occasion, what had happened to the victim was not a hate crime.

Police were not alone in assuming that bias was less likely to have happened among people who knew each other. Lawyers responsible for seeking injunctive relief under the civil rights law also discounted cases between people who knew each other. Cases involving people who had some other relationship, such as friends or neighbors, were considered problematic by those enforcing the law in Center City. A previous relationship and sustained contact over time can afford myriad opportunities for one to develop reasons aside from issues of bias to attack the victim. Cases between those who knew each other could have multiple motives, any of which could have been the reason for the attack. One assistant attorney general explained why cases between friends and neighbors did not make good cases for injunctive relief and why she discounted the use of slurs and epithets in such cases:

Often you have cases with dual motives. Maybe they used slurs, but they knew each other. They were neighbors and the incident could have been because the dog was barking. Even though a racial slur was used, we may have cut them [the perpetrator] some slack. We all have biases and we have different ways of negotiating the fact that [different] people are in our community.

In a similar vein, a different assistant attorney general replied, in response to what additional evidence she wants when she's not sure about a case:

I want to find more evidence of bias, more evidence in general. They should ask, is there a history between these two individuals? If they've never encountered each other before, that suggests two things: first, that it is bias-motivated, and second, that it's likely to be repeated.

Most of the cases the unit investigated involved attacks by people who were unknown to the victims, something that made finding the person who committed the crime more challenging. It makes intuitive sense that strangers, who are unlikely to know the victim personally, are less likely to have a reason other than bias—anger or revenge, for instance—to serve as the motivation for the attack. Perhaps the police and those prosecuting bias crimes favored cases with strangers as perpetrators rather than neighbors or friends because bias crimes committed by stranger-perpetrators make for simpler and more believable stories.

Hate Speech versus Hate Crime—Weighing Victims' Stories

A worry related to the one addressed above, that detectives seize on language as the only evidence of motivation, is that detectives will uncritically accept the victim's view of what happened and identify cases as hate crime that are really only hate speech. This is of particular concern when police are given open-ended criteria and not told exactly what weight to ascribe to victims' stories.

ABTF detectives were especially careful to weigh the victim's perception of whether a hate crime had occurred. Distinguishing between hate speech and hate crimes, the detectives held that although words of hate may hurt or inflame, they are not in and of themselves criminal. Detectives in the unit regularly acknowledged that a line exists between hate speech and hate crime. Hate speech, their conversations suggested, is wholly legal; hate crime, which involves criminal action, is what the law criminalized. Several detectives resented the unit's being called the "nyahh nyahh nyahh" unit by colleagues and disliked the implication that the unit's main focus was to police name calling. The following conversation took place in the office, while one detective was looking at an incident report and talking with another:

> *Detective 1:* A White teacher, the victim, has asked a Black student to leave the room. Evidently, the perpetrator, the student, said to the victim teacher, "What are you looking at, you fucking honkey?" [Reading directly from the crime report] "The victim thinks his constitutional rights are violated." [Looking up from the sheet] Names is not a crime.
> *Detective 2:* No.
> *Detective 1:* I'll screen this one out.

Another detective described how he weighed victims' stories with respect to bias-motivated language:

> Hate crimes are a challenge. Take an offensive term. The victim hears the term and also the offensive history. You have to remain objective. Take the swastika. That has meaning to people. The "n-word," too. Sometimes words alone don't rise to the level of a hate crime.

The detective continued, giving an example:

> A gay man is walking down the street. He hears the words "Hey, faggot." Those are just words. Or hears "Hey, White honkey." We have to look to see if he feels intimidated. It's not a crime to just use words. It's words alone in that context in a manner that may make it a hate crime. Did they threaten? Did they have intent? Someone can yell, "Faggot!" but to have intent, you need action.

The First Amendment

ABTF detectives are neither lawyers nor legal scholars. They received little or no training in what the First Amendment demands. Few detectives in the unit had even gone to college. What knowledge they had of the First Amendment came from high school civics or popular culture. Despite the detectives' lack of formal training in jurisprudence, many of their responses to questions about the First Amendment implications of their job were rather sophisticated. Like critical race theorists who argue for protections against hate speech,[6] the detectives recognized the pain of racial words to victims. At the same time, the detectives seemed clearly to understand that words—taunts, slurs, and epithets—were protected. One detective insisted:

> Racial words are very violent. Racial words may be hate incidents, but words aren't a crime. He called her a nigger? It's not a crime to say that— the First Amendment right may be violated.

Even when pressured, ABTF detectives resisted seeking civil rights charges in cases in which there was only speech and no evidence of bias motivation. In one case, a group of heterosexual men went to a gay bar and began making antigay jokes and remarks. At one point, one witness said this happened after they were told that they had no right to be in a gay bar; the men hurled a beer at the bar, and a fight ensued. Gay and lesbian organizations were quite vocal in the case, pressuring the unit to seek civil rights charges against two of the straight men. The unit refused and criminal charges were sought instead. As the detective investigating the case noted in his report, the case was one that did not merit charges, in part for First Amendment reasons:

> [M]y evaluation of the evidence to this point reveals neither of these defendants was in violation of the civil rights statutes. While both admit that they were telling antigay jokes and making inflammatory comments, they state those comments and jokes were directed to each other. This behavior is verified by [two other defendants], as well as other witnesses.While this behavior may be inflammatory in nature, it is within the First Amendment rights to speak in this manner.

The detectives did not view their actions as depriving defendants of their rights to free speech. Consistently, the response to the question about the difference between actions and behavior that infringed on a defendant's free speech rights was that hate crime involved violence and action. When asked whether perpetrators were really being punished for saying something, one detective responded:

> That's not really the case. We normally had them for something else, not just for saying something. The perp said something, then beat someone up with their fists.

Still another detective appreciated the difference between hate crime and hate speech. When asked about the free speech implications of hate crime enforcement, he responded, "People can call you a name, as long as there's no overt act, you're on firm constitutional ground. It's a very fine line." Even a detective who had a deep dislike for hate speech was clear about the protection that the Constitution gives it:

> If you call someone a nigger . . . I don't think that language should be used. But if it's used in a context where the words aren't directed at anybody. . . . [Hesitating]. It's not ok to use it at all. You can never call anybody a nigger. You can't use it when directed at someone or in a park in a crowd. Both are a problem. You say that, you might be looking for trouble. You might intimidate people, a little kid. I don't think it's OK but the Constitution allows it.

Race and the Decision to Charge

Many scholars have expressed concern that those enforcing hate crime law unfairly target minorities.[7] Though no systematic study of law enforcement bias in the area of hate crime exists, anecdotal evidence showing disproportionate percentages of minorities, particularly African Americans, charged with hate crimes provides some support for the belief that law enforcement officers disproportionately target minorities who commit hate crime.[8]

In Center City, among members of the ABTF, I observed no pattern of differential enforcement targeting minorities for hate crime charges. Figures from the unit's logs support this. In cases in which detectives sought hate crime charges, two minority groups—African Americans and Hispanics—were overrepresented as victims and underrepresented as perpetrators. In charges for racial harassment, African Americans were identified as victims in 36 percent of race-based cases the unit investigated, yet 45 percent of the requests for charges for civil rights violations were made on behalf of African-American victims. African Americans were perpetrators in just 20 percent of the race-based cases for which the unit sought charges. The detectives sought charges for Hispanics that were consistent with their representation in the victim pool; Hispanics constituted approximately 21 percent of the unit's victims, and 21 percent of the civil rights violations were sought on behalf of Hispanic victims. Hispanics were identified as perpetrators in just 4 percent of cases in which the unit sought civil rights violations.

Charges in the race-based hate crime cases on behalf of two groups, victims of Asian origin and Whites, did not match their representation in the victim pool. The disparity was largest for Whites. Whites represented 28 percent of the unit's victims in race-based cases, yet only 19 percent of charges were sought on behalf of White victims. Whites constituted 75 percent of the perpetrators in race-based hate crime cases. Thirteen percent of the unit's victims were of Asian descent, and 11 percent of the cases for civil rights violations were made on behalf of Asian victims.

The most likely explanation for the distribution of charges is the nature of bias-motivated violence. Most of the race-based cases that the unit investigated involved attacks on minorities in White neighborhoods. Consequently, the largest portion of the unit's charges for hate crimes was on behalf of minority victims. With respect to the disparity regarding Asian victims, many of the victims of Asian descent were not Asian Americans but, rather, newly arrived Asian immigrants from Laos, Cambodia, and Vietnam. The slight disparity in charges on behalf of Asian victims may have stemmed from factors noted by the victim advocate for Asian Americans: Asian victims' fear of the criminal justice system based on their experience with authorities in their countries of origin.

Choosing Not to Invoke the Law

Even if an ABTF detective determined that an incident was bias-motivated, he or she might not have invoked the law. In such situations, the detectives believed that use of the law was not appropriate or would not be successful. Their judgments about using the law were strategic. Officers explained that the battle to get civil rights violations accepted had been a hard one. Consequently, they did not want to use the law in situations in which it was not appropriate, partly because they did not want, as they called it, "to wear the law out" by seeking civil rights violations in ambiguous situations. One detective explained this succinctly: "The civil rights law has teeth. It's there to bite you on the butt. If you bring cases with lousy evidence and language, the law loses its teeth." He and his peers believed that the law would cease to be effective if they sought civil rights violations in cases in which they would not be able to get convictions. Not getting a conviction did not affect their records, for no systematic records were kept of convictions, not-guilty verdicts, and pleas; detectives in the unit just believed that it sent a bad message to perpetrators. One detective reasoned, "What good is prosecuting if you can't get a conviction? The worst message in the world is a not guilty on civil rights."

Victims and Prosecution—The Credible Victim

Among the detectives, the "good cases" were the ones with language indicative of motivation and a credible victim. A credible victim was an injured or frightened victim. Officers preferred cases that involved injuries because injuries provided physical evidence for a trial. For some, injuries and the victim's reaction to being badly hurt also made the victim's story more credible. When asked what makes someone believable, one detective responded:

> Injury. I have to put myself in the victim's position. What would I have done? Someone is throwing sticks and bottles at me? Ten of them and one of me? Would I have done that? I try to forget about being a cop and having a gun. I put myself in their position, see how they react, threatened with injury, how are they dealing with it?

Another detective said, "In one good case a victim was presumed gay and beaten unconscious. . . . There were two witnesses who watched. It was a good case. The victim had a couple of *surgeries*."[9] As the detective's comments above suggest, credible victims have to have an appropriate reaction to hate crime.

Real fear was a marker of credibility and also made for a good case. For more than one officer, a credible victim was a scared victim. In the words of one detective, a credible victim was

> absolutely petrified. I've suffered myself. My family was a victim. We were the first Hispanic family to move onto [X] Avenue. I know what it's like to have been called a "spic." Many victims experience constant vandalism and harassment. Legitimate victims are pretty scared.

Fear was not only a mechanism by which officers judged credibility, it was also good for court. One officer declared that he would never bring civil rights charges without a victim who was scared. The detectives realized that a scared victim sounded better. Another officer offered to play for the others the 911 tape of his victim; "Want to listen to a panicked victim?" he asked. After listening to the woman's frightened screams, another detective told him to get the tapes transcribed. "That 911 call will be great for the jury," she said.

Young Juvenile Offenders

Though the legal requirements of hate crime may be met, the detectives in the unit, like police officers elsewhere, tended not to invoke the law in situations where they believed its use inappropriate or unfair. One of the situations where applying the law was considered inappropriate was in cases with young juvenile offenders—generally youths younger than fifteen years old. This leniency applied only to *young* juveniles who had committed a first offense. Detectives in the unit frequently invoked the law against older juveniles, sixteen to eighteen years old, and repeat offenders who were fifteen and younger. When asked how he determined whether to go for civil rights, one detective responded:

> [Do] the case and the circumstances fit the law? Bias indicators, how many are there, but it has to fit the elements of the crime. . . . That's not to say we won't do some mediation. It depends on several factors: the age of the defendants—the younger the defendant the less likely we are to bring charges—the seriousness of the injury, and little or no property damage. If the defendants are fifteen or sixteen years old and have no criminal record, we don't go for civil rights. We don't want to hit someone with civil rights if they may have been stupid.

When asked about the weak cases for civil rights, another detective responded,

> Cases involving real young kids. I had thoughts and feelings about people when I was young too. These are twelve-, thirteen-, and fourteen-year-old kids who commit an A&B [assault and battery] using racial language. Although we'd bring it to court on the A&B, we'd try to get a plea agreement with some education.

The cases that were treated differently had all the markers of other civil rights violations—difference in identity, the perpetrator and victim were unknown to each other, use of epithets, and violence. They just involved young juveniles. Another detective talked about a case he had involving kids who had been harassing a gay man in the neighborhood and explained why he treated that incident as juvenile mischief rather than a hate crime:

> The most important bias indicators are the words used, but this varies, you have to make a case-by-case determination, for example, [Y] Street. It was a case involving a gay guy; stuff [baseballs, and so on] comes over the fence and the victim wouldn't throw it back. The perps called him a fag. There's a large gay population in that area. It was trash day, the perps started throwing trash and hitting windows. They were kids, thirteen to sixteen, getting into juvenile stuff. I don't think it was because the victim was gay; it was because of the stuff going over the wall, just juvenile mischief.

The White detectives who were dismissive in their attitude toward incidents committed by young offenders referred to such incidents as "juvenile mischief" or "kid stuff." Their choice of words suggests that they believed that such incidents were not motivated by bias. For instance, notice the statement above made by the detective who mentioned education as his preference for treating cases with twelve-, thirteen-, and fourteen-year-old kids. He did not describe them as committing civil rights violations but, rather, as committing A and B's with racial language. Comments like these imply that ABTF detectives, like detectives investigating hate crime in other cities, may have believed that age makes one less capable of racial hatred.[10] If they did indeed believe that, they departed significantly from trends in the criminal justice system, which have moved toward holding younger and younger juveniles to an adult standard.

Only White detectives manifested sympathy and concern for the lives or futures of young juveniles who had committed hate crime. Statements made by some of these detectives show that they identified with these juveniles. This may have made them hesitant to invoke the law. As the White detective quoted above remarked, "I had thoughts and feelings about people when I was young, too." In these cases, the detectives behaved like police in other contexts who do not invoke the law because they side with the offenders.[11] Sympathizing with these young men, most of whom were White, several detectives claimed that there was a high cost to young defendants of invoking the law—civil rights violations were not erased from juvenile records. Putting themselves in the place of the perpetrators, these detectives insisted that a civil rights conviction could ruin a youth's future. As one detective said:

A kid can be barred from the military if he's convicted of civil rights violations. Law enforcement is closed to him if he's even investigated for civil rights. The way the bar association is now, he might not be able to go to law school. And some of your upper-crust colleges are starting to do investigation, so that may be closed to him.

Another detective insisted, "Having a civil rights violation on a juvenile record is a heavy burden for the rest of their life." Faced with the possibility of ruining a youth's life, several detectives favored sending cases involving young juveniles to mediation or giving them warnings.

Detectives' decisions are more justifiable if their practices are adopted based on cases' probability of acceptance by prosecutors and/or assistant attorneys general (AAGs). One study of detectives investigating hate crime cases found that they reject objectionable or questionable cases as a waste of time because of DAs' orientation toward such cases.[12] There is some evidence that DAs and AAGs in Center City had similar criteria for cases that they believed to be poor vehicles for the civil rights law. In one case, an AAG refused to pursue an injunction because the victim had shown neither fear during the crime nor concern for the case. The AAG explained in a letter to the victim filed with other records of the case, "[T]he fact that you did not feel threatened or intimidated at any time during the incident presented a serious issue of whether or not we could appropriately bring a civil injunction. . . ." In another case, the unit sought civil rights charges, but the DA denied them. According to the case file, the DA refused to go forward with civil rights charges because the perpetrator had no prior record and was only fourteen years old. Instead of charges for criminal civil rights violations, criminal charges for assault and battery were filed against the perpetrator.

Conclusion: Modeling Detectives' Charging Decisions

The ABTF detectives took an interest in whether, and in what type of cases, perpetrators were charged with civil rights violations. Their interest in the former stemmed from their desire to help victims and their wish to see perpetrators punished. They were cautious about the cases they submitted because they believed that submitting anything other than real cases for prosecution weakened hate crime law. Thus, the detectives behaved strategically: guided by the constraints in the context in which they worked—the requirement for motivation under hate crime law, First Amendment limitations on hate speech, and the requirement that prosecutors approve hate crime charges—they adopted rules of thumb. These constraints and the detectives' own desire to bring successful cases led them to weed out typical non-hate crimes that came to the unit. Still, not every case that they thought was a hate crime was considered appropriate for charges. The detectives declined to enforce the law against juveniles and also in cases in which the victim did not appear to be appropriately frightened or sufficiently injured.

The diagram in Figure 7 represents the process that the detectives used to decide whether a case was appropriate for criminal or civil rights charges. Though there were exceptions, the model describes what happened in most cases for which the unit requested hate crime charges. Detectives first evaluated whether there was a difference in identity (race, religion or sexual orientation) between the perpetrator and victim. If there was none, the case was closed. If the perpetrator and the victim were of different races or one was gay and one was straight, the detectives looked for the presence of bias-motivated language—slurs or epithets—used before, during or after the crime. If there were none, the detectives looked for other bias indicators, such as whether the victim was outnumbered in the area and whether the incident was one of several that the victim had experienced. If there were no other bias indicators, the detectives might seek to bring criminal charges in the case if they found compelling reasons to do so. If not, they closed the case.

If the perpetrator used slurs or epithets, the officers checked the case against their ready list of typical non-hate crimes, and if it was a fight, a traffic accident, or a neighbor dispute, the case was closed. If the incident did not fit one of these typical non-hate crimes, they weighed whether the language used was "just words" or was indicative of motivation. Cases in which language did not indicate motivation were closed.

Once a case reached the stage where the ABTF detectives identified it as bias-motivated, they asked whether the suspect was a young juvenile committing his or her first offense, if so, they would issue a warning. In cases in which the suspect was an adult, officers evaluated the case strategically and decided to request civil rights charges if the victim had been injured or placed in great fear.

Fig. 7: Detectives' Decision to Charge in Bias Crime Cases

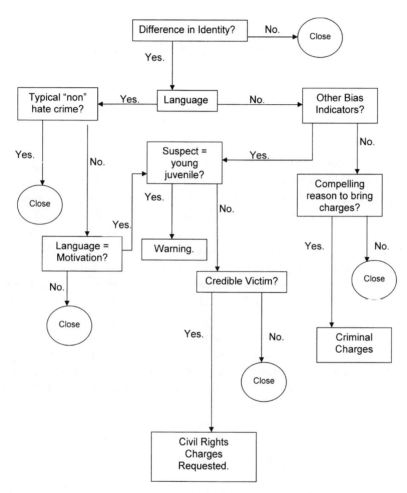

8

Prosecutors and the Courts

An ABTF detective's decision that bias crime charges are warranted does not mean that hate crime charges will be filed against the perpetrator. The police are not alone in deciding what becomes a hate crime. Charges for bias-motivated crime and civil injunctions prohibiting further bias-motivated conduct were produced by a system in which three other actors—the office of the district attorney (DA), the office of the attorney general (AG), and district court clerk magistrates—also had significant roles in determining whether alleged hate crimes would be prosecuted. Assistant district attorneys (ADAs) in the DA's office were responsible for approving civil rights charges; ABTF officers were required to obtain permission from that office if they wished to seek a complaint against a perpetrator. In lower court cases, district court clerk magistrates could approve or deny complaints brought to them by the officers. The assistant attorneys general (AAGs) in the AG's office sought civil injunctions for bias-motivated violence. Because the DA and AG offices' and clerk magistrates' determinations that a case was a bias crime followed after that of the police, each of the later actors had the ability to "correct" police interpretations, if they wished.

The current scholarship on hate crime affords little confidence that hate crime law is enforced. Anecdotal evidence, however, indicates that some enforcers, including prosecutors, find these cases difficult—especially because of the requirement that motivation must be proven—and shy away from them.[1] This chapter addresses some of the challenges that arise in bringing hate crime cases before the courts in Center City and how prosecutors deal with them. It also explores the relationship between the police and other actors in the criminal justice system, and the ability of those downstream—prosecutors and courts—to control the nature of what is actually charged as a hate crime.

Challenges of Prosecuting Criminal Civil Rights Violations

By the late 1990s, Center City law enforcement officials had two laws with which to prosecute those engaging in bias-motivated violence. The first, described in chapter 3, took effect in the early 1980s and prohibited interfering with an individual's rights under the state or federal constitutions. The second, passed in the mid-1990s, was a traditional hate crime law and prohibited property damage or assault and battery because of a person's race, color, religion, nationality, origin, sexual orientation, or disability. Cases brought under both statutes were referred to as "criminal civil rights violations."

Criminal civil rights violations were a tiny percentage of the caseload for the Center City district attorney's office. Though the office did not keep track of the number of cases filed seeking charges for criminal civil rights violations, the unit's figures suggest that the number was very small. Despite the fact that such cases were a tiny percentage of its total caseload, perhaps because they frequently attracted publicity, the DA's office paid special attention to them. The ABTF detectives were allowed to seek "ordinary" criminal complaints without the DA's approval, but they had to send requests for civil rights charges to the head of civil rights in the DA's office; the ADA in charge of civil rights there reviewed the cases at issue and made a decision.

DAs acknowledged that bias crime cases were special in requiring evidence of the perpetrator's motivation in addition to evidence that the perpetrator had committed the underlying criminal offense. They maintained that this made the cases harder to prosecute than "ordinary" criminal cases. One ADA asserted that there were no clear-cut civil rights cases, "You have to build them." Prosecutors relied on the police to find evidence of motivation, and many praised the detailed investigation in which they insisted the ABTF detectives engaged. Several ADAs who had worked with the members of the unit on cases were certain that the unit's case preparation in hate crime cases was much better than that of other police officers—such as those responsible for patrolling public transportation, or even detectives in other areas of the city. One ADA commented:

> There are many instances in which these types of cases need additional evidence. Evidence other than difference in race. We rely on the ABTF to dig into the intentions of the actor and develop a feel for motivations. I went to

training with the ABTF to convey this to line officers. Bias indicators are a jumping-off point. They don't mean a hate crime has been committed.

The real advantage of the ABTF is the procedures they have that allow for a thorough investigation before the prosecutor gets the case. The day-to-day officers' on the street response to crime does not always provide the opportunity to do as thorough an investigation.

In 99 percent of cases, other substantive criminal charges, A and B, malicious destruction of property, can be brought without having to get into looking for evidence of motivation to show to the judge or jury.

In addition to the problems presented by the requirement that cases be motivated by bias, ADAs had a troublesome time in bias crime cases getting witnesses to come forward, especially in neighborhoods like Gertown, where the prosecution of hate crime was unpopular. One ADA described a bias crime case from Gertown in which one of her witnesses had to move out of the neighborhood because she knew the defendant and had a critical piece of evidence. Pointing to the same difficulty, another ADA said that a good bias crime case was one "with lots of corroborating witnesses saying the same things as the victim and also filling in blanks when the victim is hurt and maybe on the ground. In Gertown, it's hard to get people like that to testify."

Problems with the District Courts

Even when bias crime cases had corroborating witnesses, judges were sometimes loath to convict. The most difficult judges in that respect presided over the district courts, which had jurisdiction over misdemeanor cases. Felony cases were tried in the state's high court. Several ADAs preferred trying civil rights cases in the state's high court, complaining that district court judges did not like civil rights charges. One respondent, who had worked on bias-motivated violence in both the DA's and AG's offices and was familiar with the district courts, said, "It was good to get things out of the district court because the district court was where things got bagged."

The prejudice against criminal civil rights violations that ADAs encountered when they brought bias crime cases in district courts may have stemmed from the courts' locations. The state's high court was in the city's business district but the district courts were in the neighborhoods. Gertown, Hillsdale, and other close-knit neighborhoods where bias crime cases were unpopular had district courts. Bias crime cases tended to attract significant attention. Residents and the perpetrators' supporters frequently came to watch district court proceedings. The unpopularity of the cases combined with the attention they drew may have prejudiced the district court judges against them.

One experienced prosecutor declared that judges' dislike of these cases sometimes translated to unfavorable rulings prohibiting the introduction of evidence that the prosecutor believed relevant to the issue of motivation, such as evidence of the defendant's past conduct and similar prior acts. The ADA complained that at the same time that judges prohibited the prosecution from introducing evidence regarding the defendant's history, the defendant was allowed to raise what the ADA termed "irrelevant" defenses, such as insisting that he or she committed the crime in fear of his or her life. Judges also allowed defendants to bring in evidence of good character. The ADA recalled, "In one case, we had someone testify who'd worked with the guy for two weeks and was going to testify to what a good guy he was."

Some of judges' dislike of bias crime cases may have been related to their belief that civil rights charges were duplicative of the criminal process. Perpetrators were frequently charged with "ordinary" criminal charges and then, if the ABTF investigation and the DA determined that charges for criminal civil rights violations were appropriate, these charges were added to the preexisting criminal charges. A typical example involved an incident that began when a Chinese man beeped his car's horn to get the driver of another car to move his vehicle. The second driver, a White man, yelled, "You stupid Filipinos, why don't you go back to your own country?" The White man then rammed the first driver's car. The perpetrator of the crime was charged with (and was found to be guilty of or pled guilty to) both assault and battery with a deadly weapon and criminal civil rights violations.

One ADA described judges' attitudes regarding this type of duplication, especially in light of the judges' heavy court calendars:

> Judges do not pay lots of attention if other motivation is involved. Judges don't see a lot of civil rights over time. Judges' approach is very fact based. Some take it seriously. Many are prejudiced against civil rights because they want to get rid of the civil rights charges.

He continued:

> Defense attorneys try to plead to criminal charges if the civil rights charges are dropped. Judges may see these cases as clogging up their

calendar because the defendant offers a plea, and we did have a policy of determining on a case-by-case basis. You have to look at each case. If the likelihood is that we're not going to get a conviction, it may be better to take a hit and get a stay away, restitution, and counseling. It's not something I like to do. It sends the wrong message—plead out to the substantive charges and the civil rights charges go away. I'd rather criminal charges than a "not guilty" on civil rights.

When faced with the choice of losing a case and in doing so sending a message that the defendant had not violated the victim's civil rights, the ADA chose the criminal conviction.

Selecting Cases to Win

As the ADA's remarks suggest, the challenges that civil rights violations presented for prosecutors—getting judges to accept both types of charges, proving motivation, and enticing reluctant witnesses to come forward—affected the decision of the DA's office to seek civil rights or criminal charges. The challenges, combined with the fact that perpetrators could still be prosecuted for the underlying offense, made prosecutors less inclined to take the risk of civil rights charges. The statement of one ADA in charge of approving cases suggested that he or she was more likely to bring criminal civil rights violations in cases when the chances for conviction were good. Cases involving a repeat offender—a defendant who had a history of similar attacks—fell into that category. As one ADA maintained, "An attack on an Asian is not just an inconsequential history of targeting Asians; preying on particular groups helps to tag him." Another ADA explained the importance of history in response to a question on the qualities of a good case:

> It [a good case] has intangibles not introduced at trial. The history of the defendant, FIOs (questions asked by officers) done of the defendant, information we've heard through the grapevine. All of these things could weigh me to take a charge. If there's no history, the ABTF is exhaustive in its investigation of the community. If the case is weak, the ABTF is less likely to take a chance. The ABTF is a good avenue of information. The ABTF may come to me and say we know this kid. He hangs around with a kid who beats up Latinos.

The same ADA described "pattern" cases, cases in which motivation for the attack in question is inferred from a series of similar attacks committed by the perpetrator in the past. Though "pattern" cases were not universally popular, several ADAs indicated it was easier to prove motivation in such cases. When asked about what she considered a good case, a different ADA replied, "[I]t has a repeat offender. It occurs in an area where this type of thing has happened before, the victim and the perpetrator are of different races and there is no other reason for this to have occurred."

The ADAs' emphasis on the strongest case may have had something to do with the importance of win-loss records to district attorneys' offices. Not only did such records matter for promotion, during the election campaigns for district attorney, the incumbent DA often held out his or her win-loss record. The fewer losing cases in which one sought charges, the greater the chance that the DA could broadcast a good win-loss record. One ADA responsible for approving the unit's requests for civil rights charges denied a number of the unit's requests for hate crime charges. Below, that ADA highlighted the need for "winnable" cases:

> The prosecutor's perspective is that we look at things with an eye to what is going to win. Because I'm a prosecutor or because of my experience, I look into the head of the defense. Was there a reason to fight? Did the victim steal something, or say something terrible about the perpetrator's mother? I needed to think through the defense and the impact on prosecution.

Though the ADA and the ABTF disagreed on the merits of several individual cases, they saw the same danger in taking too many cases that were not "real" civil rights violations—watering down the law. The ADA continued:

> My feeling, my view, is that I tried to make it a traditional hate crime law so as not to lose its impact or the power. I take cases that would be successful on the merits, not just add-on significance. I don't want to water down the law. I reserved charging for the strong cases.

Injunctive Relief under the Civil Rights Statute

Assistant attorneys general who were responsible for bringing civil injunctions for bias-motivated conduct under the state civil rights law faced different, though related, difficulties. The civil portion of that law was intended to allow the state attorney general to seek civil rights injunctions against perpetrators of bias-motivated violence, harassment, or intimidation. The AG's office interpreted the civil rights statute to cover actions directed at a victim because of his or her race, ethnicity, national origin, gender, sexual orientation, disability, age, or religion.[2]

Though the AG's office also sought permanent injunctions and temporary restraining orders, preliminary injunctions were the most common form of injunctive relief. Both types of injunctions enjoined the perpetrator and anyone acting with him or her from future harassment of the victim, as well as any member of the victim's group. Injunctive relief was particularly useful in cases where neighborhood residents were responsible for the harassment because they criminalized conduct that was otherwise lawful. For instance, perpetrators under injunction were prohibited from walking on certain streets or from communicating with the victim or his or her family. Though it rarely happened, violators of injunctions could face serious penalties: a defendant could be sentenced to ten years in the state prison.[3]

Like prosecutions for criminal civil rights violations, injunctions were not a common law enforcement tool in Center City. The head of the city's civil rights division indicated that the office requested between five and twenty preliminary injunctions each year. In the twelve-year period between 1982 and 1994, the office obtained injunctions in just 137 cases, an average of less than twelve injunctions a year. Because a single injunction could cover multiple defendants, the office had broader power than the number of injunctions alone suggests. For instance, in 1995 the office brought eight preliminary injunctions against seventeen defendants.

Most preliminary injunctions were decided on the basis of victim, witness, and police affidavits submitted to high court judges. According to the statute, in order for a judge to issue a preliminary injunction, the AG needed to prove by a preponderance of the evidence that the perpetrator had violated the defendant's statutory rights and that the injunction promoted (or at least would not adversely affect) the public interest. Showing that the victim's rights had been violated was not usually a problem. The harassment of the victim was easily described in the affidavits. The other requirement—that the AG demonstrate that the perpetrator was likely to repeat the conduct—was more difficult.[4]

Showing the perpetrator was likely to reoffend proved a challenge, especially in cases in which criminal charges—either criminal civil rights violations or criminal charges like assault and battery—had been sought. Similar to those adjudicating criminal civil rights violations, judges were concerned that the injunctive relief might be duplicative. If judges believed an injunction to be duplicative of the criminal process, they were unlikely to grant the injunction. One AAG explained:

> I had a case in which I was recently denied a p.i. [preliminary injunction], which I thought was the perfect case. We had a Latino man who went into Gertown and was beaten up by three kids. Actually, two were juveniles, and one has since turned eighteen. He was also called a "spic." The p.i. was denied because the judge thought the p.i. was too broad a form of relief, given parallel criminal proceedings with such actions a violation of probation. It was a new judge who really had a problem with the fact that there were parallel criminal charges. The motive seemed so clear.

When asked why judges fail to grant preliminary injunctions, the AAG continued:

> Often cases have been denied because of the condition of parole issue. . . . Judges are reluctant to give p.i.'s where juveniles are involved. They think that they are too harsh because they [the defendants] can already be punished for violating their parole if there is a parallel criminal case. You also have to prove likelihood to repeat conduct, and they [the judges] may often feel that there is not enough evidence for that.

Cases Appropriate for Injunctive Relief

Police departments, prosecutors, schools, parents, advocacy groups, and victims contacted the AG's office about incidents that they believed warranted injunctive relief. AAGs elected to pursue injunctions in only a small percentage of cases they received. Echoing considerations raised by the district attorney's office, one AAG indicated that judges' attitudes and limited resources help him make up his mind about which cases to turn away. Asked how he decides to seek a preliminary injunction, the AAG replied:

> First, do the facts as presented demonstrate a violation of civil rights law? Does additional investigation show it violates civil rights? Are there threats, intimidation in violation of civil rights? It may require additional

fact-finding. Other questions . . . is there pending criminal action or a stay away order? How will an injunction improve the situation? It should not just be duplicative of the criminal process. What is the likelihood of recurrence against this and other victims? For example, if a defendant is never to return to [the state] again, the likelihood of getting an injunction from the judge is small.

Later in the same conversation, the AAG said he was worried about the courts' perceiving of requests for injunctive relief as "piling on." The AAG said that before taking in a case in which criminal charges had been filed, he tried to determine whether the criminal process had ended. If it had, and the defendant had been convicted and sentenced, the AAG evaluated the appropriateness and severity of the sentence and whether a stay-away order had been issued. Judges would not issue injunctions in cases in which the defendant was already incarcerated. Practical considerations were important, given the scarce resources. If the judge rejected the injunction, then one of the office's very few staff members had been occupied for several weeks, to no end.

Making the Best Case

To make a good case, both assistant attorneys general seeking injunctions and assistant district attorneys prosecuting criminal civil rights violations needed to present clear evidence that bias was the reason for attack. AAGs and ADAs gave examples of cases that they had lost because the judge believed that the perpetrator was motivated by something else: revenge, drugs, or anger. As with ABTF detectives, those prosecuting bias crimes and seeking injunctions considered the context in which the crime occurred to be an important signal of the perpetrator's motivation. ADAs named the several elements that were suggestive of bias: (1) the lack of prior history between the victim and the suspect, (2) the attack's having been unprovoked, and (3) the attack's having occurred in a salient location, such as outside a gay bar.

In the vast majority of cases, the use of slurs or epithets alerted those seeking injunctions or prosecuting cases to the possibility that the incident was motivated by bias. ADAs' and AGs' reliance on language stemmed from the importance placed on it by juries and judges. Several ADAs and AAGs insisted that the use of bias language by perpetrators engaged in criminal assaults, *in a particular context*, suggested to judges and juries that the incident had been motivated by bias. Because judges and juries needed language, nearly every case ADAs and AAGs brought had language. When asked how important language is to civil rights violations, one former ADA who had prosecuted a number of criminal civil rights cases stressed that it was very important: "Unless the incident is obvious, for example, a Molotov cocktail thrown at [the] one house in the neighborhood that is [a] minority."

Another ADA responded in a similar vein:

> [I]f we get into a fight because you've taken my reindeer [picks up a toy reindeer] and I use the "n-word," then that's not a hate crime. If we're in a fight and you yell something, it's just words in the heat of passion.

As the above remarks highlight, for prosecutors, as for ABTF detectives, the context of the assault mattered. ADAs did not just assume that racial epithets and slurs indicated bias motivation. They were particularly attentive to particular types of cases, for example, those involving words uttered in the heat of passion that were indicative of anger rather than bias; they rejected such cases.

Shoring Up Cases

The importance of language as a signal to juries of motivation meant that when cases appeared to be motivated by bias but had no language or when prosecutors were unsure of the crime's motivation, they asked detectives to "verify the language." The absence of language sometimes proved fatal; one head prosecutor denied several cases that the detectives believed were bias-motivated but that lacked significant language, as well as other evidence of motivation. One such case involved a White victim who was stabbed by several Hispanics who asked, "What's up, White boy?" Witnesses said no slurs or epithets were used during the fight. The ABTF believed that the case was bias-motivated and requested civil rights charges; the DA's office refused, specifically noting the lack of language or any other indication of bias during the assault.

ADAs' preference for language affected the way in which ABTF detectives prepared cases for civil rights violations. If racial epithets were not present in the initial investigation, detectives waited to seek civil rights violations until they found witnesses to testify to the epithets used by the perpetrator. Frequently, when the detectives wished to deny that bias was involved, they pointed to the fact that language had not been used. In addition, when a detective asserted a case was bias-motivated, often the supervisor's first question was whether there was any language in the case.

The unit had had hate crime cases without language, but the detectives were forced to justify their support for such cases even when they still thought the cases were bias-motivated. In one, a detective discussed with his supervisor his belief that it was bias-motivated:

> *Detective:* A White guy dragged a lesbian who was in this club outside, and he pulled her face close to a guardrail overlooking a ledge. Then he asked her, "Do you know where you are?" After that he beat and kicked her. She was beaten pretty viciously.
>
> *Supervisor:* Was there any language?
>
> *Detective:* No, but she is a lesbian, and when he pulled her off the dance floor she was dancing with a woman and they were dancing pretty close.

In a different case, a detective justified his belief that he was investigating a bias-motivated case. He remarked:

> There's no language but the suspects have a prior history, it's a problem area, the victims are outnumbered in the area, and there's difference in race between the victims and the perpetrators.

All of these factors normally signaled to the detectives that the incident was motivated by bias. I asked, "Do you want to bring civil rights charges?" The detective responded, "Yes, I'd like that, but it depends on how the interviews turn out."

Hate Crime Charges Just for Using Speech?

In spite of all of the emphasis on language, the critics' worry that individuals are charged with hate crime violations just for using slurs or epithets is not borne out by the evidence from Center City. Both ADAs and the AAGs maintained that the usage did not necessarily signal the perpetrator's motivation. As one ADA emphasized, "Statements like 'faggot' don't mean the crime was motivated by bias." ADAs and AAGs were wary of bringing cases to court in which the perpetrator's statements were the only evidence that the perpetrator had been motivated by bias, and they took care to ascertain whether words signaled bias, or something else. Not only would the cases be lost, their offices could also lose credibility.

Like ABTF detectives, AAGs and ADAs preferred cases where the victim and the perpetrator were strangers because previous contact between the victim and the perpetrator supplied a greater opportunity for the perpetrator to develop a reason besides bias to attack the victim. One AAG explained:

> We have lots of cases where we go to interview witnesses and they say, "Don't you know what that's about?" Then they describe some prior altercation between victim and perpetrator. We can't go into court and say that a crime was motivated by race and request an injunction when it wasn't. I firmly believe in using the law appropriately, not just because racial slurs are used.

Examining the crime's setting was important because it gave a more complete picture of motivation than language alone. The same language, but in a different context, implied bias. An ADA expressed a concern similar to the one raised by the AAG above about cases in which there was not a context that suggested the incident was motivated by bias:

> Language may not be a good indication of motivation. For example, someone says, "I'm going to kick your butt, faggot," then a fight ensues. The person who was attacked is suspected of being gay, or he might have stolen something or taken a parking space. These lessen the impact of language. It might be revenge or anger. But if [the perpetrator] was unprovoked, had no prior contact, or the incident occurred outside a gay bar, then language means something. I can craft viable arguments to prosecute if that occurs. It's a very factually based determination.

As lawyers, AAGs and ADAs knew that the First Amendment protects hate speech. That protection was part of the reason AAGs and ADAs were loath to seek injunctions or bring hate crime charges in cases whose context did not suggest the perpetrator's language was indicative of bias motivation. One AAG explained, "The First Amendment is a big issue. We can't takes cases where someone just uses the 'n-word.' I can't tell you how many cases we get like that. . . . People have a right to say that."

Lawyers in both groups saw a clear distinction between cases in which perpetrators simply used hate speech, and hate crimes cases, which they prosecuted. Hate crimes were not just "verbal affronts"; they involved a perpetrator directly targeting and attacking a particular individual or individuals. None of the ADAs or AAGs interviewed found free speech arguments to be applicable in the types of cases in which their offices sought charges or injunctions. One ADA echoed others when she remarked, "It's hard to say that you're exercising free speech when you're stabbing someone." In a similar vein, another ADA said:

> It's not free speech when you've got a rock in your hand and you whip it off someone's head. That's clearly a crime. It's not like nude dancing, which is protected speech. This is hate. I don't know if that's what the Founding Fathers meant to be protected. This is hate with the threat of force, using a weapon, beating people. Anyone who makes that free speech argument doesn't know what is going on. Twelve jurors in [X County] aren't going to believe you either. It's hard to take this as free speech. It's not like speaking out against the government.

Language and Underenforcement

Perpetrators used slurs and epithets before, during, or sometimes after they committed the crime in most of the cases that the ABTF and the other law enforcement agencies in Center City forwarded to the prosecutor's and AG's offices. Attacks against individuals on the basis of race, religion, and sexual orientation may occur without the perpetrator uttering a single word, however. Ignoring the law in such cases would create a loophole that would allow perpetrators to circumvent bias crime laws simply by keeping their mouths shut.

Despite requiring that the police comb cases for language, the offices of the AG and of the DA in Center City appeared to understand that perpetrators should not be able to avoid the law by keeping quiet. Though all said language was critical, nearly every respondent in this study remembered at least one case in which injunctive relief was sought or civil rights charges were brought with no evidence of bias language used by the perpetrator.

Cases that lacked language presented greater challenges. One AAG explained:

Without language you need other facts that point to no other natural motive that can be gleaned from the situation—a random attack with others on the street, no other motive, economic or personal. I can make a good argument. One minority selected [out of a group] can tend to persuade the court. I could construct an argument with the right set of facts. It's easier when there's language. I would never want to send the message that as long as you hold language in your head, we would not prosecute you for civil rights.

When asked whether civil rights perpetrators were getting smarter, the AAG quickly replied, "No! The vast majority of cases have language. People under stress get angry; language comes out. Only much more sophisticated [individuals] wouldn't use language."

The comments of another respondent who worked in the offices of both the DA and the AG also indicate that the absence of language was something that could be rectified. The usefulness of language depended on what other evidence of bias those bringing charges had. In response to a question on the importance of language, the respondent said:

It depends on the case. Some cases, language is everything. Others, you need it for jury appeals. It makes a huge impact if they say "fucking gook." In the neighborhood, there were other incidents. A family would just move in, the only Vietnamese, and start getting their windows broken. It doesn't matter whether language was used or not.

Conflict and Cooperation Preparing Charges

Detectives are generally described as having little interest in the outcome of legal cases.[5] Once a case goes to the DA's office, the detectives' interest and monitoring of it usually ends. This was not true for most ABTF detectives. Members of the ABTF generally behaved as if they had a stake in charges being filed. Procedurally, cases in which civil rights charges were sought required the approval of the DA's office, thus the office had the ability to control whether a case the unit wanted resulted in actual civil rights charges being issued.

It is important to note the unidirectional effect the requirement for approval of charges had on police discretion and the enforcement of hate crime law. The discretion of police regarding the cases that received charges was limited; their discretion *not to enforce the law* remained intact. The DA's office did not review all cases reported to the unit, only the cases in which the unit thought charges were warranted. Thus, the DA's office could ratchet down enforcement of the law only by denying charges. Cases that the ABTF "broomed," deactivated, mediated, or in which it issued a warning were invisible to the DA's office. Of course individual ADAs were aware of cases in which the unit filed criminal charges but not civil rights charges. Practically, however, this did not provide a "check" on the detectives' decisions that incidents were not bias crimes. The detectives in the unit maintained that ADAs received the case file so close to the first court appearance that it would have been nearly impossible for an ADA to review the case and then request the additional ABTF investigation needed for civil rights charges. Thus the DA was unable to ratchet up enforcement of the law in cases in which detectives believed that the use of the law was not warranted.

For most of its history, the unit had had good relations with the DA's office, but having a stake in whether charges were filed led to conflicts between the ABTF and the office under one ADA who refused to issue civil rights charges in some of the cases the unit requested. Over a two-year period, the unit's records showed that of fifty cases in which charges were requested, twelve charges (24 percent) were denied. The percentage was especially significant to detectives accustomed to having all requested charges approved. Tension between the office and the unit was exacerbated not only by the denials but also by the fact that the ABTF publicly endorsed in one DA's race the opposing candidate, who went on to lose the election. Detectives in the unit insisted that the denials of civil rights charges were motivated by the incumbent DA's desire to appease Whites in Gertown, an important part of his constituency. An ADA in the office attributed the denials, instead, to differences in the unit's and the DA's standards for acceptable cases.

Despite a brief period of tension between supervisors in both offices, individual ABTF detectives experienced little friction in dealing with the individual ADAs prosecuting cases; once a case had been approved for charges, the two offices had the same goal: successful prosecution. The detectives were also in a position to help the ADAs, many of whom were inexperienced in handling cases with civil rights charges because there were very few criminal civil rights charges and these were often assigned to different ADAs.[6] In comparison to ADAs who might never have prosecuted a civil rights case, the experienced detectives were repeat players. ABTF detectives developed knowledge of the civil rights law as a consequence of often having to present legal arguments when seeking complaints in front of clerk magistrates unfamiliar with the civil rights law. An ADA also had far less knowledge of facts of the case than the investigating detective. Thus, the normal situation in which prosecutors explain the legal standards to police officers to ensure that their testimony conforms to the law was occasionally reversed in the unit, when ABTF detectives spoke at civil rights training for ADAs and prepared "packets" on the civil rights law for inexperienced ADAs.

The unit's relationship with the AG's office fluctuated with the level of cooperation that the unit was given for the charges it sought. Some assistant attorneys general were more deferential to the unit than others. Detectives assigned to the unit not long after the civil rights law was passed praised the lawyers in the AG's office for seeking injunctions when the DA's office was hesitant to approve criminal civil rights charges. The former was credited for its willingness to take chances and pursue charges in difficult cases in which there was no certainty that an injunction would be issued. At other times, detectives argued that the AG's office was more interested in appearing liberal on civil rights issues rather than actually controlling bias crime.

The ability of the AG's office to increase enforcement of the civil rights law in ways that detectives in the ABTF considered impractical created tension between the two entities. An example of this occurred when in response to an incident that occurred in Gertown the ABTF requested an injunction covering several individuals. The AG's office agreed that injunctions were warranted but sought, and was granted, an injunction covering many more people than the unit had originally requested. The AG's office believed that its response in the case showed that the office was not affected by politics—specifically the need to appease those in Gertown. One AAG asserted proudly, "The attorney general was explicit about bringing cases based on the facts of the law. No politics. I never had a single hate crime case turned down. I decided to bring more injunctions, draw a broader net. I think the police were surprised."

ABTF detectives were surprised and a few were angered by the AG's actions. The ABTF was responsible for enforcing these very complicated injunctions that barred the perpetrators from coming within one hundred feet of the victims' residence or that of other perpetrators. Enforcement would require the arrest of the perpetrators in violation. Neighborhood size and number of perpetrators rendered the injunctions susceptible to violation. The injunctions themselves made the community angry and increased tension in a neighborhood that was already difficult to police. The detectives insisted that when the perpetrators were in violation and the unit went to court, judges refused to sanction the defendants. In Gertown, one detective declared, "They laughed and we had egg on our face. After that they started hating us." One detective even noted in his reports that some of the defendants' families subjected ABTF detectives to verbal abuse, directing profanity at the detective at a court hearing. The unit detectives were discomfited by the additional animosity the injunctions created and believed that the AG's overzealousness had landed the unit in a trying situation.

Getting Past Clerk Magistrates

Seeking a Criminal Civil Rights Complaint

After the prosecutor approved charges for criminal civil rights violations, the ABTF's final hurdle before an individual could be charged involved getting complaints past district court clerk magistrates. In Center City, detectives in the ABTF were responsible for performing the first step in the criminal process, applying for a complaint, the formal written charge against the defendant, in front of a district court clerk magistrate, or as detectives referred to that person, "clerk." Technically, because in most cases the suspect had not been arrested on hate crime charges, the detective was seeking a warrant for arrest or a summons to be drawn up. Clerk magistrates were responsible for "issuing process," the formal terminology for approving the detective's application. They were the employees of the neighborhood district courts and were not required to be (and in many cases were not) lawyers.

The detective's application for a complaint was supposed to convey the basic information about the crime with which the defendant was to be charged. It contained the defendant's name and identifying details, the date and location of the offense, the offense charged, and the particulars of the case, such as the victim's name and the weapon the perpetrator used in the crime. There was also an "other remarks" section that the detectives often used to supply a narrative description of the crime, including how the victim was assaulted and what the perpetrator said. The "other remarks" section of one fairly typical application for a complaint in which charges for both assault and battery, and misdemeanor civil rights violations had been requested read:

> At approximately 10:15 on 1/25/96, the victim put money into a pay telephone outside variety store in [X area]. Victim dialed number to call taxi, and W/M standing nearby told her, "I'm using this phone. I'm waiting for an important call. Use the phone across the street Nigger." W/M grabbed victim on her shoulder with one hand and grabbed phone receiver with other. W/M continued to push and grab victim and would not let go. When victim hit W/M with phone on his hand, he backed off, calling her a "cocksucker."[7]

Once the complaint application was prepared, court procedures required the detective to request a hearing in front of the clerk magistrate. Such hearings were informal and were not held in a courtroom. In the hearing the clerk magistrate was supposed to interview both the police officer and the suspect. Generally, only the victim, the police officer who signed the complaint, and the suspect were present. Though attorneys could attend, they were not often present. The hearing was not supposed to be an adversarial process. For instance, if a lawyer were present, he or she had no right to question or cross-examine participants.[8]

The burden of proof was quite low in the hearing. The clerk magistrate had only to determine whether there was probable cause to believe a crime had been committed and that the defendant had committed the crime. The complaint standards gave the clerk magistrate wide discretion to take on a range of roles, from acting as a mediator and settling the matter informally before the criminal process even began, to assuming a traditional legal role and issuing process.[9] Legally, the clerk magistrate had the option to deny the application for a complaint, to issue process, or to hold the complaint in abeyance for a set period of time. If the complaint were denied, the police officer could ask for a hearing in front of a judge. If the application were granted, the clerk magistrate would issue either a summons or an arrest warrant, depending on the likelihood of the defendant appearing. If the charges were held in abeyance, barring further incidents, at the end of the time period the application was withdrawn.

Clerk Magistrates' Practices

Even before the civil rights law was passed, ABTF detectives had conflicts with the clerk magistrates. The former insisted that the latter denied applications for criminal charges against perpetrators because they did not view the harassment of minorities as a problem. The detectives argued that this was political—a desire to protect constituents. One detective contended that clerk magistrates were in denial about what was happening in the neighborhoods:

> They had to pass the civil rights law because of the clerks of court. To them everything was an isolated incident; there was no pattern of harassment. . . . All protected their constituents; they decide their docket and when they come in and when they leave.

> They denied "member of a protected group." No one knew the law. They considered the law an unnecessary add-on penalty. We passed the law because we were sick of people getting slaps on the wrists for breaking people's windows.

> The clerks weren't educated in the ways of the civil rights law. Every neighborhood had its own clerks. They didn't think that their neighborhood had problems. It's hard to say these problems are occurring in your neighborhood.

Even after the civil rights law had been in use for a few years, ABTF detectives had difficulty getting charges approved. Clerk magistrates would often deny charges because they did not really understand the civil rights law or were not knowledgeable about it. In one case, not long after the second hate crime law was passed, a clerk magistrate denied hate crime charges because he had not known that sexual orientation was a protected category. The ABTF officer insisted that the law had been changed, yet the clerk magistrate still denied charges. The clerk magistrate later learned that the detective was correct, and found probable cause to issue the complaint.

Other clerk magistrates denied charges because they felt that the unit should not bring cases against White perpetrators. They consistently blocked its efforts to enforce the law, either by denying charges and letting the perpetrators off with a warning or by holding the charges in abeyance, thereby preventing the officers from appealing the decision. One civilian who worked in the ABTF in its early days recalled how clerk magistrates who disliked the unit's activities treated the complaints:

> Rather than issuing charges or denying them, they'd hold them in abeyance. If they don't deny, it can't be appealed. . . . They'd screw

around with our hearing date. We'd appear, and they'd say they'd had the hearing two days ago, and for us to seek new complaints. We'd have to keep going back in. The clerk would say, "This is happening to my people," and they'd duck and duck charges. Finally, they gave in with the DA's office and the police there; you can't duck all the charges. It was a huge problem in the beginning.

Some clerk magistrates were open in their opposition to the enforcement of civil rights law against White perpetrators. One accused a detective who had applied for hate crime charges as well as ordinary criminal charges (as was the standard practice) of "overkill." Another clerk magistrate used racial slurs when he asked a detective whether the unit ever requested that any charges be brought against minorities who attacked Whites. One detective, who accused clerk magistrates of racism, discussed their parochialism:

> They'd say this isn't a crime. They didn't have to say anything, they wouldn't grant the complaint. Everybody had connections, [the perpetrators were] the sons of firefighters, police officers—their constituents. It was very frustrating.

Echoing the above comments, another detective explained clerk magistrates' reasons for denying complaints in civil rights cases:

> They'd give some excuse. "It's just a simple A and B" [assault and battery]. Especially in [X area]. In Gertown, it was that good old boy shit. We did the paperwork. Before granting the complaint, they'd want to reduce it to lesser charges. Then we knew they had the upper hand in court. I know what constitutes a civil rights violation. They'd want us to show the chapter and section. Nine out of ten times they lived in the neighborhood. I knew they knew them because you'd get into the courtroom and they'd [the perpetrator] be walking in and say, "Hey Joe, this fucking cop busted me for breaking this gook's windows." And they still wanted to take a reduced charge.

The ABTF officers reacted with defiance toward clerk magistrates. In their reports, they noted their fury regarding clerk magistrates' racist comments and lack of impartiality. They continued to bring the same types of cases but used strategies in an attempt to get around clerk magistrates' denials. After a number of denials, one supervisor began bringing an assistant attorney general with him as an observer when he went to argue at hearings. Tired of the use of racial slurs by clerk magistrates, the same supervisor brought a Black detective to court. On one occasion, another supervisor wrote a letter to the judge of one court, complaining that the use of racial slurs by one clerk magistrate signified a lack of objectivity in the case. After that case, the ABTF succeeded in getting that clerk magistrate removed from future hate crime cases.

Conclusion

The power to decide whether the law would be invoked in hate crime cases in which the ABTF believed doing so was warranted lay outside the unit, in the hands of ADAs, AAGs, and district court clerk magistrates. The DA's office could, and at times did, exercise its power by withholding approval of complaints. Even when the DA's office gave its approval, clerk magistrates could deny the application for a complaint. The DA's and AG's offices, like the unit, worried about cases being denied and rejected cases they believed they could not get past those making decisions downstream: juries and judges.

Though the actions of courts and those preparing cases affected how the police prepared cases, the police evaluation of whether an incident was a bias crime was still crucial. The police were on the frontlines and controlled the range of cases that other actors saw. This did not mean that police completely controlled the case outcomes. Once the police made their decision, the clerk magistrates and DA could still decide that hate crime charges would not be issued. But because the first decision belonged to the police, and the later bodies only reviewed the cases that the police brought to them, police decisions and police discretion were critical.

9

Conclusion

This book describes in great detail the significant discretion that police officers have to define hate crimes and, in doing so, to name social reality. This power, I argue, is largely unrecognized by both opponents and supporters of hate crime legislation. The power of the police is not, however, what has prevented legislatures from passing hate crime laws. Instead, the political and intellectual debate on hate crime is dominated by three main concerns: (1) that hate crime legislation is special protection for minorities; (2) that hate crime legislation will be enforced in a way that violates the First Amendment; and (3) that hate crime law is redundant. The concerns are important but must be addressed empirically in order to settle the debate.

My study of the enforcement of hate crime in Center City shows that these objections should not prevent passage of hate crime legislation. Below I recap each of these arguments and provide responses based on the data from Center City.

1. "Special Protection" for Minorities

This argument typically insists that because hate crime legislation contains the categories "race," "gender," and "sexual orientation," it affords special protection for racial and religious minorities, gays, and lesbians. Echoing concerns similar to those raised in affirmative action debates, this argument also maintains that under hate crime law, crimes against Whites could not be prosecuted as hate crimes. To treat victims differently, this position contends, creates a hierarchy of victimhood in which the pain of particular victims is considered more serious than the pain of others.[1] A corollary of the special-protection argument, advanced by legislators, is that hate crime legislation that punishes antigay and -lesbian bias crimes constitutes an endorsement of homo-sexuality.[2]

The problem with the special-protection argument is that race, gender, and sexual orientation are categories, not groups of people. Hate crime legislation with these categories protects everyone who has a race, everyone who has a gender, and everyone who has a sexual orientation so long as they are attacked because of their status. In other words, hate crime laws punish attacks on everyone. In Center City and nationally, minorities and gays and lesbians constitute a large percentage of the victims of bias-motivated attacks. Nevertheless, in Center City and elsewhere, large numbers of White or nonminority victims of bias-motivated crime benefit from the investigation of hate crimes perpetrated against *them*. In 1999, the FBI received reports of 781 victims of anti-White crime.[3] After African Americans, Whites were the largest racial group victimized.[4]

Hate crime legislation that includes sexual orientation provides a remedy for crimes against gays, lesbians, *and* heterosexuals, so long as the individual has been attacked *because of* his or her sexual orientation. Heterosexuals are attacked because of their sexual orientation. One of the ABTF's cases involved a man attacked because he was heterosexual. Several other cases involved heterosexual men who were attacked because perpetrators believed they were gay. These cases were treated as hate crimes because attacks like these are prohibited under hate crime statutes that reach conduct based on one's *actual or perceived* sexual orientation.

Of course, it matters little that bias crime legislation is designed to protect everyone if those enforcing the law do so differentially, investigating crimes against one particular type of victim and concluding that bias-motivated attacks against that type are the only *real* hate crimes. For example, some people believe that bias crime laws will be enforced only when minorities are the perpetrators. In Center City, I found no pattern of differential enforcement. Although most of the perpetrators in the cases the unit investigated were White, officers did not adopt the perspective that there was a stereotypical hate crime or a stereotypical victim. The ABTF investigated and brought charges on behalf of Black, Latino, Asian, White, Jewish, and gay and lesbian victims of hate crime.

This did not mean that Asian, Black, and Latino victims did not receive a significant portion of the hate crime unit's services. Most of the cases the unit investigated and the majority of the cases in which the unit requested charges were on behalf of victims of color. This was not because of a constructed notion of what "real" bias-motivated violence looks like but, rather, stemmed from the nature and history of bias-motivated violence in Center City. Asians, Blacks, and Latinos were frequently the target of bias-motivated violence, often on the occasion of integrating formerly all-White neighborhoods.

The data from Center City provide no support for the oft-cited assertion that police will use hate crime laws to single out minorities for abuse. Most of the cases the unit investigated and most of the charges it sought were against White perpetrators who had attacked victims of color.

2. Hate Crime Legislation and the First Amendment

Politicians and legal scholars alike worry that enforcers of hate crime law will fail to distinguish fairly or accurately between hate speech and hate crime as they enforce hate crime legislation. Often this objection is accompanied by an argument that echoes John Stuart Mill—all that is needed to erase bias-motivated intolerance is more speech.[5]

Critics of hate crime legislation express uncertainty about whether enforcers can accurately identify perpetrators' motivation and instead are arresting individuals for using hate speech. ABTF detectives were surprisingly conservative in their use of hate crime law. They adopted a complex series of routines that helped them identify bias motivation. The process involved an initial screening, followed by filtering mechanisms that required detectives to remove whole categories of cases likely motivated by a variety of other emotions—anger, resentment, and jealousy—and then a detailed examination of the perpetrator's motivation. Not every case in which the detectives found the perpetrator to have been motivated by bias resulted in hate crime charges. Though the presence of injured victims and fifteen-year-old or older perpetrators was not required for invoking the law, the detectives preferred cases with injured victims and disliked cases with very young perpetrators. The detectives' decisions not to enforce the law against very young perpetrators raises the specter of underenforcement of hate crime law; failure to enforce the law in this context suggests that the detectives may have eliminated cases that were problematic from a First Amendment perspective.

The detectives' conservative use of the law and the elaborate system of identifying bias indicates that critics' predictions of prosecution of protected speech have not come to fruition in Center City. This is true in part because the types of cases the critics imagine—cases involving pure hate speech, conversations, remarks, racist jokes—are rarely reported to the police, and when they are reported, are quickly discarded. The actual hard cases from a First Amendment perspective are cases in which slurs or epithets are used during the commission of a crime. The rigorous system of inquiry into motivation that detectives practice makes it highly unlikely that cases in which protected speech serves as evidence survive until the charging process. In the unlikely event that such cases do make it through, they are caught by prosecutors, who use the law sparingly and are alert to the danger of prosecuting individuals just for using hate speech.

3. Hate Crime Legislation as Duplicative of the Criminal Law

One of the most frequent objections to hate crime legislation often comes in the wake of a particularly gruesome hate murder. An objection of this nature is often phrased in the following manner: "We already have protections for murder, why do we need protection for hate crimes?" "The man who killed James Byrd already got the death penalty, what else are we going to give him, 'death plus'?" There is also an empirical side to the objection that has to do with the police. "James Byrd's and Matthew Shepard's murders have been aggressively investigated by a homicide squad. These types of crimes get investigated."[6]

There is an element of truth in several of these statements. Though all homicides are not investigated with the same level of intensity, solutions to homicide are pursued energetically and persistently. A former ABTF detective put it in these terms: "Every cop longs to work in Homicide." Homicide is a plum assignment, and detectives work hard to get there and harder to stay. But as chapter 4 highlights, the crime of homicide is an exception to the general rule. Though homicide is aggressively investigated, the vast majority of *other* crimes in this country are not investigated at all.

Most hate crimes are not homicides. According to the FBI's Hate Crime Report, in 1999 law enforcement agencies identified only 17 hate murders out of 9,031 offenses. Most of the hate crimes identified as hate crimes were simple assaults and intimidation.[7] Center City's experience mirrors that of the rest of the country. Most of its hate crimes are low-level crimes—simple assault, harassment, threats, and vandalism—crimes normally given the lowest priority.

The passage of hate crime laws that track the criminal law for low-level offenses is not duplicative. It signals that we, as a society, particularly disdain the selection of an individual for criminal attacks because of race, religion, ethnicity, or sexual orientation. Like the term *hate crime*, which has captured public attention, the passage of hate crime statutes singles hate crime out for special legal treatment. By doing so, we create an institutional incentive for police departments to allocate special resources for hate crime investigation. The news media will report more on bias-motivated violence if there are laws specifically punishing hate crimes, and police behavior relative to this type of crime will become the focus of a variety of social and political actors.

Police must be given incentives to treat hate crime differently because hate crimes have been shown to have a terrible effect on victims, greater than do other crimes of a similar violence level. Without intervention, police will treat hate crime like other crimes in the crime classifications into which they fall—assaults and vandalism—and hate crimes will not be investigated. Critics are right. We do not need hate crime legislation for the Matthew Shepards and James Byrds. We do need it, however, for the thousands of individuals each year who are victimized and revictimized by "low-level" bias-motivated harassment.

Why Hate Crime Law Worked

My finding that police were able to walk the fine line between policing hate speech and policing hate crime is unexpected, given most of the existing literature on the police. Scholars argue that police officers enforce the law only minimally and do their best to avoid constitutional protections when they can. Other scholarship on the relationship between the police and minorities—gays, lesbians, and people of color—suggests, contrary to what I found, that police officers use their discretion in ways that are abusive. Identifying incidents as bias-motivated required ABTF detectives to respect the stories and experiences of racial minorities and gays and lesbians, groups that traditionally have been treated quite poorly by the police.

My findings that police officers enforce hate crime law are even more surprising in light of my discovery of the perils of enforcing hate crime legislation. I found that if hate crimes are occurring as a result of move-in violence, as they have in many cities in across the country, enforcing hate crime legislation can pit the police against communities like Gertown that are mobilized against the enforcement of hate crime law. Given the racial attitudes of many police departments, as evidenced by the difficulties minority officers face and the prevalence of race-based arrest and detention policies, detectives who take the side of people of color who are victims of hate crime may face ostracism and obstacles from their fellow police officers.[8]

So why the counterintuitive results? As I argued in chapter 5, residents mobilized against the law failed to stop its enforcement primarily for two reasons. First, hate crimes are high-visibility events, and residents' demands that hate crime laws not be enforced were not ones that the city's political climate could allow the police department to fully accommodate. Thus, higher-ups in the department had to settle for putting pressure on the unit rather than removing its funding, or limiting the number of detectives assigned to it.

If the hate crime unit does well, as the ABTF did, and hate crimes increase, police departments and city officials may pressure it to reduce the number of hate crimes it reports to avoid negative comparisons with neighboring cities and towns that do not investigate hate crime. This puts additional pressure on hate crime units not to enforce the law.

Detectives who face the challenges of community pressure may indeed behave unexpectedly if their unit can create a culture that places a premium on service to crime victims. ABTF detectives operated in a context dramatically different from that of patrol officers, hence, the difference in the two groups' treatment of minorities is unsurprising. In the ABTF, institutional culture, combined with the job police had to perform, provided a means to develop an orientation toward victims that helped them resist both departmental and community pressure. The detectives dealt with many individuals who had been horribly frightened. They developed a desire to help such persons in part because of unit procedures—interviewing victims only in their homes, requiring officers to check on victims between court appearances, and requiring them to take victims back and forth to court. These practices were largely followed and fostered a relationship between the victim and the investigating detective, ultimately leading to "conversion"—a commitment to investigating civil rights cases and helping hate crime victims. The ABTF also had resources to make it financially rewarding for detectives to stay in the unit. The officers' desire to help victims and their willingness to bear the personal and professional costs of doing so is less surprising in light of unit culture, conversion, and significant resources.

Policy Recommendations

This book has described the way that hate crime law is enforced in a single city. I do not suggest that detectives in other places are engaged in the same routines that characterize the work of the Center City hate crime detectives. The aim of the work is not to describe how all hate crime detectives are enforcing the law. Rather, it is to identify difficulties that are likely to arise in other environments as officers struggle to balance competing pressures created by institutional, legal, and community forces as they seek to enforce hate crime statutes. My theory describes the ways in which street-level bureaucrats in Center City dealt with competing issues. Although my model cannot predict what officers everywhere will do with the pressures that they face enforcing hate crime legislation, it may well apply to cases in which officers share similar institutional procedures for processing hate crime.

I close with two policy recommendations; the first addresses the accountability of those on the ground, and the second focuses on hate crime law.

1. Increase Visibility and Change Incentives in Order to Increase Accountability

Ground-level enforcers of the criminal law—police, prosecutors, court magistrates—are powerful, not so much for their control over final outcomes but for their low-visibility power not to enforce the law. Ground-level enforcers can and do decide which cases will be thrown away—that is, which cases will not get investigated,[9] which cases do not get prosecuted,[10] and which complaints are "junk."[11] Even if ground-level enforcers are not the last word, the power to filter is significant, especially when it limits the range of decisions available to enforcers above them. We cede the power to street-level bureaucrats in exchange for flexibility in the application of the law.

My results from Center City suggest that if we are unhappy with the decisions that ground-level enforcers make as they cope with ambiguity in the law, there are two things we might do. First, we can follow the lead of those in Gertown and increase the visibility of police decisions not to enforce the law. When Gertown residents believed White victims were not getting justice, they demanded accountability. Departmental higher-ups responded by putting pressure on the unit. This did not stop the enforcement of hate crime law in Gertown, but it did mean that officers took measures to ensure that White victims received attention. This implies that the invisibility of the nonenforcement decision is one thing that gives street-level bureaucrats their power.

The second thing we might do to curb street-level bureaucrats' nonenforcement is to create incentives to enforce the law. The ABTF did that by making victim service a part of the job. For instance, one of the reasons that police so flagrantly disobey the law in the Fourth Amendment context is that departments place more emphasis on catching suspects than on conducting constitutional searches. If police officers are caught doing the wrong thing they do not get punished; prosecutors—not the police—just lose the evidence needed for conviction. Even in the unlikely event that police officers feel the loss of the conviction, the only incentive the loss creates for them is to still "make the collar" but hide their illegal actions better the next time. The implications of shifting incentives may hold for other street-level bureaucrats as well.

2. Enact Hate Crime Law

In this book, the terms *hate crime* and *civil rights violations* are often used interchangeably; this is in part because of the structure of the law in Center City. Many of the charges the unit brought against perpetrators of hate crimes were brought under the state's civil rights statute. To talk about hate crimes as civil rights violations *better* reflects the empirical reality of hate crime violence in Center City and elsewhere. The rights to equal access to housing and public accommodations are bedrock civil rights. In Center City, much of the ABTF's activity was concerned with policing neighborhoods in which residents were resisting housing integration. A common response to minorities moving into neighborhoods has been "White flight," but not everyone who wishes to leave has the means. Some of those who cannot afford to leave stay and fight, attempting to "crime-out" the newcomers. As stated earlier, "move-in" violence is not just a Center City phenomenon; it has been identified in New York City, St. Louis, Chicago, the suburbs of Maryland, and other places as well. As Blacks and other minorities integrate formerly all-White areas, they experience harassment and violence. This is also true for gays and lesbians, as perpetrators restrict their safe movement to and from places of public accommodation.

Casting hate crime as an issue connected to hate speech is a mischaracterization that ignores the empirical basis of many of the incidents investigated by the police. The cases that the ABTF investigated suggest that hate crimes arise as White residents try to protect "their" neighborhoods from outsiders. This is clear from the language used in these crimes. "Go back to where you belong," "Go back to China," "Gertown is for us," "No niggers in Hillsdale" are taunts that commonly accompanied the assaults and other harassment in many of the ABTF's cases.

The vast majority of the unit's cases did not involve mere name calling, or even garden-variety bigots airing their views. Hate crimes were not ordinary muggings with slurs attached. The hundreds of cases investigated by the ABTF were the stories of perpetrators whose intention was not to express views but, rather, to drive people out of "their" neighborhood or off the street because the perpetrators did not like their victims' race, religion, or sexual orientation. In Center City, the detectives and defendants knew that hate crimes are not about hate speech. Enforcers of hate crime law rarely saw their jobs as implicating the First Amendment, and defendants almost never asserted their First Amendment right to use slurs or epithets. Thus, enforcers and perpetrators realized that although defendants' criminal actions were not protected, defendants retained their right to hate.

In order to guarantee equality in housing and travel, we need hate crime legislation and bias crime units. Low-level crime, the category into which most hate crimes fall, is the type of crime most frequently overlooked by police. Special laws punishing bias-motivated conduct encourage police departments to pay attention to low-level, bias-motivated crime.

The enforcement of hate crime laws can be better accomplished with separate centralized bias crime investigative units. Important qualities for an effective unit include (1) racial, gender, and sexual orientation diversity; and (2) adequate personnel resources to allow space and time for thorough investigation and training. The perspective offered by a diverse group of officers expands any unit's ability to reach out to victims from a variety of backgrounds. Since a small number of hate crimes may be reported in a given area of the city, aggregating the city's hate crimes and assigning all of them to a single centralized unit is more likely to provide detectives with more investigative experience, enabling the development of specialized techniques and expertise. Centralized units for hate crime may also be better equipped to allow the creation of norms that encourage detectives to investigate low-level crimes and provide victim service.

It is unclear whether police enforcement of hate crime law in centralized units is more effective at stopping hate crime or deterring hate crime perpetrators. The evidence from Center City is inconclusive. Between 1979 and 1993, roughly half of the years showed an increase in the number of incidents reported over the previous year's figures. The other half showed a decrease. A better measure of the value of police units may be in the victim services provided. Enforcing hate crime in Center City, and elsewhere, involves listening to victims' stories and attempting to address the harassment they have faced. Listening to victims and investigating hate crimes is one way, albeit a small one, of officially recognizing that racist, anti-Semitic, and antigay and -lesbian violence is real, and harmful.

Research Methodology—A Peek behind the Curtain

Researchers' "confessional" tales demystify our fieldwork and us by showing what we did in the field.[1] Police researchers' confessional tales rarely see the light of day; they are absent from most of our books or reduced to a single line that obscures more than it reveals. Thus, how one achieved access, what it was like in the field, and the choices that the researcher made are safely veiled. The reader is thus prevented from gaining valuable insights into how the research was conducted, and other researchers are deprived of models for further research.[2] The scholarly value of exhibiting one's research methodology and the interest that has greeted my story—one of a young African-American woman studying cops—encourage me to provide further details about the story behind my research. I have appended a confessional tale to my book that offers a (tiny) peek behind the curtain.

Mea Culpa: *The Choices I Made*

In designing this research, I was forced to make a series of unusual choices, especially regarding the length of time spent in the field and site selection. I offer an explanation because my choices—while typical for those who have done fieldwork studies of the police—might perplex other researchers, like those conducting fieldwork studies of other governmental institutions (such as Congress) or those who have done ethnography of groups of people (such as the Mashpee). In an ideal world with unlimited access to police hate crime units, I might have made other choices, but the particular question I chose, as well as the special difficulties of doing police research, led me to a particular course. I elaborate more on my choices, my research design, and some of the difficulties of police research below.

The research on which this book is based was designed to create a comprehensive model of decision-making in bias crime cases that incorporates official procedure, organizational norms, experience, and certain environmental conditions that police face as they enforce hate crime law. The environmental conditions include the role of political considerations within the police department, the local political structure, the structure of the law in the jurisdiction, the legal culture, and the role of community-based actors—anti hate crime activists and community members.

Why Choose the CCPD? Weighing Access and Fit

In order to fully appreciate the environmental conditions that police encounter, my research design required that I observe the police, conduct interviews with a variety of individuals including police officers, and also have access to the police department's case files. I chose the Anti-Bias Task Force (ABTF), the hate crime unit of the Center City Police Department (CCPD), for two reasons. First, unlike other police departments I approached, the CCPD was willing to provide the full level of access outlined in the research plan. Second, CCPD's hate crime unit had been in place for a number of years. Hate crime units vary in overall investigative activity devoted to hate crime. For a project focusing on the behavior of police officers that enforce hate crime law, it was important that the research site have developed a number of procedures worked out over time in the area of bias crime. For instance, I contacted one hate crime unit that appeared willing to cooperate but had investigated just five hate crimes in three years. The Center City unit's tenure, in addition to its level of activity (that is, the number of crimes referred and investigated each year), also facilitated the collection of large amounts of data (including time series data) in a short period of time. This is important to police researchers who may be given access for only a limited period.

I cannot attribute my being granted access on my second attempt to anything other than sheer luck—I was prepared when I encountered a splendid opportunity. After having been denied access in a department where I had contacts, I happened to meet the director of research of the

CCPD at a conference. He reluctantly agreed to make suggestions relative to my letter to the head of the department and allowed me to use his name. I sent my letter to the commissioner, who forwarded it to the head of the unit. After a brief in-person meeting with me a few weeks before the project was scheduled to begin, the head of the unit approved the project, and I was "in."[3]

I read the Center City Police Department's allowing my access as neither atypical nor unusual. The long list of observational studies of the police testifies to the fact that it is not at all rare for police departments to allow researchers access.[4] Hate crime does not appear to be a special area of police sensitivity to research. I approached five police departments. None found the idea of this type of study repugnant. One provided me with internal departmental reports but at the last minute, for reasons that were never explained, reneged on a promise of full access. Another department responded positively to my inquiries about conducting the research but backed off when the chief of police closed the department to researchers. Evidently, that department had allowed *so many* research projects that they were creating a disruption.

Though my research design and the difficulty of obtaining access to any department prevented me from selecting the "average" city or "average" police department (if these truly exist), the size, professionalization, and experience of CCPD officers is fairly typical. With between 1,500 and 2,500 officers, the CCPD is among neither the country's largest nor its smallest police forces.[5] The CCPD does not, as some police departments have begun to do, require those applying for a job as a police officer to possess a two-year college degree. Thus, it cannot be argued that officers in Center City are better educated than most police officers.

Researchers have eschewed single-case studies like mine in favor of a comparative approach, studying as many sites as possible for a short period of time. The drive to make studies comparative has been criticized on the grounds that the selection of a broad number of sites requires prior knowledge about details in each site that researchers may not possess. It may also lead to a preoccupation with idiosyncratic rather than more important broad theoretical issues.[6] Those who are theoretically or practically limited to a single-case study may try to maximize the "generalizability" of the research—the extent to which the findings in the site studied can be said to apply to other sites with similar characteristics—through the selection of a site that contains characteristics, such as population, geographic size, resources, and institutional procedures, that are similar to those of other sites.

I could have limited my time in Center City and pursued access to other sites. The site I chose takes a particular structural approach to hate crime investigation that does not exist in every department that investigates hate crimes in this country. The Anti-Bias Task Force is a centralized detective unit. Had I studied more departments, I might be able to discuss the implications of experimentation in investigation. For example, had I studied departments in different cities, I could have evaluated the different ways departments investigate hate crime—decentralized groups of detectives in neighborhood precincts (Los Angeles), one single officer (Seattle), or referring hate crime to special investigations units (Atlanta).

To fully understand the environment, I chose instead to focus only on Center City, concentrating the hours of observation, more than five hundred in all. I got to know the officers and history of the unit, I collected hundreds of pages of documents, and I interacted with the hate crime law enforcement community. As a result, I was able to supply critical details about police processes and law enforcement in this context, which provides an important knowledge base and allows groundbreaking preliminary theory building.

With respect to the question of representativeness of the site, I question whether one could identify a single unit that was representative of all bias units given the wide variations in how police handle bias crime.[7] More important, the aim of the work is not to describe how all hate crime detectives are enforcing the law. Rather, it is to identify difficulties that are likely to arise as officers struggle to balance competing pressures created by institutional, legal, and community forces as they enforce hate crime legislation. I have developed a theory that describes the ways in which street-level bureaucrats in Center City deal with competing issues that arise. My model cannot predict what officers in every unit will do with the pressures, but it may well apply to cases in which officers share similar institutional procedures for processing hate crime.

One pressure is the barrier to hate crime investigations created by departmental culture and politics. The Center City Police Department has a culture on race similar to that of other police departments. Like many departments in this country, that in Center City has a majority of White officers. Like police departments in other cities, there was a great deal of racial tension in the department that frequently threatened to upset relations between Black and White officers within the department and between White officers and the minority community.[8] In addition, as chapter 6 describes, Center City police officers outside the unit frequently dismissed hate crimes as "unimportant," "not police work," and "not worth investigating," as have police officers studied in other departments. Given that the CCPD shares a culture on racial issues with other departments, as well as a culture regarding the importance of hate crime investigation, my findings regarding departmental barriers to hate crime investigation may be widely applicable—irrespective of the way in which a department investigates hate crime.

How Long Is Long Enough? Balancing Access and Depth

Like many who study the police, I had to balance the widespread notion that I should spend a year or more on-site learning about the culture of the institution and the reality of conducting police research. The conventional wisdom about conducting ethnographic fieldwork is that a longer period of time allows one's research subjects to forget that one is there—one can "blend into the wallpaper." It simultaneously allows the researcher to learn the culture more fully.

Extended access was not a luxury that I, nor many police researchers, can afford. First, police departments view providing access to researchers as expensive, something that costs the department. Thus, departments are often unwilling to allow researchers to have access over a lengthy period. Four of the police departments I contacted about the possibility of conducting this research raised the issue of the cost to the department in terms of hours that would have to be expended explaining the job to researchers. Three departments indicated that they rejected the proposal outright because they believed that the six weeks that I wished to spend in the department was too much. In the department that I studied, I asked for twelve weeks; eight weeks were approved. I ended up spending more than five months observing the unit.

Another reason that it may be better to plan to get in and out as quickly as possible is that the level of access to police sites is individually negotiated with each head, as well as being contingent on the person who extended access remaining in his or her position. Staffing shifts are frequent in police departments. With change in the leadership of the unit or department, one's access can likewise change, end, or have to be renegotiated. The head of the unit I was studying was transferred the last week I spent in the unit. Access that I needed in order to clean up the data set had to be renegotiated with a new head who was somewhat less supportive of the project but agreed nevertheless.

I am not convinced that had I been able to stay in the unit longer, much would have been gained. Because I planned to collect data for only a short period, the time I spent in the unit was intense. Initially, I asked for the opportunity to observe detectives in the office three times each week. After a few weeks, however, I began coming into the office nearly every day, including weekends. The unit operated with a day shift and night shift from 9:00 A.M. until 1:00 A.M. the following morning. It was important that I observe officers on both shifts, so most days I came to the office in late morning and stayed until late evening. Over the course of five months, I observed detectives on more than sixty occasions, occasionally for more than ten hours at a stretch.

Data Collection

In order to capture a range of police procedures and police interactions, as well as to verify salient issues, data collection was triangulated.[9] Data were drawn primarily from three sources: semistructured interviews, secondary source documents (the department's records and notes taken from the unit's case files), and participant observation of ABTF detectives. I describe each below.

Interviews

I interviewed fifty individuals—a selection of thirty current and former ABTF detectives (approximately 80 percent of whom had spent at least one year in the unit), fifteen lawyers who had prosecuted hate crime cases or sought injunctions, and five victim advocates. The victim advocates represented the Asian American community; the African American community; the gay, lesbian, bisexual, and transgendered (GLBT) community; and the Jewish community. Most respondents were selected using the snowball method. Someone in the field volunteered a name, and, if the referent had the appropriate level of experience, I asked how to contact that person and generally interviewed him or her. At the end of each interview, I asked for suggestions of good people with whom to speak. The interviews were semistructured, with a standardized questionnaire used for each group and follow-up questions where appropriate. The vast majority of interviews were approximately forty-five minutes long.

My interviews and field observations were based on notes, rather than tape recordings. Before I entered the field, I made the conscious decision not to tape-record interviews because of advice from other police researchers who said police officers are very suspicious of tape recorders. My belief that my respondents, especially the police officers, would be more hesitant were I to use a tape recorder were confirmed in the field when at the end of her interview one subject remarked that as a cop, she would never have "talked to a tape recorder."

All things being equal (though I do not assert that they are), tape recorders more accurately capture every word than does note taking. Regarding the accuracy of my note taking, I did have some previous relevant experience taking notes during in-person interviews; I conducted twenty interviews before doing the research in Center City. I also attempted to mitigate the data loss as much as possible. As soon as each interview ended, I immediately sat down and "filled in" the missing data. The interviews were typed up later that evening.

Case Files and Other Documentation

I also examined written reports and other documentation concerning the unit's investigation of each incident located in the unit's case file. Reports produced by the department helped provide an institutional history of the unit and the historical context for the bias crime classification in the time period prior to my observation. The materials were added to the research design so as to provide a more thorough understanding of the development of innovation in bias crime identification and observation over the unit's history, as well as to provide a systematic database for the treatment of cases over time. Analyzing the case files containing officers' reports and impressions of an incident not long after it occurred also provided a check on the officers' interview accounts and completed the interview-observation-records triangulation of the data.

Analyzing the unit's case files also served an instrumental purpose that turned out to be exceedingly important. I was permitted to read files in the office. Spending long hours collecting these data provided excellent "cover" for casual observation of the detectives at work. It gave me something to do in the office while I observed the detectives as they went about their tasks in the office—writing up reports, assigning cases, making decisions about how to proceed, and telephoning victims. As they were working, I was working too. It kept me quiet, occupied, out of the way, and unobtrusive, allowing the detectives to function normally.

I was given access to all of the unit's case files in their entirety for the years 1980-1997, inclusive. The files contained police department records associated with each incident, such as detective reports, transcripts of interrogation, and information from other agencies, such as court judgments against perpetrators. I sampled incidents from approximately seven hundred case files, 27 percent of the total number of cases investigated. I also examined selected files from 1980 (the first year information was available) and from 1984 through 1997. For each of the cases I read, I noted on a form that I devised a brief description of the incident; the language used by the suspect prior, during, or after the commission of the crime; the detective's determination as to whether the crime was bias-motivated; and the legal outcome of the case.

My research also involved collecting other written documents, including legal briefs and documents, from cases investigated by the unit; newspaper articles written about the unit and cases handled by the unit; and videotapes used by the unit in training sessions. All of these outside sources were at various points used to enrich or problematize research subjects' accounts.

A Note on Police Statistics

There are many ways to get a sense of the outcomes that emerge from the decisions that police make about enforcing hate crime law. In this book, I have discusses several. For instance, one can look at what they do. Chapter 4 describes the percentage of cases the police actually investigate and the extent to which they investigate them, the level of investigation. Much of the book analyzes what I learned about what the detectives do by watching them, asking questions, reading their reports, and observing their practices.

Like most police researchers, in addition to the data I collected, I present some statistics compiled from police data, specifically from the unit's logbooks. In chapter 7, for instance, I use the unit's records, detailing when criminal or civil rights charges are requested. The logbooks for each year consist of a chart that lists basic information about each case, including race of victim, race of perpetrator, location of incident, date of referral to the unit, investigating officer, and status. The status of a case indicates whether it is under active investigation, the action taken, and whether criminal charges, civil rights charges, or an injunction were sought. Alternative dispute resolution, mediation, is also noted in the logs. If the investigation is abbreviated because the victim refused to prosecute, that too may be noted. The logbooks are kept by the unit's detective clerk and are supposed to be updated periodically though the year.

Though statistical measures of how often the law is invoked or how many people or institutions are in compliance are often considered good descriptions of how law works or how well it is working,[10] I caution readers to refrain from drawing too many conclusions from the statistics from the logbooks about how hate crime law works in Center City. I found the statistics created by the police on what gets charged to be the least reliable measure of the decisions that police make enforcing hate crime law.

Though there are advantages to using the logbooks—the most obvious is that they present a comprehensive picture of all types of cases—there are drawbacks as well. In comparing the logbooks against my sample taken from the actual case files, I found them very accurate for some things, such as data on race of victims and perpetrators, but very inaccurate for other things, such as whether the investigating detective thought an incident was racially motivated. For example, all the logbooks contained the notation "non-racial," indicating that some cases were racially motivated and others were not. Comparing the cases marked "non-racial" in the logbooks, I noticed that detectives often failed to say whether they thought an incident was bias-motivated. A large percentage of cases were simply moved to inactive status without explanation.

I found other inconsistencies. In some years it seemed that every case that did not have a criminal action, mediation, or an injunction (roughly 75 percent of the cases) was marked "non-civil rights." The likelihood of that many cases being deemed non-racial was contradicted by several officers' testimony that frequently they just did not know whether an incident was bias-motivated or not. I thus interpreted the label "non-civil rights" or "non-racial" not to be a judgment based on the facts of the case but, rather, a label that the detective clerk affixed to cases that had been moved to inactive status with no criminal or civil action.

I do not fault the unit's record keepers for the gaps and silences in the data on charging and the outcome of legal cases. ABTF detectives are not professional record keepers; they are detectives. Their job and focus had much more to do with scrupulous documentation of individual cases of bias-motivated harassment rather than with the outcome of legal cases that they had turned over to prosecutors and other legal officials. My reliance on the police data on charging is lessened by my familiarity with its inadequacies.

Participant Observation: Hanging Around Observing Detectives

In order to capture the interpretive work in which officers in the unit were engaged, it was necessary to observe officers at work. Thus, as in many studies of police practices, a central portion of the research project involved observation of police practices.[11] Most of this observation took place in the office because most of the detectives' work involved the writing of reports based on their field investigation. The detectives' reports are composed in the unit's office, which is located at main headquarters.

In addition to observing detectives in the office setting, I was also able to observe them in the following situations: in training sessions on civil rights law; in their outreach efforts in high schools; while they conducted neighborhood surveillance; during investigations/interviews with victims; while they were taking part in dispute resolution (court and mediation); and in interagency planning sessions. I thought it important to see everything I could; I asked questions as often as I felt appropriate; and I asked to accompany officers wherever they were going.

Many of the observations were made during activities in the context of what are commonly considered "traditional" police functions—investigation, surveillance, and court appearance—but there were some very valuable experiences that were not. This is true in part because, in connection with their jobs, the detectives engaged in a number of other activities—they visited schools to talk about hate crime, they ran mediations in ethnic disputes, and they conducted in-service training at the academy. Rather than restrict observation to the activities most likely to yield information about hate crime classification, I recognized the value early in the research of just being there, observing, even if the occurrence did not fit into what I considered traditional police work. "Hanging around" at times when it was unlikely that anything important would happen meant not only that I would be there on the off chance that it did, but it also maximized the times I was able to talk with them informally about their work.

In the unit I experienced little formality and a marked absence of characteristic divisions that normally exist between subject and researcher. After I had been observing the detectives for a short period of time, they "loosened up" and began to include me in meals and tell me stories about themselves. They also offered more explanations regarding their activities. My youthful appearance may have led officers to consider me less of a threat (several detectives called my dissertation my "paper"), and may have also led them to believe I had much to learn. They took pains to take me places—to court, to trainings, and on investigations—to expose me to parts of the job they considered significant. In an attempt to present their job as they saw it, they told "war" stories (sometimes the same one more than once) and introduced me to people.

Each encounter with the unit was written up as part of my daily field notes. The notes consisted of a narrative description of what had happened that day, as well as my impression of the events I had observed. Often, the typed notes composed at the end of the day were based on brief notes quickly jotted down during the day or evening as events were happening. Discreetly jotting down a word or two as events were happening was possible when I was in the office, where I was often already taking notes, but not in court, in interviews with victims, or on investigations. For events outside the office, I carried a tiny notebook that allowed me to write a few words about an incident that would jog my memory when writing a more detailed account back in the office for incorporation into the day's field notes.

Building a Rapport

Because my time in the field was limited, I came into the unit frequently, which may have made it easier for detectives to get used to my presence. It was clear to me that I did blend in. One officer who had been suspicious of my presence early in the study commented a month or so later during her interview, "I can't believe I'm telling you this. I can't believe it. It's like you've become part of the wallpaper." Another detective said frequently, "You're one of us, you're one of us, Jeannine." A third, an especially hard-boiled detective, said to me, when I told him I was preparing to leave, that I need not go. He was quite serious when he said that I could stay, join the police academy, and become a police officer.

It is not just their comments that made me think I was "in"; their actions were indicative too. They stopped treating me as special and telling me where items could be found, and started telling me about cases and their personal lives. I am not naïve enough to think that the ABTF detectives considered me a sworn detective. Still, their behavior suggests that I fell into a category somewhere between "outsider" and "detective."

Such close contact with the members of the unit let me worry less about not being able to learn the culture than becoming so immersed in it that I "went native." Though I took daily field notes to guard against the danger of losing my perspective over time, the prospect was still a concern. In the end, I strove for a balance between leaving before I could really appreciate the culture and getting so far in that I was no longer able to be objective. I tried to balance all of the competing considerations by taking the advice of a longtime police researcher, who told me it was time to exit when I had stopped "learning things."

The role that my race and gender played in my access to individuals and developing a rapport with them is rather complex. When I conducted the research I was relatively young looking; I am an African American woman. The largest group of individuals in the unit was White men, yet there were several people of color, including three African American women. I developed a rapport with detectives who were Black and White and with women and men. My best, most open informants were an African American woman and a White man. I think I developed a rapport with a variety of detectives, both African American and White, for different reasons. My race and gender may have suggested to some of the Black detectives that I would be more open to their side of the story. White detectives may have felt that I was open to what they had to say because of my willingness to listen to their stories without judgment (or perhaps without comment). Still others saw me being taken aside by particular detectives and felt the need to tell their side of the story.

Notes

NOTES TO CHAPTER 1

1. See *Black's Law Dictionary* (1999) 378.

2. See Diana Struzzi, "Determining the Hate in Crime: Grayson County Interracial Case Puts a Spotlight on How Hate Crimes Are Defined," *Roanoke Times and World News*, 17 August 1997.

3. Ibid.

4. Joseph A. Goldstein, "Police Discretion Not to Invoke the Criminal Process: Low-Visibility Decisions in the Administration of Justice," *Yale Law Journal* 69 (1960): 554.

5. See, e.g., Alison Mitchell, "Police Find Bias Crimes Are Often Wrapped in Ambiguity," *New York Times*, 27 January 1992, B2; Ellen Nakashima and Marisa Osorio Colon, "In Effect Since 1990, State's Hate Crime Law Brings Few Convictions," *Hartford Courant*, 19 July 1993; Aurelio Rojas, "Turning a Blind Eye to Hate Crimes: Most Attacks in California Go Unprosecuted," *San Francisco Chronicle*, 22 October 1996, A1.

6. See, e.g., Paul Duggan, "Gay Youth's Death Shakes Colorado City," *Washington Post*, 1 September 2001, A03; Adam Nossiter, "Gay Men's Slaying: Hate or Robbery?" *New York Times*, 13 October 1994, A20; Paul Duggan, "Man Is Charged in NW Slaying; Robbery, Anti Gay Bias Cited by Police as Possible Motives," *Washington Post*, 27 March 1993, B1.

7. See, e.g., Aurelio Rojas, "State's Tolerant Image Tarnished: Hate Crime Report Suggests Tense Climate," *San Francisco Chronicle*, 18 July 1996, A1; Nossiter, A20; Duggan, "Man Is Charged in NW Slaying."

8. See Rojas, "Turning a Blind Eye to Hate Crimes."

9. See Samuel Walker and Charles M. Katz, "Less Than Meets the Eye: Police Department Bias-Crime Units," *American Journal of Police* 14 (1995): 32.

10. See, e.g., Samuel R. Cacas, "Asians under Attack: Law Enforcement Reluctant to Acknowledge Hate Crimes," *Human Rights* 21 (Fall 1994): 34.

11. Chuck Wexler and Gary J. Marx, "When Law and Order Works," *Crime and Delinquency* 23 (1986): 205.

12. James B. Jacobs and Barry J. Eisler, "The Hate Crimes Statistics Act of 1990," *Criminal Law Bulletin* 29 (1993): 113.

13. Federal Bureau of Investigation, U.S. Department of Justice, Hate Crime Statistics (Washington, D.C., 1994).

14. Kevin Berrill, "Anti-Gay Violence," in *Bias Crime*, Robert J. Kelly, ed. (1993) 161.

15. See Lu-in Wang, "The Transforming Power of 'Hate': Social Cognition Theory and the Harms of Bias-Related Crime," *Southern California Law Review* 71 (November 1997): 47–136.

16. See Howard Ehrlich, Barbara E. K. Larcom, and Robert Purvis, "The Traumatic Impact of Ethnoviolence," in *The Price We Pay: The Case Against Racist Speech, Hate Propaganda, and Pornography*, Laura Lederer and Richard Delgado, eds. (New York: Hill and Wang, 1995) 62–79; and Luis Garcia and Jack McDevitt, "The Psychological and Behavioral Effects of Bias and Non-Bias Motivated Assault," Report for the National Institute of Justice, U.S. Department of Justice, December 1999.

17. Ehrlich, Larcom, and Purvis, 62–66.

18. Ibid.

19. Garcia and McDevitt, 96–97.

20. Ibid.

21. For a discussion of the passage of state hate crime legislation, including the influence of advocacy groups, see Valerie Jenness and Ryken Grattet, "The Criminalization of Hate: A Comparison of Structural and Polity Influences on the Passage of 'Bias-Crime' Legislation in the United States," *Sociological Perspectives* 39 (1996): 129–154.

22. Bureau of the Census, *County and City Data Book, 1994*, Table C.

23. Ibid.

24. See Heart of Atlanta Motel, Inc. v. United States, 379 US 241 (1964) and Katzenbach v. McClung, 379 US 294 (1964). *Heart of Atlanta* affirmed the constitutionality of the Civil Rights Act of 1964 based on Congress's power to regulate interstate travel.

25. See Jones v. Alfred Mayer Co., 392 US 409 (1968). This case affirmed the right of all citizens to inherit, purchase, lease, sell, hold, and convey real and personal property.

Notes to Chapter 2

1. See N.Y. Penal Law § 485.05; Cook County State Attorney's Office, *A Prosecutor's Guide to Hate Crimes*, IV–2 (1994).

2. The Model Penal Code defines homicide as the killing of one human being by the act, procurement, or omission of another. Model Penal Code § 210.1 (1962). A human being is guilty of criminal homicide if he or she pur-

posely, knowingly, recklessly, or negligently causes the death of another human being. Criminal homicide within criminal codes includes murder, manslaughter, and negligent homicide. Homicide, however, is not always a crime.

3. Jack Kuykendall, "The Municipal Police Detective: A Historical Analysis," *Criminology* 24 (1986): 175–201; Michael Lipsky, *Street-Level Bureaucracy* (1980); Kenneth Culp Davis, *Police Discretion* (1975).

4. Lipsky, *Street-Level Bureaucracy*, 13.

5. Ibid., 40.

6. Jerome H. Skolnick, *Justice without Trial* (1967) 73. For another example, see Aaron V. Cicourel, *The Social Organization of Juvenile Justice* (1968) 323 (describing police officers' labeling of juvenile delinquents as stemming from departmental policies, organizational rules, and codes).

7. Wayne R. LaFave, "The Police and Non-Enforcement of the Law—Part II," *Wisconsin Law Review* (March 1962): 203–204.

8. See Goldstein, 543, 573–577; James Q. Wilson, *Varieties of Police Behavior* (1973) 37–39, 225–226, 297–299; and LaFave, 210.

9. LaFave, 218–222.

10. Skolnick, *Justice without Trial*, 9, 11.

11. LaFave, 217–38.

12. See Jerome H. Skolnick and James Fyfe, *Above the Law* (1993), 125.

13. LaFave, 204. For another example, see Wilson, *Varieties of Police Behavior*, 84 ("[F]or most officers there are considerations of utility that equal or exceed in importance those of duty or morality, especially for the more common and less serious laws."); and Richard J. Lundman, "Demeanor or Crime? The Midwest City Police-Citizen Encounters Study," *Criminology* 32 (1994): 631, 648.

14. Egon Bittner, *Aspects of Police Work* (1990) 19–28; Wilson, *Varieties of Police Behavior*, 17–34; and Skolnick, *Justice without Trial*, 1–22.

15. Skolnick, *Justice without Trial*, 10–11.

16. See Peter K. Manning, *The Narc's Game* (1980) 79; Wilson, *Varieties of Police Behavior*, 84 (describing the decision to arrest as the result of discretionary balancing of net gains and losses for all parties involved); Egon Bittner, "The Police on Skid Row: A Study of Peace Keeping," *American Sociological Review* 32 (1967): 712 (describing the use of law to solve practical problems involved in keeping the peace on skid row); Lundman, 647 (describing extralegal factors, such as demeanor, that shape the police exercise of discretion); and Robert E. Worden, "Situational and Attitudinal Explanations of Police Behaviors: A Theoretical Reappraisal and Empirical Assessment," *Law and Society Review* 23 (1989): 667.

17. LaFave, 187.

18. Ibid., 197–199. See also David H. Bayley, *Forces of Order* (1991) 98–115.

19. LaFave, 192.

20. Ibid., 192–193.

21. William B. Sanders, *Detective Work* (1977) 13.

22. Ibid., 6–29.

23. See Richard V. Ericson, *Making Crime* (1981).

24. Ibid., 94.

25. United States Department of Justice, National Institute of Law Enforcement, and Criminal Justice Law Enforcement Assistance Administration, *The Criminal Investigation Process* (April 1977) 20.

26. Lu-in Wang, *Hate Crimes Law* (2000) § 10–2.

27. Ibid.

28. See Terrence Sandalow, "Opening Address: Equality and Freedom of Speech," *Ohio Northern University Law Review* 21 (1995): 831, 843; Craig Peyton Gaumer, "Punishment for Prejudice: A Commentary on the Constitutionality and Utility of State Statutory Responses to the Problem of Hate Crime," *South Dakota Law Review* 39 (1994): 1, 24; and Robert Riggs, "Punishing the Politically Incorrect Offender Through 'Bias Motive' Enhancements: Compelling Necessity or First Amendment Folly?" *Ohio Northern University Law Review* 21 (1995): 950 (arguing that *Mitchell* and *R.A.V.* cannot be reconciled); Susan Gellman, "Hate Crimes after *Wisconsin v. Mitchell*," *Ohio Northern University Law Review* 21 (1995): 865; and Steven G. Gey, "What If *Wisconsin v. Mitchell* Had Involved Martin Luther King, Jr.? The Constitutional Flaws of Hate Crime Sentence Enhancements," *George Washington Law Review* 65 (1997): 1014 (arguing that *Mitchell* was incorrectly decided).

29. 505 U.S. 377, 396 (1992).

30. St. Paul, Minn., Legis. Code § 292.02 (1990). It provided:

Whoever places on public or private property an object, appellation, characterization or graffiti, including, but not limited to, a burning cross or Nazi swastika, which one knows or has reasonable grounds to know arouses anger, alarm or resentment in others on the basis of race, color, creed, religion, or gender commits disorderly conduct and shall be guilty of a misdemeanor.

31. See Matter of Welfare of R.A.V., 464 N.W.2d 507, 510–511 (Minn. 1991).

32. 315 U.S. 568, 572 (1942).

33. See R.A.V., 505 U.S. 377, 391.

34. Ibid.

35. Ibid., 392.

36. Ibid.

37. Ibid., 396.

38. For evidence of the confusion, see, e.g., State v. Plowman, 838 P.2d 558 (Oe. 1992) (upholding Oregon statute); State v. Wynant, 597 N.E.2d 450 (Ohio App. 1992) (striking down Ohio statute); State v. Mitchell, 485 N.W.2d 807 (Wis. 1992) (striking down Wisconsin statute), rev'd Wisconsin v. Mitchell, 508 U.S. 476 (1993).

There is some evidence that there was police confusion in this area as well. See Katia Hetter, "Enforcers of Hate-Crime Laws Wary after High Court Ruling," *Wall Street Journal*, 13 August 1992, B1 (describing law enforcement officials as wary about enforcing hate crime laws after Supreme Court's decision in *R.A.V. v. City of St. Paul*).

39. 508 U.S. 476 (1993).

40. Ibid., 476, 479–480.

41. Wis. Stat. § 939.645 (1996).

42. 169 Wis.2d 153, 158 (1992).

43. 508 U.S. 476, 481.

44. 169 Wis.2d 153, 158, 163 (1992).

45. 508 U.S. 476, 485–487.

46. Ibid.

47. Ibid.

48. Ibid., 488.

49. Ibid., 486.

50. 503 U.S. 159 (1992).

51. Ibid., 167.

52. Phyliss B. Gerstenfeld, "Smile When You Call Me That! The Problems with Punishing Hate Motivated Behavior," *Behavioral Sciences and the Law* 10 (1992): 270.

53. See, e.g., Susan Gellman, "Sticks and Stones Can Put You in Jail, but Can Words Increase Your Sentence? Constitutional and Policy Dilemmas of Ethnic Intimidation Laws," *UCLA Law Review* 39 (1991): 359; and Martin Redish, "Freedom of Thought as Freedom of Expression: Hate Crime Sentencing Enhancement and First Amendment Theory," *Criminal Justice Ethics* (Summer/Fall 1992): 30.

54. See James B. Jacobs and Kimberly Potter, *Hate Crimes* (1998) 128; Gellman, "Sticks and Stones," 359; Gerstenfeld, 279.

55. See Gellman, "Sticks and Stones," 349; see also James Morsch, "Comment, The Problem of Motive in Hate Crimes: The Argument against Presumptions of Racial Motivations," *Journal of Criminal Law and Criminology* 82 (1991): 671 (arguing prosecutors are prohibited by the First Amendment from using the accused's beliefs because liberal admission may chill freedom of expression).

56. Gellman, "Sticks and Stones," 356.

57. Ibid., 356–357.

58. See ibid., 361, note 134; Gerstenfeld, 279; Barbara Dority, "The Criminalization of Hatred," *Humanist* (May/June 1994): 38–39.

59. Gerstenfeld, 279.

60. See Linda Greenhouse, "Defining the Freedom to Hate While Punching," *New York Times*, 29 December 1992.

61. Gellman, "Sticks and Stones," 360; see also Nat Hentoff, "No: Equality among Victims," *ABA Journal* (May 1993): 45.

62. Gerstenfeld writes, "Unless the defendant is an avowed member of the Ku Klux Klan, or another hate group, it might be difficult to determine his motive. One can imagine prosecutors canvassing the defendant's neighbors and co-workers to discover how many times he made racist comments or told an ethnic joke," 270.

63. Jacobs and Potter, *Hate Crimes*, 98.

64. Ibid.

65. Ibid.

66. See Gellman, "Sticks and Stones," 361.

67. James B. Jacobs, "Rethinking the War against Hate Crimes: A New York City Perspective," *Criminal Justice Ethics* (Summer/Fall 1992): 56 (describing motivation as complicated and at minimum encompassing ideas about unconscious as well as conscious desires).

68. See Gregory M. Herek, "Psychological Heterosexism and Anti-Gay Violence: The Social Psychology of Bigotry and Bashing," in *Hate Crimes*, Gregory M. Herek and Kevin Berrill, eds. (1992); Wang, "The Transforming Power of 'Hate,'" 47.

69. See Jack L. Levin and Jack McDevitt, *Hate Crimes* (1993) 49, 65, 75, 89.

70. Ibid., 49–53.

71. Ibid., 65.

72. Ibid., 75.

73. Ibid., 89.

74. Ibid.

75. Ibid., 173.

76. Ibid.

77. Ibid., 171.

78. Ibid., 171–172.

79. See James B. Jacobs and Jessica S. Henry, "The Social Construction of a Hate Crime Epidemic," *Journal of Criminal Law and Criminology* 86 (1996): 384; for another example, see Susan E. Martin, "Investigating Hate Crimes: Case Characteristics and Law Enforcement Responses," *Justice Quarterly* 13 (1996): 469 (reporting that "victims of bias crime reacted more strongly to their victimization than did victims of comparison crimes").

80. Lu-in Wang, "The Complexities of 'Hate,'" *Ohio State Law Journal* 60 (1999): 812.

81. Ibid.

82. Ibid.

83. Elizabeth A. Boyd, Karl M. Hamner, and Richard A. Berk, "Motivated by Hatred or Prejudice: Categorization of Hate-Motivated Crimes in Two Police Divisions," *Law and Society Review* 30 (1996): 827.

84. Ibid.

85. Ibid., 827–829.

86. Ibid., 832–839.

87. Ibid., 840–845.

88. Ibid., 845.

89. James A. Garofalo and Susan Martin, "Bias-Motivated Crimes: Their Characteristics and the Law Enforcement Response," Report for the National Institute of Justice, U.S. Department of Justice, January 1993, 49–50.

90. See "Police Seek Motive in Shop Fire," *Los Angeles Times*, 21 April 1992; "Vandals Leave Trail of Racist Graffiti; Homes, Cars Damaged in Joliet Neighborhood," *Chicago Tribune*, 6 September 1999; "Lake Forest Park Hit with Racist Graffiti; Police Unsure Whether Vandalism Was Hate Crime or Prank," *Seattle Times*, 12 May 2001.

91. See Jacobs and Potter, *Hate Crimes*, 93; and "Revision to Hate Crime Law Is Offered," *Austin American Statesman*, 2 April 1995.

92. For an example of police behavior in this regard, see LaFave, 191–192.

93. Witness the hundreds of papers and books written on the countermajoritarian difficulty. Perhaps the most famous of these is Alexander M. Bickel, *The Least Dangerous Branch* (1962).

Notes to Chapter 3

1. Laura Lederer, "The Case of the Cross-Burning, An Interview with Russ and Jones," in *The Price We Pay: The Case against Racist Speech, Hate Propaganda, and Pornography,* Laura Lederer and Richard Delgado, eds. (1995) 27–31.

2. Brian A. Reaves and Andrew L. Goldberg, *Law Enforcement Management and Administrative Statistics, 1997*, xix.

3. Pub. L. 90–284, Title VII, § 804, 82 Stat. 83 (1968).

4. See Shelley v. Kramer, 334 U.S. 1 (1948) (restrictive covenants outlawed); Jones v. Alfred Mayer, 392 U.S. 409 (1968) (racial discrimination in the sale or rental of private property illegal under 42 USC § 1982).

5. U.S.C. § 245 (b) (5) (1998 and Supp. 1V 1992).

6. Margalynne Armstrong, "Protecting Privilege: Race, Residence, and Rodney King," *Law and Inequality* 12 (1994): 361. See also Reynolds Farley,

Sheldon Danziger, and Harry Holzer, *Detroit Divided* (2000) 145–149; and Arnold R. Hirsch, *Making the Second Ghetto* (1983) 40–67.

7. J. Anthony Lukas, *Common Ground* (1996) 508–521.

8. Douglas Massey and Nancy Denton, *American Apartheid* (1993) 90.

9. Ibid., 90–91. For more discussion of this phenomenon, see Reginald Leamon Robinson, "The Racial Limits of the Fair Housing Act: The Intersection of Dominant White Images, the Violence of Neighborhood Purity, and the Master Narrative of Black Inferiority," *William and Mary Law Review* 37 (1995): 69.

10. Levin and McDevitt, *Hate Crimes*, 246.

11. Donald Green, Dara Z. Strolovitch, and Janelle S. Wong, "Defended Neighborhoods, Integration, and Racially Motivated Crime," *American Journal of Sociology* 104 (September 1998): 397.

12. Ibid.

13. See Jonathan Rieder, *Canarsie* (1985) 171–172; Thomas Sugrue, *The Origins of the Urban Crisis* (1996) 230–258; and Howard Pinderhughes, "The Anatomy of Racially Motivated Violence in New York City: A Study of Youth in Southern Brooklyn," *Social Problems* 40 (November 1993): 489.

14. See Pinderhughes, 489.

15. Kuykendall, 183.

16. *Center City Daily News*, 27 September 1982.

17. *Grangeville Star*, 25 November 1979.

18. Letter to mayor dated May 8, 1980 (ABTF files).

19. *Center City Daily News*, 27 September 1982.

20. CCPD Special Order, April 7, 1978.

21. In order to protect the confidentiality of informants, the text of the law is described in detail rather than quoted in full.

22. Levin and McDevitt, *Hate Crimes*, 5.

23. Center City District Court, Standards of Judicial Practice, "The Complaint Procedure," § 3.00.

NOTES TO CHAPTER 4

1. The unit's log is arranged around single incidents that happened to an identified victim. Frequently, when detectives in the unit began investigating a case, they discovered that other incidents had occurred and began investigating those as well. Such incidents were not represented in the unit's log.

2. Ericson, *Making Crime*, 7–11.

3. Setsuo Miyazawa, *Policing in Japan* (1992) 1.

4. See John E. Eck, *Solving Crimes* (1983) 96–118. This confirms an earlier study of detectives that found the vast majority of detective cases were handled in a single day. See Peter W. Greenwood, Jan M. Chaiken, and Joan Petersilia, *The Criminal Investigation Process* (Lexington, MA: C.C. Health, 1977).

5. Ericson, *Making Crime*, 81.

6. See Eck, *Solving Crimes*, 99–121.

7. Garofalo and Martin, 36.

8. See Ericson, *Making Crime*, 41. Skolnick, *Justice*; and William B. Sanders, *Detective Work* (1977), 36.

9. Boyd, Hamner, and Berk, 835.

10. See, Sanders, *Detective Work*, 79

11. Ericson, *Making Crime*, 89; see also Eck, *Solving Crimes*, 96; Sanders, *Detective Work*, 80.

12. Sanders, *Detective Work*, 80.

13. See, e.g., ibid., 129.

14. Ericson, *Making Crime*, 69.

15. See, e.g., ibid., 102.

16. See ibid., 103.

17. Wilson, *Varieties of Police Behavior*, 225–226, 297–299.

18. Center City Police Department, "General Considerations and Guidelines for Interviewing Witnesses."

19. Ibid.

20. See Ericson, *Making Crime, victim-complainants* is the widely used term in his study. Skolnick, *Justice without Trial*, also uses the term *complainant*.

21. Ericson, *Making Crime*, 85.

22. Center City Police Department, Neighborhood Disturbances Unit, "Key Points on Bias Crimes."

23. See Boyd, Hamner, and Berk, 839.

24. This is a pseudonym.

NOTES TO CHAPTER 5

1. LaFave, 218.

2. Ibid., 219.

3. *Center City Daily News*, 28 February 1992.

4. *Center City Daily News*, 29 January 1988.

5. *Grangeville Star*, 13 December 1987.

6. Ibid.

7. *Grangeville Star*, 26 February 1988.

8. *Bayview City Herald*, 29 January 1988.

9. *Grangeville Star*, 13 December 1987.

10. *Center City Daily News*, 28 February 1992.

11. *Gertown Voice*, 4 April 1996.

12. *Gertown Voice*, 21 July 1994.

13. *Gertown Voice*, 4 April 1996.

14. *Center City Daily News*, 28 February 1992.

15. *Gertown Voice*, 20 April 1995.

16. Ibid.

17. *Center City Daily News*, 23 August 1990.

18. *Center City Daily News*, 21 October 1993.

19. See Frederick Lawrence, *Punishing Hate: Bias Crimes under American Law* (1999) 23; and Peter Finn, "Bias Crime: Difficult to Define, Difficult to Prosecute: New Laws and Techniques That Are Putting Violent Bigots behind Bars," *Criminal Justice* 3 (Summer 1998): 19.

20. *Center City Daily News*, 7 June 1993.

21. *Center City Daily News*, 24 February 1990.

22. See Arlene Levinson, "Small Town Smoldering," *Las Vegas Review Journal*, 17 August 1997, A17; Chris Burritt, "Town Rocked by Grisly Slaying Insists the Crime Wasn't Racial," *Atlanta Journal and Constitution*, 24 August 1997, 19A; and Ed Vulliamy, "Horror and Fear Haunt Streets of Race-Murder Texas Town," *The Guardian*, 12 June 1998.

23. See Pinderhughes, 486.

NOTES TO CHAPTER 6

1. Ericson, *Making Crime*, 78–81, 167.

2. Skolnick, *Justice without Trial*, 219.

3. Boyd, Hamner, and Berk, 833.

4. See ibid., 834.

5. LaFave, 207–210.

6. See Garofalo and Martin, 44.

7. This is a pseudonym.

8. See Boyd, Hamner, and Berk, 826–829.

9. See ibid.

10. Eck, *Solving Crimes*, 252. Eck indicates the Greenwood and Petersilia study of detectives also found little difference between specialist detectives and generalist patrol officers. See Greenwood, Chaiken, and Petersilia, *The Criminal Investigation Process*.

11. Ibid., 252–253.

NOTES TO CHAPTER 7

1. See Goldstein, 573.

2. For a description of due process punishing defendants, see Malcolm Feeley, *The Process Is the Punishment* (1992).

3. See David Sudnow, "Normal Crimes: Sociological Features of the Penal Code in a Public Defender Officer," *Social Problems* 12 (1964).

4. See Susan Martin, "A Crossburning Is Not Just an Arson: Police Social Construction of Hate Crimes in Baltimore County," *Criminology* 33 (1995): 314. Martin's study of verified and unverified racial, religious, and ethnic incidents investigated by police in Baltimore County, Maryland, found that unverified incidents more often than not had a history of conflict between the parties.

5. See Lisa Frohmann, "Convictability and Discordant Locales: Reproducing Race, Class, and Gender Ideologies in Prosecutorial Decision Making," *Law and Society Review* 31 (1997): 531–555.

6. See, e.g., Mari J. Matsuda et al., *Words That Wound* (1993).

7. See, e.g., Jacobs and Potter, *Hate Crimes*, 194; Gerstenfeld, 284; and Gellman, "Sticks and Stones," 387.

8. See Frederick Lawrence, *Punishing Hate* (1999), 21.

9. Emphasis added.

10. Compare Boyd, Hamner, and Berk, 837.

11. See J. David Hirschel and Ira W. Hutchinson, "Female Spouse Abuse and the Police Response: The Charlotte, North Carolina, Experiment," *Journal of Criminal Law and Criminology* 83 (1992): 80–81.

12. Boyd, Hamner, and Berk, 839.

NOTES TO CHAPTER 8

1. Finn, 20; Jacobs and Potter, *Hate Crimes*, 102–103; Richard Barbieri, "DA Files First Ever Suit to Stop Hate Crimes," *American Lawyer* (29 March, 1991): 1; Linda Bean, "Prosecuting Bias Cases: A Delicate Balancing Act," *New Jersey Law Journal* (27 September 1993); Migdalia Maldonado, "Practical Problems with Enforcing Hate Crimes Legislation in New York," *Annual Survey of American Law* (November 1993): 555–561; Geoff Boucher, "Case Will Test Definition of Hate Crime," *Los Angeles Times*, 25 July 1996; and David Reyes, "Coalition Urges More Prosecutions of Hate Crimes," *Los Angeles Times*, 9 September 1994, B1.

2. See State Attorney General's Office, *Comprehensive Model Enforcement and Prevention Program To Combat Hate Crimes and Civil Rights Violations* (September 1994): 5. The AG's office used the civil rights statutes broadly and in areas unrelated to bias-motivated conduct—to enjoin blockades of abortion clinics, in cases in which breaches of contract interfered with an individual's First Amendment rights, and to support the right to collect signatures on a private property.

3. Ibid., 17.

4. Ibid., 8.

5. William B. Sanders writes that detectives viewed their jobs in terms of "clearing cases." Clearing a case requires only catching or identifying suspects; conviction is not necessary for clearance. See, e.g., Sanders, *Detective Work*, 80.

6. In interviews, ADAs reported that an ADA who was considered experienced in the jurisdiction might have had ten criminal civil rights cases, one or two of which might have gone to trial.

7. Application for Complaint, ABTF files.

8. Center City District Court, Standards of Judicial Practice.

9. Ibid § 3.

Notes to Chapter 9

1. See, e.g., Gail Heriot, "Problems with Hate Crimes Laws," *San Diego Union Tribune*, 5 July 2000, B11; Richard Cohen, "The Trouble with Hate-Crime Laws," *Washington Post*, 19 October 1999, A19; Nat Hentoff, "No: Equality among Victims, *ABA Journal* (May 1993): 45; and Testimony of Robert H. Knight before the Senate Judiciary Committee, 11 May 1999.

2. See, e.g., arguments made by legislators opposed to hate crime legislation in Lawrence, *Punishing Hate*, 19.

3. United States Department of Justice, Federal Bureau of Investigation, *Hate Crime Statistics 1997* (1999) 7.

4. Ibid.

5. See, e.g., David Rohn, "Beware of Compelling Unity," *Indianapolis Star*, 17 July 1999. In this editorial, Rohn advises that discussion is a better way to end the hatred that provoked the Benjamin Smith and other bias-motivated killers. He writes, "Hatred should be combated with reason and compassion. Let truth and falsehood grapple."

6. See, e.g., Linda Chavez, "Focus on Laws, Not Motives," *Denver Post*, 16 July 1999; and Steve Stephens, "Liberals Dressed in Conservative Clothing Push Hate Crime Law," *Columbus Dispatch*, 19 October 1998.

7. United States Department of Justice, *Hate Crime Statistics 1997*, 7.

8. For a historical description of the difficulties faced by Black officers, see W. Marvin Dulaney, *Black Police in America* (1996). For examples of harassment and discrimination of minority officers, see Jennifer Goldson, "Black Police Group Wants Plainfield Chief to Quit," *The Star Ledger* (Newark, NJ), 2 September 1990; and Thomas Zolper, "Black and Latino Caucus Blasts State Police, Organizational Bias Seen," *Northern New Jersey Record*, 31 August 1999.

9. See Ericson, *Making Crime*.

10. See Lisa Frohmann, "Discrediting Victims' Allegations of Sexual Assault: Prosecutorial Accounts of Case Rejections," *Social Problems* 38 (1991): 213–224; and David Sudnow, "Normal Crimes: Sociological Features of the Penal Code in a Public Defender Officer," *Social Problems* 12 (1964).

11. See Barbara Yngvesson, "Making Law in the Doorway: The Clerk, the Court, and the Construction of Community in a New England Town," in *Law*

and Community in Three American Towns, Carol Greenhouse, Barbara Yngvesson, and David Engel, eds. (1994).

NOTES TO THE APPENDIX

1. See John Van Maanen, *Tales of the Field: On Writing Ethnography* (Chicago: University of Chicago Press, 1988) 73, 81.

2. For a discussion of this, see Ericson, 29.

3. For more on the issue of access, especially for police research, see Jeannine Bell, "Breaking through the Yellow Tape," in *Gaining Access: A Practical Guide for Field Researchers,* Martha Feldman, Michele Berger, and Jeannine Bell, eds. (forthcoming).

4. See, e.g., Skolnick, *Justice*; Ericson, *Making Crime*; Steve Herbert, *Policing Space: Territoriality and the Los Angeles Police Department* (Minneapolis: University of Minnesota Press, 1997); and Manning, *The Narc's Game.*

5. See Reaves and Goldberg, Law Enforcement Management and Administrative Statistics, 1997.

6. See Feeley, *The Process Is the Punishment*, xxviii.

7. See Walker and Katz.

8. For a discussion of the racial tensions in police departments in both the North and the South, see W. Marvin Dulaney, *Black Police in America* (1996).

9. For a discussion of triangulation, see Michael W. McCann, *Rights at Work: Pay Equity Reform and the Politics of Legal Mobilization* (Chicago: University of Chicago Press, 1994) 16–18.

10. See, for example, Gerald Rosenberg, *The Hollow Hope: Can the Courts Bring About Social Change?* (Chicago: University of Chicago Press, 1991). One of the measures that Rosenberg heavily relies on to argue that the Supreme Court was unable to effect social change is the number of southern schools that complied with its decision in Brown v. Board of Education, 349 U.S. 294 (1955).

11. See Sanders, *Detective Work*; Manning, *The Narc's Game*; Ericson, *Making Crime*; and Skolnick, *Justice Without Trial.*

Bibliography

Armstrong, Margalynne. "Protecting Privilege: Race, Residence, and Rodney King." *Law and Inequality* 12 (June 1994): 351–380.

Bayley, David H. *Forces of Order: Policing Modern Japan.* Berkeley: University of California Press, 1991.

Bickel, Alexander M. *The Least Dangerous Branch: The Supreme Court at the Bar of Politics.* Indianapolis: Bobbs-Merrill, 1962.

Bittner, Egon. *Aspects of Police Work.* Boston: Northeastern University Press, 1990.

———. "The Police on Skid Row: A Study of Peace Keeping." *American Sociological Review* 32 (1967): 699–715.

Boyd, Elizabeth, Karl M. Hamner, and Richard Berk. "Motivated by Hatred or Prejudice: Categorization of Hate-Motivated Crimes in Two Police Divisions." *Law and Society Review* 30 (1996): 819–850.

Cicourel, Aaron V. *The Social Organization of Juvenile Justice.* New York: Wiley, 1968.

Cook County State Attorney's Office. *A Prosecutor's Guide to Hate Crimes.* 1994.

Davis, Kenneth Culp. *Police Discretion.* St. Paul, MN: West, 1975.

Dority, Barbara. "The Criminalization of Hatred," *Humanist* (May/June 1994): 38–39.

Dulaney, W. Marvin. *Black Police in America.* Bloomington: Indiana University Press, 1996.

Eck, John E. *Solving Crimes, the Investigation of Burglary and Robbery.* Washington, D.C.: Police Executive Research Forum, 1983.

Ehrlich, Howard, Barbara E. K. Larcom, and Robert Purvis. "The Traumatic Impact of Ethnoviolence." In *The Price We Pay: The Case against Racist Speech, Hate Propaganda, and Pornography,* edited by Laura Lederer and Richard Delgado. New York: Hill and Wang, 1995.

Ericson, Richard V. *Making Crime: A Study of Detective Work.* Toronto: Butterworths, 1981.

Farley, Reynolds, Sheldon Danziger, and Harry Holzer. *Detroit Divided.* New York: Russell Sage, 2000.

217

Feeley, Malcolm. *The Process Is the Punishment: Handling Cases in a Lower Criminal Court.* New York: Russell Sage, 1992.

Finn, Peter. "Bias Crime: Difficult to Define, Difficult to Prosecute: New Laws and Techniques That Are Putting Violent Bigots behind Bars." *Criminal Justice* 3 (Summer 1998): 19–48.

Garcia, Luis, and Jack McDevitt, "The Psychological and Behavioral Effects of Bias and Non-Bias Motivated Assault." Report for the National Institute of Justice, U.S. Department of Justice, December 1999.

Garofalo, James A., and Susan Martin. "Bias-Motivated Crimes: Their Characteristics and the Law Enforcement Response." Report for the National Institute of Justice, U.S. Department of Justice, January 1993.

Gaumer, Craig Peyton. "Punishment for Prejudice: A Commentary on the Constitutionality and Utility of State Statutory Responses to the Problem of Hate Crime." *South Dakota Law Review* 39 (1994): 1–48.

Gellman, Susan. "Hate Crimes after Wisconsin v. Mitchell." *Ohio Northern University Law Review* 21 (1995): 863–870.

———. "Sticks and Stones Can Put You in Jail, but Can Words Increase Your Sentence? Constitutional and Policy Dilemmas of Ethnic Intimidation Laws." *UCLA Law Review* 39 (1991): 333–396.

Gerstenfeld, Phyliss B. "Smile When You Call Me That! The Problems with Punishing Hate Motivated Behavior." *Behavioral Sciences and the Law* 10 (1992): 259–285.

Gey, Steven G. "What If Wisconsin v. Mitchell Had Involved Martin Luther King, Jr.? The Constitutional Flaws of Hate Crime Sentence Enhancements." *George Washington Law Review* 65 (1997): 1014–1070.

Goldstein, Joseph A. "Police Discretion Not to Invoke the Criminal Process: Low-Visibility Decisions in the Administration of Justice." *Yale Law Journal* 69 (March 1960): 543–594.

Green, Donald, Dara Z. Strolovitch, and Janelle S. Wong. "Defended Neighborhoods, Integration, and Racially Motivated Crime." *American Journal of Sociology* 104 (September 1998): 372–403.

Herek, Gregory M., and Kevin Berrill, eds. *Hate Crimes: Confronting the Violence against Lesbians and Gay Men.* Newberry Park: Sage Publications, 1992.

Hirsch, Arnold R. *Making the Second Ghetto: Race and Housing in Chicago, 1940–1960.* Cambridge: Cambridge University Press, 1983.

Hirschel, J. David, and Ira W. Hutchinson. "Female Spouse Abuse and the Police Response: The Charlotte, North Carolina, Experiment." *Journal of Criminal Law and Criminology* 83 (1992): 73–119.

Jacobs, James B. "Rethinking the War against Hate Crimes: A New York City Perspective." *Criminal Justice Ethics* (Summer/Fall 1992): 55–60.

Jacobs, James B., and Barry J. Eisler. "The Hate Crimes Statistics Act of 1990." *Criminal Law Bulletin* 29 (1993): 99–123.

Jacobs, James B. and Kimberly Potter. *Hate Crimes: Criminal Law and Identity Politics*. New York: Oxford University Press, 1998.

Jenness, Valerie, and Ryken Grattet. "The Criminalization of Hate: A Comparison of Structural and Polity Influences on the Passage of 'Bias-Crime' Legislation in the United States." *Sociological Perspectives* 39 (1996): 129–154.

Kelly, Robert J., ed. *Bias Crime: American Law Enforcement and Legal Responses*. Chicago: Office of International Criminal Justice, University of Illinois at Chicago, 1993.

Kuykendall, Jack. "The Municipal Police Detective: A Historical Analysis." *Criminology* 24 (1986): 175–201.

LaFave, Wayne R. "The Police and Non-Enforcement of the Law—Part II." *Wisconsin Law Review* (March 1962): 179–239.

Lawrence, Frederick. *Punishing Hate: Bias Crimes under American Law*. Cambridge: Harvard University Press, 1999.

Lederer, Laura J. "The Case of the Cross-Burning: An Interview with Russ and Jones." In *The Price We Pay: The Case against Racist Speech, Hate Propaganda, and Pornography*, edited by Laura Lederer and Richard Delgado. New York: Hill and Wang, 1995.

Levin, Jack L., and Jack McDevitt. *Hate Crimes: The Rising Tide of Bigotry and Bloodshed*. New York: Plenum Press, 1993.

Lipsky, Michael. *Street-Level Bureaucracy: Dilemmas of the Individual in Public Services*. New York: Russell Sage, 1980.

Lukas, J. Anthony. *Common Ground: A Turbulent Decade in the Lives of Three American Families*. New York: Vintage, 1996.

Lundman, Richard J. "Demeanor or Crime? The Midwest City Police-Citizen Encounters Study." *Criminology* 32 (1994): 631–647.

Manning, Peter K. *The Narc's Game: Organizational and Informational Limits on Drug Law Enforcement*. Cambridge: MIT Press, 1980.

Martin, Susan E. "A Crossburning Is Not Just an Arson: Police Social Construction of Hate Crimes in Baltimore County." *Criminology* 33 (1995): 303–326.

Massey, Douglas, and Nancy Denton. *American Apartheid*. Cambridge: Harvard University Press, 1993.

Matsuda, Mari J., Charles R. Lawrence, Richard Delgado, and Kimberlé Williams Crenshaw. *Words That Wound: Critical Race Theory, Assaultive Speech, and the First Amendment*. Boulder: Westview, 1993.

Miyazawa, Setsuo. *Policing in Japan: A Study on Making Crime*. Albany: State University of New York Press, 1992.

Morsch, James. "Comment, The Problem of Motive in Hate Crimes: The

Argument Against Presumptions of Racial Motivations." *Journal of Criminal Law and Criminology* 82 (1991): 659–689.

———. "Demise of the First Amendment? Focus on RICO and Hate Crime Legislation—Shield from Terrorism? or National Gag Order? Eighteenth Annual Law Review Symposium. *Ohio Northern University Law Review* 21 (1995).

Pinderhughes, Howard. "The Anatomy of Racially Motivated Violence in New York City: A Study of Youth in Southern Brooklyn." *Social Problems* 40 (November 1993): 478–462.

Reaves, Brian A., and Andrew L. Goldberg. *Law Enforcement Management and Administrative Statistics, 1997: Data for Individual State and Local Agencies with 100 or More Officers*. Washington, D.C.: Bureau of Justice Statistics, 1999.

Redish, Martin H. "Freedom of Thought as Freedom of Expression: Hate Crime Sentencing Enhancement and First Amendment Theory." *Criminal Justice Ethics* (Summer/Fall 1992): 29–41.

Rieder, Jonathan. *Canarsie: The Jews and Italians of Brooklyn against Liberalism*. Cambridge: Harvard University Press, 1985.

Riggs, Robert. "Punishing the Politically Incorrect Offender Through 'Bias Motive' Enhancements: Compelling Necessity or First Amendment Folly?" *Ohio Northern University Law Review* 21 (1995): 945–957.

Robinson, Reginald Leamon. "The Racial Limits of the Fair Housing Act: The Intersection of Dominant White Images, the Violence of Neighborhood Purity, and the Master Narrative of Black Inferiority." *William and Mary Law Review* 37 (Fall 1995): 69–159.

Sandalow, Terrence. "Opening Address: Equality and Freedom of Speech." *Ohio Northern University Law Review* 21 (1995): 831–844.

Sanders, William B. *Detective Work: A Study of Criminal Investigations*. New York: Free Press, 1977.

Skolnick, Jerome H. *Justice without Trial: Law Enforcement in Democratic Society*. 2d ed. New York: Wiley, 1967.

Skolnick, Jerome, and James Fyfe. *Above the Law: Police and the Exclusive Use of Force*. New York: Free Press, 1993.

Sugrue, Thomas. *The Origins of the Urban Crisis: Race and Inequality in Postwar Detroit*. Princeton: Princeton University Press, 1996.

United States Department of Justice, Federal Bureau of Investigation. *Hate Crime Statistics 1994*. Washington, D.C., 1995.

———. *Hate Crime Statistics 1997*. Washington, D.C., 1999.

United States Department of Justice, National Institute of Law Enforcement, and Criminal Justice Law Enforcement Assistance Administration. *The Criminal Investigation Process: A Dialogue of Research Findings*. Washington, D.C., April 1977.

Walker, Samuel, and Charles M. Katz. "Less Than Meets the Eye: Police Department Bias-Crime Units." *American Journal of Police* 14 (1995): 29–47.

Wang, Lu-in. *Hate Crimes Law*. St. Paul: West Group, 2000.

———. "The Transforming Power of 'Hate': Social Cognition Theory and the Harms of Bias-Related Crime." *Southern California Law Review* 71 (November 1997): 47–136.

———. "The Complexities of 'Hate.'" *Ohio State Law Journal* 60 (1999): 799–900.

Wexler, Chuck, and Gary J. Marx. "When Law and Order Works." *Crime and Delinquency* 23 (1986): 205–217.

Wilson, James Q. *Varieties of Police Behavior: The Management of Law and Order in Eight Communities*. New York: Atheneum, 1973.

Worden, Robert E. "Situational and Attitudinal Explanations of Police Behaviors: A Theoretical Reappraisal and Empirical Assessment." *Law and Society Review* 23 (1989): 667–711.

Yngvesson, Barbara. "Making Law in the Doorway: The Clerk, the Court, and the Construction of Community in a New England Town." In *Law and Community in Three American Towns*, edited by Carol Greenhouse, Barbara Yngvesson, and David Engel. Ithaca: Cornell University Press, 1994.

Index

Advocacy groups, victim, 13, 27, 73, 107–12, 119, 151, 167; Anti-Defamation League, 108; Gay and Lesbian Anti-Violence Project (GLAP), 107; interviews with, 196; LEGAL, 107; National Association for the Advancement of Colored People, 32, 107; relations with ABTF, 107–10

Anti-Bias Task Force (ABTF): contact with victims, 39, 121; conversion of, 127–29, 130, 186; criteria for selection of, 44, 122; criticisms of, 89, 90–91, 98, 104, 130–31; diversity of, 44, 122, 186–90, 194–95; function of, 29, 37–40, 49; level of investigative activity, 54–57; log, 49, 55–57, 139, 198–99; mission of, 123; morale in, 90–91, 106–7, 120–21; origins of, 8, 36–37; personal and professional costs to, 120–121; political pressure, 97, 98–100; pressure to reduce crime, 98–100, 125–26, 186; relations with prosecutors, 173–76; resources, 43, 130, 187, 189–90; response to victim advocacy groups, 107–10; size, 43–44; structure, 37–40, 132, 133; unpopularity with other officers, 114–117, 120. *See also* Detectives

Anti-Semitism, 23, 28, 145

Attorney General, 45, 139, 160, 166, 180, 187; relationship with ABTF, 175–76

Bias crimes. *See* Hate crimes

Bias indicators, 69, 72–74, 109, 111, 141, 143, 144, 146–47, 155, 162, 170

Boyd, Elizabeth, et. al., 23–24, 132

Byrd, James, 1, 6, 105, 184, 185

Case files, 197–98; contents, 55; length, 54

Cases: "brooming" of, 59, 60, 100, 174; building strong, 168; detectives' personalization of, 71; group discussion of, 64; load, 132; numbers investigated, 99; pattern, 164–65; screening of, 59, 81, 100, 174 183; statistics, 50; types investigated, 50–52

Center City: demographics, 7–8; housing integration, 33–36, 40; placement of hate crime, 39–40; school desegregation, 33; segregation, 31–33

Center City Daily News, 7, 90, 102

Center City Housing Office (CHO), 35, 85, 86

Center City Police Department (CCPD), 29; professionalization, 193; size, 193

Center City Tribune, 7, 102

Chaplinsky v. New Hampshire, 17–18

Charging decision, 138–39, 163, 164, 169, 157–59; 173–76, 199; duplication of charges, 160, 185; and juveniles, 155–157; options, 134–40; and race, 4, 152–54

Civil rights charges, 12, 68, 101; distribution of, 153. *See also* Civil rights violations; Criminal civil rights violations

Civil rights law, 40, 45, 47, 161. *See also* Criminal civil rights violations; Hate crime law; Injunctions

Civil rights violations, 138–39, 153–58, 164, 169–70, 172, 176, 188; decision to seek charges for, 140–41; difficulty of prosecution, 161; evidence of motivation, 79, 141, 143–45. *See also* Civil rights charges; Civil rights law; Injunctions

Community: ethnicity and, 32, 39, 91, 153; homogeneity of, 32; loyalty towards, 95,

About the Author

Jeannine Bell, who holds both a J.D. and a Ph.D. from the University of Michigan, is an associate professor of law at Indiana University, Bloomington, and an adjunct professor of political science. She teaches courses in the area of criminal procedure, law and society, and the First Amendment.